A
Doctor
at All Hours

Dr. Kellogg at the age of 41, in 1888.

A
Doctor
at All Hours

The Private Journal of a Small-Town Doctor's Varied Life

1886--1909

by David S. Kellogg, M.D.

Edited by Allan S. Everest

The Stephen Greene Press

Brattleboro, Vermont

1970

Designed by R. L. Dothard Associates, printed and bound in the United States of America by The Book Press. Library of Congress Catalog Card Number: 70–114413 International Standard Book Number: 0–8289–0112–0

Foreword

Here is the story, told in his own words, of a most uncommon doctor's life in the sparsely settled northeastern corner of New York State during the last decade and a half of the 19th Century and most of the first decade of the 20th. It is the story of David Sherwood Kellogg, a Plattsburgh physician with a large rural practice. He reveals himself, his family life, his professional experiences, and his crowding cultural interests with engaging grace, candor, and frequent humor in these pages, excerpted largely from his previously unpublished journal and occasionally from other writings he did with no thought of publication.

Beginning with the second day of January, 1886, the journal entries take Dr. Kellogg from his vigorous prime, at the age of thirty-eight, nearly to the day of his untimely death, in 1909, when he succumbed to an increasing burden of care and illness two months after his sixty-second birthday. Passages that have been omitted were either repetitious or devoted to the daily weather, which practicality obliged him to keep a sharp eye on but whose moods he viewed with poetic appreciation. He could even revel in a savage thunderstorm.

Other small-town doctors may have been Dr. Kellogg's equals in devotion to duty, in compassion, and in physical endurance. They, too, could have told of being always on call and of riding behind a faithful horse at any hour of the day or night to the remote bedsides of suffering patients, through hub-deep mud or drifts higher than a horse's back. Few, if any, of his contemporaries in the medical profession would have been able, however, to match his fascinating array of avocational pursuits. He was a tireless recorder of folklore and local history, a born naturalist, an enthusiastic mountain-climber, an explorer of ancient forts, a self-taught authority on glacial geology, a respected amateur archeologist, a voracious reader and a haunter of bookshops, a collector of old blue chinaware, and an assiduous frequenter of scientific and literary symposiums. Still, despite these manifold activities, Dr. Kellogg was a rather frustrated intellectual, admiring learned and literary people above all others but ruefully finding himself always short of their lofty level. "It is humiliating to me," he confided to his journal one day in 1887, "that people know so much more than I do." This was unjustified disparagement of his own considerable attainments.

Dr. Kellogg left a large body of manuscripts other than this journal. He enjoyed writing and liked frequently to exercise his fondness for it, mostly by generating stories and sketches for his children: tales of his boyhood on a Vermont farm, schooldays during the Civil War, bygone Thanksgivings, and local ghost stories. Avidly he interviewed many elderly citizens of his locality who were reputed to have long memories and a good sense of detail, and he wrote down their reminiscences. Many of the most interesting of these interviews have been published in a booklet called *Recollections of Clinton County and the Battle of Plattsburgh, 1800–1840*, which I edited and which was published in 1964 by the Clinton County Historical Association. A few are reprinted in part here, where journal entries pertain to the interviews that produced them.

The Doctor was among the first to explore the many Indian sites of his beloved Champlain Valley, salvaging their treasures before they were dissipated or destroyed, recording his finds with an eager satisfaction that will touch every collector's heart. "What fun it is to search, and find!" he once exclaims.

"I have visited so many places to look for, and to get, relics," he wrote in the journal on March 18, 1890. "I can truthfully say I have looked the whole lake shore over from Rouses Point to Port Kent. I do not think there are many rods in that whole distance I have not travelled over." Although not a trained scholar in archeology or the glacial era, he was locally considered to be an authority and delivered numerous lectures on both subjects in New York, Vermont, and Canada.

Dr. Kellogg was an early promoter of studies of the Champlain Valley. He offered prizes to students for essays on local history, believing that "the pride of locality is a good subject for an exhaustive treatise." He was instrumental in commemorating the local battle sites of the War of 1812 with permanent markers. The Plattsburgh Institute, of which he was a prime mover, met twice a month for several winters to hear and discuss papers on local and national history as well as scientific subjects.

Dr. Kellogg loved to hunt for antique blue china in out-of-the-way country stores or farmhouses, but his favorite search was for old books and manuscripts, as well as the best in contemporary literature. His reactions to the books he read reveal tastes, culture, and sensibilities typical of the literate New Englander of his day. He was the devoted head of a large family, an ardent Republican who could sometimes discern the hand of God at election time, and the friend of people on all levels of life. He was sympathetic and understanding in the homes of the poor, intellectually responsive in the company of men such as William Dean Howells.

Dr. Kellogg was born in Essex, Vermont, on October 21, 1847. He received his A.B. degree from the University of Vermont in 1870 and, after a period of teaching, his M.D. degree from the University in 1873. After interning in Hartford, Connecticut, he settled in Plattsburgh in 1874.

In the following year he married Elizabeth Smith of Burlington, whose mother thereafter was on call for many a family crisis. His pride in their five children is evident through the journal. The Doctor also brought up and educated, with affectionate interest, the three children of his sister Fannie and her husband, Osceola Kyle, after the death of both parents. In his journal he makes frequent mention, too, of Philo Pierson, who had worked on the Kellogg farm in Essex for many years.

"I have for years had a great desire to write a book," Dr. Kellogg confessed one day in his journal. "I should like to write one that would interest people and that would do them good. But one not accustomed cannot sit down and write by mere force of will," he continued. "If he does so his efforts will amount to nothing. He must have something to say, some good point to make." This informal record of his busy life, which he never expected would be seen outside the family, perhaps fulfills his hope better than if he had written a book "by mere force of will."

We wish to thank Mr. Theodore Chase for his help in the development of this publication and Mrs. George V. Bobrinskoy for compiling the index.

Plattsburgh, New York   ALLAN S. EVEREST

The Kellogg homestead in Essex, Vermont as it appears today.

The Doctor's Circle

Bessie	*his wife*
Mrs. Smith	*his mother-in-law*
Robert	*his eldest son*
Nelson (Nello)	*his second son*
Elizabeth (Elspeth) (Bessie)	*his only daughter*
David	*his third son*
Francis Fellows	*his fourth son*
Helen Kyle	*his niece*
Theodora (Theo) Kyle	*his niece*
Francis Kyle	*his nephew*
Mary Griffin	*his sister*
Henry Griffin	*his brother-in-law*
Philo Pierson	*his father's farmhand*
Fly	*his favorite horse*
No. 2	*his spare horse*
Belmont	*his Fly's successor*

DECEASED SISTER'S CHILDREN

(bracket grouping Helen Kyle, Theodora (Theo) Kyle, and Francis Kyle)

1866 Jan. Have just finished "Wilhelm Meister's apprenticeship" on Mr. Emerson's recommendation—or suggestion. I shall read his Travels when the book comes from Northampton. What a silly fool Wilhelm Meister was. If his Travels do not exhibit him in a more favorable light I shall have a permanent disgust for him. How he was always falling in love with the last woman. She was always the most charming one of her sex. He fell in love so many times it became a second nature to him. He got into a habit of it. I hope he marries Natalia

A reproduction from Dr. Kellogg's Journal—January 2, 1866.

1886

In the opening year of Doctor Kellogg's journal, Plattsburgh, where he had lived since 1874, was a village of six thousand inhabitants, trying out its first electric street lights. It was a railroad center on the New York-to-Montreal run, as well as on the route to popular Adirondack resorts, like Paul Smith's. Lake Champlain, which it fronted, was a highway of travel, and Plattsburgh was a port of call for all lake steamers. It was also an old military town, with a permanent garrison at the Barracks.

As the year begins, the Doctor has built up an extensive practice and has recently become thirty-eight years old. His wife, Bessie, is thirty-six. So far, they have three children: Robert, who is seven; Nelson, four; and Elizabeth, two.

The Doctor's initial journal entries quickly acquaint us with this warm-hearted, dryly humorous man and his chief enthusiasms. He reveals himself as a sensitive observer of both man and Nature, with an original mind, a scientist's ready curiosity, and a touch of poetry in his soul.

In this year, he admiringly reads Goethe, Tolstoi, and General Grant for the first time; pokes around historic forts; happens upon a rich new source of Indian relics; doggedly studies German; and elicits dramatic first-hand recollections of the War of 1812 from local old-timers whom he interviews for that purpose. Though bone-weary from sick calls that have kept him from sleep, he still can rejoice at a panoramic view of Lake Champlain on a frosty fall day at dawn and the ringing chorus of frogs that accompanies his jog home at first light of an April morning. With customary scientific interest, he also describes in detail the peaceful death of one of his patients, and concludes that "the end of life is as marvelous as the beginning."

JAN. 2—Have just finished *Wilhelm Meister's Apprenticeship* on Mr. Emerson's recommendation, or suggestion. What a silly fool Wilhelm Meister was. If his *Travels* do not exhibit him in a more favorable light I shall have a permanent disgust for him. How he was always falling in love with the *last* woman. *She* was always the most charming one of her sex.

The Doctor's mother and father, Evalina and Nelson Kellogg, taken some years after their marriage in 1835.

He fell in love so many times it became a second nature to him. He got into a *habit* of it. I hope he marries Natalia and that she leads him a life. He deserves it. Still there are so many wonderful things in the book! It was really worthy of the genius of Carlyle to translate it. Goethe does not make the sexual relations a prominent, but an incidental, feature of life. Some of his best characters get into what might be called pretty doubtful conditions. Yet they all seem to think them justified or at any rate unavoidable.

Of course I have no knowledge or appreciation of his talk on theatres. It seems to me that a man who thinks a theatre the greatest thing in the world—the man who thinks that in *acting* are the most real things in life—must be disappointed if he ever comes to himself. There are *real* things enough to move one's soul without depending upon things not real.

2

A tremendous snowstorm from the North is raging. Our
sleighing of December was all gone and this may give us more. Yesterday
the thermometer reached zero for the first time this winter. What a luxury
it is to stay indoors "fast by an ingle bleezing finely" and see the storm
without, *raving* and *rustling*.[1]

On Wednesday of this week the wife of Mr. Smith M. Weed was buried.[2]
The stores, banks, and saloons were nearly all closed. I believe, though,
the Vilas Bank was not closed. Of course it was some consolation to the
family to know how greatly she was esteemed, but after all this general
closing looked more like toadyism than real affection. Some said the drygoods stores ought to go into mourning for the loss of their best customer.
Yet Mrs. Weed was a kindhearted woman and there was enough real
mourning felt for her to make it unnecessary to have any sham.

JAN. 13—Pension Day. One would-be pensioner, in his "subjective
symptoms," said he had typhoid fever while in the army which resulted in
the loss of his "smellage." He also said that he "felt something fluttering
in his stomach like a fish's tail and after that he had the blind staggers."

Nelson yesterday began to have a bank account. He put $1.32 into the
Merchant's National Bank and has a bank book with the amounts recorded
in it. He feels very rich.

My attention has been called to the *Sentinel's* account of the funeral of
Mrs. Weed. It says, "The large funeral procession was formed and moved
to the grave in Riverside Cemetery, there to rest until the resurrection
morn."

JAN. 19—This morning a little before eight I heard ice cracking on the
lake. I was at the house, 52 Court Street. The sound was not unlike the
rumbling of a heavy wagon down street, but there was more resonance
and harmony.

Last night I began to write down the folklore, weather lore, aphorisms
and so on that I could think of. When I got to the house the family supplied
many more. Today Mrs. Myers and many others have told me some and
tonight I have written in a book 344. Most of these are probably used
wherever the English language is spoken. Still a very few of them are
local. I took them down as people remembered them, not as they were in
books. Quite a number of them are quotations from poets, but I presume
the origin of many of them never will be known. Many of them explain
themselves.

*The following are examples of the 566 sayings eventually collected and
recorded by the Doctor:*

"An elephant has stepped on my purse."

"One boy is a whole boy, two boys are half a boy, three boys are no boy at all."

"He that would thrive must rise at five. He that hath thriven may lie till seven."

"Beware of the man of one book."

"When the youngest is married first, the oldest has to dance in the pig's trough."

"Rub a wart with a leaf, throw the leaf down, and the one who picks up the leaf will have the wart and yours will go away."

"If the fools should all die, there would be no rich men left alive."

"Clean stove, empty gut."

"Who has cobwebs likes kisses," (i.e., one lazy enough to let cobwebs stay is sentimental).

JAN. 25—I came across a reference in Peter Esprit Radisson's "Travels" to a former Indian village at Dead Creek, I think.[3] After *carrying* past a "Rappid Streame" in the Richelieu they stayed at night at a village which I believe to have been at St. Valentin (Isle aux Noix). The next day they came to a large lake six leagues wide and at night they camped on a "fine sandy bancke" where it seems there was, or had been previously, a village. This, if my conjecture be true, is a reference to this "fine sandy bancke" at the Creek, which is a mile in length and is a much *finer* sand bank than any between here and Isle aux Noix. And yet this reference throws us back to only 1653, a date which in England or Ireland or Scotland would be considered recent.

It is said of my grandmother that she was accustomed to go half way to one of the neighbor's and meet this neighbor to pray with her. One of my aunts suggested that, as on one occasion they stayed so long together, it would be a good thing *to take them a lunch*. When I was a small boy my training led me to believe it was sinful to throw a stone on Sunday or even to slide down the footpath in front of the kitchen door on the way to the barns.

On Pike's Cantonment one winter during the last war with England, some 2,500 or 3,000 soldiers lived in log huts all winter, but in Platts-burgh today there are hardly ten persons who know where this place is. It is not remembered that an epidemic killed off rapidly the men and that it was thought that the disease was caused by their coming from the Caro-linas to this cold climate. Yet after a time they found that the whiskey given the sick ones contained a large quantity of copperas put there by some British emissary to poison our men. As soon as they stopped giving the whiskey the epidemic ceased. (This isn't the first epidemic caused by whiskey.) I have looked in vain for the place where these soldiers, said to have been two or three hundred, were buried.[4]

JAN. 30—The pride of locality is a good subject for an exhaustive treatise. The tendency towards organizing, searching and recording as done in the various historical, genealogical, geological, antiquarian societies and numerous others is an illustration of the pride of locality. Almost every such society had its beginning in a matter of local interest. Every place has its history, its romances, its pleasant spots, its natural scenery, its geology, its natural history and its everything to make it interesting and worthy of study. Thoreau said they need not go to the Arctic regions to find red snow, for they had it in Concord.

I have sent $1.50 for Bessie and me to go to a concert tonight by Blaisdell's orchestra. I expect to hear some music that will please me, some that will not interest me, and some that will be positively disagreeable. If I can hear as much harmony as the cracking ice or the telegraph wires' music when I strike the pole with my cane coming downtown nights, I think I shall be satisfied. I have been trained to very little in artificial music, for which I suppose I ought to feel myself humiliated.

JAN. 31—Well, my concert expectations were realized. The music was of course "fine." "The celebrated singer, Alta Pease of Boston" was quite hoarse but did not sing *distressingly* loud. The full orchestra writhed and twisted and brought forth sounds in good time and fair harmony; but I would rather hear Bessie sing "There's nae Luck about the House" or "Lord Ronald" than the whole of their music. I shall still use my telegraph wire music and feel downtrodden for want of such as Blaisdell's orchestra, and I shall not think the less of the cracking ice chorus.

FEB. 4—I have borrowed "Lt. Hadden's Journal" and "Hadden's Orderly Book."[5] The accounts given here of Burgoyne's expeditions are very fascinating. A map is given showing the location of the British and American fleets at the Battle of Valcour Island, October 11, 1776.[6] The American fleet at this battle "consisted of 3 row galleys, 2 schooners, 2 sloops, and 8 gondolas, carrying in all 90 guns." The British fleet "carried only 87 pieces of ordnance including 8 howitzers." It seems that the contests lasted a large part of the afternoon. Seventy of the Americans were killed or wounded.

FEB. 18—What a comprehensive affair history is! How long it takes to make it, how short, often to write it. Someone has said that the life of every person is worth writing, if properly described. Alas, we, many of us, will only have an epitaph for our history, which may be as complete as the one Hawthorne found in England,

> Poorly lived and poorly died,
> Poorly buried and no one cried.[7]

If the events of Champlain Valley history were written, this town alone could scarcely contain the books that could be written. The romantic (seen at this distance) excursions, the hardships, the enjoyments of the early settlers of Canada, the beauty of the forests primeval as God had made them, all add delight and charm to the history of New France and the valley of Lake Champlain.

FEB. 19—Am reading Carlyle's *Life of John Sterling*. Evidently T.C. didn't greatly admire Coleridge, perhaps because Coleridge talked so fast Carlyle couldn't get a word in edgewise. It seems that after Sterling came under Carlyle's influence he admired Coleridge less and Goethe more. Sterling's letter to T.C., criticising *Sartor Resartus,* is capital. T.C. would have done well to heed that criticism instead of calmly looking down on to Sterling with a peculiarly patronising expression, as much as to say, "Wait until you are older, sonny, then you'll see this thing differently."

FEB. 24—Today there was an explosion in the dynamite factory at the Maine Mill.[8] It seems that the dynamite in the vats exploded. The building covering these and the engine was utterly demolished. Large stones of a ton weight or more were thrown several hundred feet. The report was heard in all parts of the village and at Cumberland Head. I was in Dr. Lyon's office and we all thought some heavy dry goods box had been thrown over upstairs. The brick building just east was not much damaged. There are 2,000 pounds of nitroglycerin in this building, which did not explode.

FEB. 25—Today went on a special train to Mooers to attend the funeral of Dr. C. H. Bidwell. It seems that one week ago last Tuesday he went into the country two or three miles and from that place he found he must go on some ten miles farther. The day was quite warm and he had not on his usual winter coats. He did not get back home until into the night. He took a severe cold, had pericarditis with effusion, pneumonia and oedema of the lower extremities. Dr. Bidwell was a man much respected, and greatly loved by his friends.

FEB. 26—Today we got notice from the pension department that our claim for examinations for pensions for the quarter ending September 30, 1885 had been allowed. So next week probably, I shall have $201.00 apiece.[9]

Old Mr. Noel, a man of 83 years, walked with me 5 miles one morning along the Richelieu. He made his sons stay at home and work. I met also an old one-legged man, Martin by name, at St. Valentin. He told me that he lost his leg in the Papineau war.[10] I asked him if he got a pension. He shrugged his shoulder (as Frenchmen do, using the "Frenchman's muscle") and said: "No. I was with Papineau. I thought Papineau was right." That was all he got for *his* patriotism.

What Thackeray says in *Vanity Fair* about how the immediate relatives even after the funeral will do, was somewhat illustrated yesterday after Dr. Bidwell's funeral. Two of Dr. Charles' brothers were on the train. One of them sat with the doctors in one end of the car, smoked, laughed and joked, and seemed to enjoy himself. Madame Bidwell seemed anxious that her mourning apparel and false teeth should look well. Mr. and Mrs. Hall, the especial friends of the deceased, appeared cheerful and happy. The different doctors told stories, smoked and did not present any subjective symptoms of great grief. The other mourning friends showed no indications of being bowed down with sorrow.

It is better to have it so. Struggling and working remain to the living. To the departed, peace and quiet belong. It does not benefit our deceased friends to have us make great ado over them. If we can, we must in a measure forget them. Life is for the living and not for the dead. But the recollection, the recalling to mind, of our dear ones is a great comfort to us. It is thus that their influence remains with us. What it *is* as things *are* is what concerns me. That we do not know the day of our death or of the death of our friends must be considered the greatest blessing imaginable.

FEB. 27—Tonight, coming down, I imagined I could hear the frogs. That may have been a case of "telepathy," but I am more inclined to think it a case of vivid imagination. Some one has said that a person never gets to be so old that he does not expect to live to hear the birds sing at least *one* more spring.

MAR. 6—The real things of life are stranger than the imaginary. Many a thing seems terrible in the distance which, close at hand, is bravely borne. The fear of death is often greater than the real. Carlyle says, "Terrible indeed to all men is death. Rightly of old called king of terrors."[11] There seems to be an instinct in every animal which makes him love life and fear death. Yet men, when told they must die, take it calmly and look on death as an event that must come to all. "I want to get well but I'm not afraid to die" is a common expression among the sick.

MAR. 8—Read yesterday Emerson's essay on "Books." He gives a good list of good books which one should read. Just think of one getting acquainted with the *best* minds of all ages, not the ordinary "no-account" minds, but the *best*.

MAR. 9—I received notice last night of my appointment as "a corresponding member of the New England Historic Genealogical Society." Tonight I have been looking up my ancestry for the N.E.H.G.S. and find that I had a good many grandparents. The Thomas Sherwood who came to Boston in 1634 is so much my grandfather that I am afraid I shall be disrespectful to him when I address him. Just think of having to say g-g-g-g-g-g-grandfather. How hard it must be for the individual who traces his line continuously back to Adam. He would need to be a monumental stammerer. I should like a composite photograph of the whole line. I could find then where my square hands come from, also my beginning bald head and my six feet of height.

MAR. 10—It has been a busy day, especially in examining pensioners. My fingers feel as if they wouldn't write any more. A woman whom I attended today in her tenth confinement told me that she should name her baby "Enough."

MAR. 11—Bobbie, Nello and Baby Bessie have whooping cough. Bob and Bessie cough a great deal.

I received last night a letter from a cousin of my father, Harvey F. Aubrey of Brooklyn, N.Y., giving, so far as he could remember, the names of the Kelloggs and Aubreys. Mr. Aubrey himself is 82 years of age. I quote from Mr. Aubrey's letter the

Aubrey-Castle Incident

"You also wished to learn something of the family of Aubrey that you have lately come across, the same who took part in the Revolutionary War. Now all I know is what I remember my father saying that his father, John F. Aubrey, was born in France or Germany, was educated in Germany as a Surgion and Physician, came to this country early in the Revolution, that he married a Miss Woodworth.

"In 1775 my father was born, that soon after he went with the army and was taken by the Indians, and it was reported all were killed. My father was named after his father, John F. Aubrey. After awhile my father's mother married Mr. Abel Castle in Essex, my father then a little boy living with his mother and stepfather, Abel Castle.

"In about 9 or 10 years by some strategy Dr. Aubrey got clear from the Indians and made his way to find his wife and child. He heard that she was married again and was told where he could find her. The first she knew he walked in Mr. Castle's house, and there met his wife and 3 chil-

The Doctor's mother, Evalina Kellogg, in 1886 at the age of 78. She died in California in 1897

dren. My father said there was a great time, his mother fainted, Mr. Castle came in and the two husbands met. Of course no one was in fault. The whole matter was talked over, neighbors consulted and the matter was left to the wife which man to live with. She having 2 or 3 children by Castle, she decided to live with him. Whether there was any legal separation or not I can't say but presume there was.

"Dr. Aubrey went to the South part of Vermont and there married and raised a family. My father remained in Essex with the Castle family, became a carpenter by trade and farmer. He married one of the daughters of David Kellogg, sister of your Grandfather Russell Kellogg."

MAR. 20—Yesterday Bess and I called on Dr. and Mrs. Wilson, the new surgeon at the Barracks. Dr. Wilson was for part of a year in the Egyptian army. He said the first thing the Kedhive (if that is the way to spell it) did was to detail eighteen wives to him.

1886 MAR. 24—This morning news came of the death in New York of Mr. S. F. Vilas, our "richest man." It is suggestive to hear the comments made on him. One man says, "He couldn't take any of his money with him." One of his employees said, "God had blessed them by removing this old man this morning."

After all, there have been much worse men than Mr. Vilas. He is said to have done always as he agreed, but his agreements usually tended to his own benefit. It is said that when a young man peddling (that is the way he began to make his money) he used to buy a lot of little cheap whistles, ten for a cent, and give one to the school children whom he met in exchange for their dinner. He also is said to have slept often under his cart in order to save the expense of a night's lodging. He had a faculty of making things pay that he had anything to do with. He once had considerable to do with the plank road west of here. He looked after the tolls, made people pay who dodged the toll gates, and got the road stock up to where it was worth something and sold it.

Once when in business with Messrs. Crosby and Orvis, they bought a cheese together for their own individual use. They divided it into three equal parts and Mr. Crosby and Mr. Orvis each took his part home. Mr. Vilas put his piece into a drawer in the back part of the store and left it there until it was almost a nuisance from its decomposing odor. His partners asked him why he didn't take it home with him. He said, "You see, my wife's mother is at our house and she is dreadful fond of cheese. She is going away in a few days. Then I will take the cheese home."

He is said to have been accustomed to go into the kitchen and tell the servant, "When you make tea, take a little pinch every time and you will soon save enough for a whole drawing." He is said to have been in the habit of examining the milk in the pans to see if the servants were drinking any of it. One girl arranged the pans so that when he tipped one up, he spilled the whole over on to himself.

The capital stock of his bank is $100,000. He owns $95,000 of this and $1,000 more as one of the directors. It seems that he, in interest, loans and discounts, credited the bank with the *legal rates only*. The amount *above* the legal rates he kept himself, i.e. he had 96/100 of the whole anyway, but the other four directors only shared in the legal rates of profit. A government bank examiner found this out and compelled him to pay the usurious amounts taken from the other directors to these directors. This had been going on for years. He settled with three of these directors by paying them $1,000 each. The fourth one wanted more. I don't know how that has been settled, if at all.

Last fall when he hired a new man, he told him to let him know when he went out to feed the cow. Well, they took a pail full of food out from

10

the house and set it down near the cow. The bovine made a dive for it and began to eat ravenously. Mr. Vilas then began to gesticulate frantically in front of the cow and to pretend to try to drive her away from the pail. He turned to the man and said he did that "to make the cow think I am going to take the pail away. She then will keep her nose in the pail and eat and won't take it out and spill any and waste it."

MAR. 26—I saw the first robin today. He was scolding like fury. So I conclude it must have been a "lady bird."

APRIL 19—The ice went out of the broad lake Friday, April 16. The [steamer] *Williams* came to Port Kent Saturday, April 17. Monday, April 19, the steamer came to Plattsburgh for the first time. The ice is not all out yet.

APRIL 20—This morning at 12.15 o'clock I had to go out onto the State Road. I came home this morning about 5. The frogs' music was tremendous. I heard the first frog this spring April 12. This morning and today it seemed as if there were thousands making harsh, monotonous frog music.

APRIL 24—Already at 3 in the morning the robin is singing. He seems to see the "first sweet dawn of light" before it actually appears in the east. What a wonderful horoscope is his! He must have more than human knowledge to know when to begin his matin. The rooster, the artificial index of civilization which is also artificial, is bolder in his morning call than the robin. A large fire may make him sing because he thinks morning has come, but a robin cannot be deceived in that way. He may cry fear, but he knows that morning is not a burning building.

APRIL 27—I had to give evidence in court today on which a man was sentenced to prison for four years. He had struck another man a severe blow, unprovoked. To think of four years being taken out of a man's life when one at best has so few to live.

MAY 1—Bought a new cow on Thursday, April 29. She is said to be four years old. I gave $30 for her.

MAY 20—Nelson said the other day that Daniel had been eating onions and for that reason the lions wouldn't eat him. He claimed he learned that in Sabbath school, but he has a strong imagination.

MAY 21—An old man came into my office to consult me today. I asked him how old he was but he did not know. He had been given away three or four times when a child and so could not tell.

11

1886   MAY 26—The most of the street electric lights are lighted tonight for the first time.

Have finished the second volume of Part First of Count Leo Tolstoi's *War and Peace*. It really seems as if this were something new in literature. The description of the Battle of Austerlitz is especially his own. Tolstoi's philosophy in these volumes is mostly healthy.

Have also read a large part of General Grant's *Memoirs*. Grant's sayings ought to be collected and published in a separate volume. "Few events in men's lives are brought about by their own choice." "That story like many others would be good if it were only true." I quote these from memory, so they may not be accurate. Grant's estimate of men seems to have been pretty fair and just. It seems as if his nature softened and that he looked on all mankind with affection before his death. Perhaps this was only a revealing of his *real* nature.

It seems to me that all noble men, when looking over the experiences of their lives and of the lives of their fellow mortals, are inclined to be lenient toward the slippings of themselves and of their fellows. The great human heart of mankind is generous, lenient and forgiving. We may criticize General Grant's course in many ways, especially while he was President, but probably few men could have improved on him. He was a hero, as much as Washington, Lincoln, John Brown. These all would have been deified had they lived in the times when men believed in different gods on earth.

JUNE 13—A patient of mine, J. H. Lunt, died on Friday of last week. The upper entrance to his stomach was closed so that for a week he had not swallowed anything. His thirst was fearful. He would hold a tumbler of ice water in his hand, look at it and say, "Two dollars a swallow if I could only drink that. Fifty dollars if I could drink the tumblerful without hurting me." That was in reality the experience of Tantalus.

JUNE 26—Theo and Francis left for Northampton on the 17th to be present at Helen's graduation. We expect them home tonight. Mother, aged 78 last February, and Mary left their home in Spring Valley, Minnesota, the 22nd, and reached Plattsburgh the 24th. Mother does not in any manner appear tired or the worse for her journey.

JULY 2—Have read *Anna Karenina* by Tolstoi. It is a powerful book, but not good for young people. Kitty, in my opinion, is by far the best character in the book. Levin is also a good character. Anna herself didn't know her own mind and was *insane*. Tolstoi doesn't admit or insinuate even that he thinks Anna insane, but he has succeeded in portraying a type of insanity in his description of her which would have been better

12

if he had called it by its real name. It may exist in real life, i.e., his account of her resembles what occurs too often if it occurs once, even; still, her mind was diseased, unhealthy. Of course everyone must feel sorry for her. The impulse that forced her on must have been a terrible one.

Have also read the second part of *War and Peace*, i.e., "The Invasion." That follows well after "Before Tilsit." I am anxious to get more of this historical novel. I like it better, I think, than Anna Karenina. I may not always think so.

JULY 13—The medical society of Clinton County held its semiannual meeting at Lyon Mountain. We had a special train which left Plattsburgh at 10.30 a.m. and arrived home at 7.20 p.m. We got to Lyon Mountain exactly at 12 and went directly to a mine opening. Many of us went down about 200 feet. Next we returned to a public hall where the papers were read by title. We adjourned to the hotel for dinner and then all went to "Ralph's" on Chateaugay Lake. The day was delightful and everyone seemed to enjoy himself to the utmost. Twenty-four men of us rode to "Ralph's" in one long side-seated wagon. Our combined weight was 3,990 pounds. At every attempt on the part of the horses to trot there was a lurch of the wagon to one side or the other which made it seem as if we should all spill out, but we didn't.

JULY 31—Have finished Tolstoi's *War and Peace*, Part III, Vol. 2. It makes me feel awed, so much power and strength are displayed. Prof. George H. Perkins made me a flying trip yesterday.[12] It is agreeable to meet a gentleman who is real and not shoddy.

AUG. 9—At the last commencement of the University of Vermont at Burlington, at the alumni meeting, steps were taken toward getting a fund among the alumni for the college library.[13] I, J. E. Goodrich and Elihu B. Taft were appointed a committee to bring the matter to the alumni. We have had a circular letter printed and today I have mailed 402 of these letters. Last Thursday I sent out 50, making in all to date 452. I hope they will be productive of much money to the fund, but fear they won't.

AUG. 16—Last Friday Bess and I took the cars for Crown Point. We went to Mr. Viall's hotel at Crown Point village and after an excellent dinner we took a horse and buggy to the site of the remains of the old forts at the north end of Crown Point. We visited three distinct forts and saw at least one cluster of earthworks which we did not visit.

It seems that Fort St. Frederick was on the most northerly part of this point. Peter Kalm says of this fort: "The English call this fortress Crown Point, but its French name is derived from the French Secretary of State, Frédéric Maurepas, in whose hands the direction and management of the

French court of Admiralty was at the time of the erection of this fort." Fort St. Frederick now is a mass of ruins. The outlines are still plainly visible. The stone and earth walls are large, and still it is the scene of desolation.[14]

The 12th of August, 1759, the English under General Amherst began to build another fort south by west of this and within a few rods of it. This fort is in an excellent state of preservation. Inside are the remains of three large stone barracks, one of which is wonderfully preserved. This one stands two stories high, with five large chimneys quite perfect. This barrack I estimate to be about 150 feet long and 25 feet wide.

The second barrack is similar to the first, but smaller. The third one is almost wholly gone. It is said that some fifteen years ago, while building a kind of dock for a railroad, this barrack was demolished, the stone being used for filling in. Thus do modern barbarians continue the work of ancient vandals. To the southwest of this fort is seen a high mountain, which is probably the one Major Robert Rogers ascended when he looked down into the old fort and saw what the enemy was doing.

We did not have time to examine the works on the eastern shore south of St. Frederick, where the old windmill stood. A family living near the forts had a large number of relics from their vicinity, such as nails, spoons, keys, bullets, one cannon ball. They also had two iron supports said to have been used on the boots while walking on the ice, like the following.

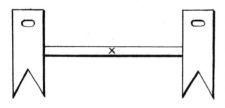

This represents the irons said to have been used by the soldiers while walking on ice. The horizontal piece X the sole rested on. The four lowest points stuck into the ice. The two holes in the end pieces were supposed to contain a cord fastened over the top of the boot.

We got back to Viall's about 8.30 p.m., where we had a capital supper. After breakfast we took the conveyance to the depot and went on a train to Fort Ti. We went down the track and found along the margin of the lake an immense quantity of flint that had been brought there by Indians. We found perhaps 15 hammer stones and nearly 100 arrow and spear points and knives, all made of the flint which occurs so abundantly in nodules in the limestone from Ti to Crown Point. This flint is mostly dark.

Later on we went over to the extreme southeast angle of the promontory, between the outlet of Lake George and Lake Champlain. We found some good spearheads and arrow points and other stone relics but pretty soon we fell in with a couple of modern specimens in the shape of small boys with a boat. When they found I was looking for arrow points, they said,

"We can jist shovel 'em right up over there on that point where the cattle are," pointing across the river to Wright's Point. I tried to make a bargain with them to row me over, but after consulting together they concluded to let me name my own price. I told them I would give them fifty cents, which seemed ample. The arrow points and other stone relics *were* plentiful on Wright's Point.

We took the steamer *Vermont* at 2 p.m. for Burlington. The next day Bessie, I and Bob, who had been with his grandmother, Mrs. Smith, came home on the steamer *A. Williams.* Our whole trip cost us a little more than $21.

SEPT. 7—This evening I spent an hour with Dr. Cleveland of the Poughkeepsie Insane Asylum. He and three or four other men are a committee appointed by the Governor of New York to examine different sites for a new Insane Asylum to report to the next legislature. We hope the new asylum will come here, but are uncertain about it as yet. Ogdensburg also wants the asylum. These commissioners were at the Fouquet House. Yesterday they were taken around by citizens and shown the various sites in this vicinity. They seemed to be quite favorably impressed.[15]

SEPT. 9—Helen S. Kyle, my niece who was graduated from Smith College last June, left Tuesday of this week to teach in Miss Cram's school in Burlington, Vermont.

SEPT. 14—Saturday evening Bess, Bob and I started for St. Johns [St. Jean, Quebec]. We got to the St. Johns Hotel about 10. The next day, Sunday, it rained nearly all day. Bob and I, however, took a walk in the rain and visited some old forts made of earth just south of the village on the Richelieu. We could not learn when these works were made, but probably they have been made over by various armies in various wars.[16]

Yesterday, September 13, we visited Chambly. Alexander Bertrand, U.S. Consul to St. Johns, was with us. We went down to Chambly on the east side. We saw the eel traps, which are walls of stone in the shallow rapids of the Richelieu, V-shaped. At the extremities of the angles of the V's were boxes into which the eels passed on their route from Lake Champlain to the sea. The boxes were taken up every morning and were emptied of about 10 barrels of eels daily. These are sent chiefly to Saratoga, where they are called "Richelieu trout." Certain persons have the exclusive right to take eels in this place in this manner. They pay their government a considerable sum for the privilege. I was told by Mr. Bertrand that the government survey showed that there was a fall of only five inches on the Richelieu between Rouses Point and St. Johns. The fall between St. Johns and Chambly must be more than 90 feet.

1886 We crossed the bridge at Chambly and went directly to the old fort. Fortunately the fort stands in many respects as formerly. "The Government" has made an appropriation of $5,000 for the preservation of this noble and interesting historic building. The south, west and north walls have been put into shape like their original, I suppose. The eastern wall is not yet completed.[17] M. Joseph O. Dion, our very polite and intelligent director whom we met at the fort, told us that formerly there was a plateau extending eastward from the fort 80 feet to the river. Now the river runs close to the base of the eastern wall.

In the northeast part of the fort we were shown what was formerly a dark, small enclosure. In this place, it is said, prisoners in the Papineau War, 1837–38, were crowded. Mr. Bertrand said his grandfather was confined there. The English soldiers burned his house and barn and destroyed all his property, as if it had been the lair of a wild beast.

A little toward the northwest, a few rods from the fort, is the old cemetery in which were buried the soldiers and some Americans. M. Dion had found the names of some of them in the register and had them painted in black on white boards. One was an American General Thomas who, I believe, died there of smallpox in 1776.[18] M. Dion wanted Bessie to plant a willow in the fort, which she did. M. Dion said he hoped to have a monument in the yard to the memory of the dead soldiers. Not much earth could be taken up which does not contain human bones, M. Dion said.

Thomas Heffernan of Plattsburgh told me that on the night of the 3rd of July 1855 he climbed the old flagstaff in Chambly fort and nailed the American flag onto the staff. They had to shoot down the flag the next day, as no one dared climb it. A reward of ten dollars was offered the next day for the apprehension of the one who put up the flag, but no one got the reward.

SEPT. 22—It is fair time, the first time the new fairgrounds on Boynton's farm have been used. John Martin and I put in two large cases of Indian relics. The Plattsburgh *Telegram* with its usual brilliancy speaks of them as *"Indian Relicts."*

SEPT. 24—A letter from Prof. J. E. Goodrich tells me that he has purchased from Houghton, Mifflin & Company $500 worth of books. I suppose this may in part be attributed to the efforts in regard to the Alumni Library Fund. I sent out in all 525 circulars to alumni.

OCT. 1—Our hired girl, Mary Knowles, left us today to be married. She has lived with us since December 11, 1882. I have paid her in all $588, of which $6 was interest. She lost only 30 days' time and that was while her father was sick. She was a good, faithful woman in all respects and earned every cent of the wages I paid her.

16

OCT. 5—Five years ago today I made my first discovery of relics at the mouth of the Big Chazy River. Mr. John E. Hyde and I visited the mouth of the Little Chazy and followed along the coast for some distance. We found an occasional chipping, which abundantly satisfied me. At length we found some broken arrow points. But after getting to the mouth of the Big Chazy, what a sight met me. There, on both sides of the river were more relics than I had ever found at one time or place before. Arrow points, spearheads, axes, hammers, cores, one fine perforated tablet and all the stone remains of an Indian village. I never experienced greater genuine pleasure.

The wind blew from the northwest terrifically. This blew the water off-shore and so made more relics appear. A little before dark the wind went down and the water returned and was at least four inches deep where before it was dry. We hunted till it was so dark we could not distinguish a stone from a stick and then gave up. I visited the same place several times that fall and afterwards and found many hundreds of stone implements and weapons. The ground at the mouth of the Big Chazy is mostly clay. As there is very little sea there and still some current from the river, the earth has gradually disintegrated, allowing the stones to drop down and remain and not be washed away.

OCT. 7—A report published in the *Morning Telegram* today stated that some divers from Boston were at Port Jackson, and were going immediately to work to investigate the *Royal Savage*, Arnold's boat sunk near Valcour Island in October 1776. I communicated with John Martin at the Customs House and he thought nothing could be done. However, the United States law was very clear on that subject, the penalty being imprisonment and a fine of not over $5,000. So Emmet Armstrong and I, John Martin and Charles H. Spear, both deputies from the Customs House, John Henry Myers and Colonel George F. Nichols started for Valcour. The deputies went by order of William Reed, collector of customs at this port.

There was one diver and he was then partly in his diving apparatus. He had on a covering continuously over his body and extremities as far up as his neck. Around his neck was a kind of iron band. Over his whole garment the diver put something like pants and frock and also he put on mittens and heavy shoes weighted with iron. Then his copper headpiece, something like a large iron kettle with glass on four sides, was fastened on to the iron neck piece. To this headpiece was fastened a rubber tube not unlike inch garden hose, which was fastened to an air pump on the scow. As soon as the headpiece was fastened on, the men began to pump and immediately the diving garment began to swell out on all sides. After this was full, with two ropes in his hands—one for signal and one for tying around any material he might get hold of—he was let down into the water with a rush. The pump was kept constantly in motion while he was under water, and we could easily trace his path by the bubbling of air to the surface. He was then in about 35 feet of water.

While we were at the house for lunch the men rowed their scow up south, where the remains of the *Royal Savage* lie. We followed them after lunch and saw the diver bring up what was probably a piece of a gun carriage. Then we rowed alongside and Mr. Martin asked who was in charge of that expedition. One of the strangers said that Captain Duncan, the diver, was. Then Mr. Martin told him he was sent there by the Collector of this district, that that was United States property he was handling, and read the law on the subject to him, warned him to desist and not take any of it away with him. The diver said he had had a good deal to do with the United States, that he had been in the business a good while. After some further conversation we pulled away. The strangers on the scow had said they were getting these things to sell, that they were not sent by any society, that some people would pay a large price for these relics. I hope they will not return. He only got a few pieces of timber, some shot and a spoon.

OCT. 21—Those men who plundered the *Royal Savage* are said to have returned again for plunder on two different nights. The U.S. District Attorney, Hon. Martin I. Townshend, has been instructed to take the matter in hand and to proceed against these fellows. He has telegraphed Assistant U.S. District Attorney William V. S. Woodward, who happened to be in town, to make investigations. Witnesses will be subpoenaed to the United States Court in Auburn the last week in November, and Captain Duncan will probably be indicted.

OCT. 26—Went to Rand Hill this morning, starting about 4.45 a.m. A man came for me, Mr. Darius Whitman, at 4.20 a.m. He had on a buffalo coat. I harnessed Fly, having put on my overcoat, rubber coat and mittens. It was exceedingly dark but I had my lantern under the wagon. Almost every step of the way was uphill. When I got to Mr. Whitman's at 7, there was about an inch of snow on the ground and it was daylight. I remained there about an hour.

On my return my view of Lake Champlain was grand. Although cloudy and stormy in places, I could see from Trembleau Mountain at Port Kent to Wool's Point on the North. I also could see five different white long rolls of smoke from as many locomotive engines. Two on the Dannemora Railroad, one on the Ausable, one towards Port Kent and one in Beekmantown.

18

OCT. 29—Tonight Nello fell and cut himself badly in the center and upper part of his forehead. The gash was 1½ inches long, horizontal, just at the edge of the hair. I had to sew it up. He was very brave about it. After he found I really had to hurt him he did not put his hands up at all, but held them down very bravely.

I went up to call on Mr. John Bailey this afternoon and to get from him some personal reminiscences of Plattsburgh in early times. His recollections are exceedingly interesting and valuable.

"My grandfather, Captain Platt [Mr. Bailey recalled], raised the first company of soldiers on Long Island for the Revolution. He lived on Long Island for the Revolution and afterwards moved to Poughkeepsie. He brought a family of Negro slaves to Plattsburgh about 1790. One of the female slaves was given to Mrs. Benjamin Mooers. Another female, called Isobel, was given to my mother. There were also slaves in other families in Plattsburgh. A law was passed freeing the slaves gradually (*1799*). Isobel was given her freedom before her time was out, because she was so much excited about being a free woman that we thought it better to hire our work done than to try to get the work out of her. Her daughter Rose, who was about my age, married Azel Soper and was for years cook at the Cumberland House. Isobel was very black, but Rose was half white.

"Hazen Mooers, a nephew of General Benjamin Mooers, kept a grocery store near the Barracks. The Barracks were then wooden buildings, opposite the fort at the bend of the river. An order came from the commanding general that no spiritous liquors should be sold within half a mile of the Barracks. One day a colonel, whose name I forget, came down and accused Hazen Mooers of selling his soldiers liquors: 'I think you've been selling my soldiers rum. You sell my soldiers rum—they get drunk—we catch 'em—we shoot 'em. *You are guilty of murder, by God, sir!*'

"I remember when James Monroe, President of the United States, was in Plattsburgh in 1817. He was given dinner on the turnpike, I think near where the east branch of the Chazy River crosses the turnpike, 15 or 16 miles from here. I remember seeing General Wool here in this house on a visit several times between 1845 and 1850, after the Mexican War, I think. He was the artillery officer here in 1814—Major Wool—who advanced and met the British at Culver Hill in Beekmantown. He retreated and made stands along in various places. The last stand was at the corner of the road south of the late Zephaniah Platt's, where it meets Boynton's Lane. Major Wool couldn't have fired more than two or three charges at most for the enemy was right upon him. I have seen General Scott here on reviews, in 1847, I think (*1848?*). I saw him with his adjutant, Colonel Robert E. Lee, at Fouquet's.

"One of Judge Zephaniah Platt's daughters married Peter Brinkerhoff of New York City. She gave the site for the Academy, and Brinkerhoff Street was named for her. Margaret Street was named after Margaret Smith. Cornelia Street was named after Cornelia Smith, a sister of Margaret. Cornelia married "Jack" Bleecker. He was the black sheep of the family. He was a wonderful man in everything excepting being a good man. He was better at a game of cards than he was at a Bible lesson."

NOV. 2—Election Day. I suppose that never before was so much money used here to buy voters with. Votes sold for from five to twenty dollars. As the Democrats had the most money their entire county ticket was elected. Mr. Smith M. Weed had his son, George S. Weed, elected member of Assembly. It is said Mr. Weed spent $30,000 out of his own pocket. It is said the Republicans sent enough money into Peru to give every voter in that town ten dollars apiece, and into Champlain to give every voter in that town six dollars apiece. It was most shameful. Men who were worth good farms took ten dollars for their votes. The Republicans are said to have spent $1,800 in buying votes in the single district over the river, and the Democrats in the same district over $3,600.

NOV. 5—Today my wife and I took a horse and buggy and drove to Champlain to see Mr. Moses Mooers, aged 92. Mrs. Mooers, his wife, was born January 4, 1800, and both had vivid recollections of the early part of this century, which I took down in writing. Mr. Mooers seemed pretty vigorous for a man of his years. He had a very perceptible cataract in his right eye, and walked with a cane. His wife is bent nearly double from a curvature of the spine.

"My name is Moses Mooers [he opened the interview]. I was born in Haverhill, New Hampshire, July 15, 1794. My father's name was Moses Hazen Mooers. He was a brother of General Benjamin Mooers. My father came to Point au Roche from New Hampshire when it was a howling wilderness of wolves about here, somewhere about the year 1800. I have lived on this place 70 years, having come here in 1816. I married Catherine Shute in Champlain February 22, 1820.

"We both remember the Battle of Plattsburgh very distinctly. The British went on the direct road through East Chazy to Plattsburgh. In the first place they sent out Indians and Voltigeurs to explore the route. When they came out I was at my brother's about one and a half miles south of here on this road. He had taken his place of old General Benjamin Mooers and kept bachelor's hall. He had one cow and a lot of milk in pans. These Indians and Voltigeurs came in and drank out of the pans all the milk they wanted. They impressed me and my horse to show them the way. The road was filled with trees, and they were mad at me because they thought I had misled them, but I hadn't. A lieutenant rode my horse. He was very gentlemanly and gave it back to me, and fifty cents for my services. This was perhaps a week before the battle. I had gone about three miles south with them, and they all came back with me.

"(By Mrs. M.) Before the British came in, the Indians went down the Champlain River and destroyed all the canoes and boats there. The Voltigeurs were awful looking creatures. They had some kind of leather caps, with cows' tails fastened on to them behind. Their chins were smooth, but they had beards across their faces on a line with their mustaches.

"(By Mr. M.) Before the British came, we heard so much talk about the Indians coming that a company was raised and put up north in Champlain on guard. I was one of them.

"The rolling of the British cannon and ammunition wagons made a noise like distant thunder. When they went back in the night there was the same noise. It had rained and the road to Plattsburgh was a bed of mud a foot deep. I started for the battle, but when I got as far as Point au Roche I heard the battle was over. We both heard the cannon distinctly at the time of the battle. I have the idea that they did not have so many cannon when they went back as when they went out. I suppose there were cannon sunk in Dead Creek. I think the British came back both the roads they went out in. They came back in a hurry.

"(By Mrs. M.) You don't know what rejoicing there was among the inhabitants of this town after the British had gone back. We heard the Indians were coming and would do worse than ever. We heard that when the people on Cumberland Head saw the British retreating they shouted and blew horns and showed signs of rejoicing so much that the British fired a cannon at them.

"Many of the British deserted. Some to my father's, William Shute's. They had laid in the woods and stayed until the British had retreated. Some were Irish. One of them was the first Irishman I ever saw. A company at or near Plattsburgh is said to have tried to desert in a body, but our soldiers misunderstood them and fired into them. After a time they came down and laid their guns down flat on the edge of the river. Then our men understood them and did not fire. One of the deserters told us that we were a different people from what they supposed us to be. They had been told they were going to fight the 'heathen Yankees'. When they got here they found that we talked just as they did. They said we were their own brothers and sisters. One said he had an uncle in Philadelphia."

NOV. 12—Today there was a serious fire in Baker's planing mill. The north upright part was all on fire inside. Their whistle blew and immediately the fire alarm sounded. The hose carts were drawn down through the mud by horses, the men sitting in a wagon and holding on to the ropes.

NOV. 13—I attended my German recitation today. I wonder if I shall ever be able to learn German well.

NOV. 18—I was with Mr. Steven D. Boynton last night when he died. He lay breathing heavily, but a little after eleven there was a change. I held my finger on his pulse for about three minutes at the last. His heart seemed suddenly to beat slowly and more slowly like a wheel stopping. The pulse hesitated for a minute as if uncertain whether to stop or go on, as if it were surprised and amazed at the prospect of so great a change. Slowly it vibrated, then seemed entirely gone, but returned again for a few more feeble strokes, after which it was at rest forever.

I could not see what left him, to make so wonderful a transformation. In his external physical appearance there was no apparent difference. His bones, his muscles, his entire body were there, the same, but something had left him, something invisible which had produced a mighty difference. He was no more the same than water is the same as stone, than darkness is the same as light. Mystery of mysteries, the end of life is as marvelous as the beginning. Both are forever unknowable.

DEC. 20—Theo and I went to hear Mr. Hall preach at his—the Peristrome Presbyterian—church.[19] It was a sermon to the young men of the Railroad Association. Some of his expressions are the following:

"Young men might do well to deport themselves in a kindred atmosphere." "Superb specimen of the supremely sublime." "Affected a faultless fulfillment." "Plucked from the wrath of this sinister league." In spite of all such as this, however, Mr. Hall is a most admirable man in all places excepting in the pulpit.

The electric light apparatus is now so arranged that it can be run by a steam engine in case there is not water enough or if the anchor ice[20] runs too much. This change was completed so that the engine could be used for the first time last Saturday night.

I recovered my "King's Arm" one week ago yesterday. I bought it six years ago of the General Couch estate for two dollars. Since then it has been in the possession of Mr. Armstrong or his son. This flintlock musket was carried by Sergeant Samuel Couch at the Battle of Lundy's Lane in 1813. My old sabres of the War of 1812 are now three in number. I hope to get more in time.[21]

DEC. 26—Yesterday was Christmas and a merry one with the children and also with the grown-up people. Bob and Nello and Baby Bessie "got just what they wanted." Santa Claus brought me a nice large rosewood armchair, Volume II of *Diary and Letters of Thomas Hutchinson,* and some

A view of Brinkerhoff Street as seen from the Doctor's office window. From there he noted numerous human incidents in the passing scene.

other things. I got for Bessie on her thirty sixth birthday, December 18, Professor Morse's book on Japanese homes. Also for myself the four volumes of Motley's *United Netherlands*, which I am now reading.

I saw one day last week a funny sight on the street. A little man, one cool morning, was walking along rapidly, followed by his four little children, hand in hand and two by two, with the father in front in the center. The children were talking among themselves and gobbling in an excited manner. The little shavers had to run and be pulled along in order to keep up. Their faces were all interest and smiles. They all were utterly oblivious of the presence and apparently of the existence of any other human beings than those in their own company. A happier family I never saw, and the cause of their happiness was evident. Their father had a *real live turkey with feathers on,* which he was taking home for Christmas in his arms.

DEC. 28—Went to Pointe au Roche again today and also to Ingraham's. At Ingraham's I visited Mr. Simeon Doty, who was born in Hoboken, New Jersey, July 15, 1797. His recollections of the old times were pretty fair. He helped to bury the dead on Isle St. Michel (Crab Island) after the battle in 1814.

"At the time of the battle of Plattsburgh [said Mr. Doty] I was in Captain Joseph Hazen's company and in North Hero. Our captain went over first on Sunday and we could not go then. We went over on Monday. On our way we saw the fleet. We went to Crab Island. I helped

23

bury the dead there. They were broken up and smashed up a great deal. I went on to the fleet in a skiff. I saw the British Commodore, his aide and his *Miss*, all dead. The colors were laid over them. The decks were not cleared off but were bloody. My brother fainted when he saw the blood and the dead.

"A rooster is said to have crowed on one of our boats about the time the British struck their colors. The cannon roared like thunder all of the time. They fired terribly fast. Spring cables were used to turn the vessels round with. The vessels were anchored at each end and when they fired from one side they "sprung" the vessels round and fired from the other side, which was already loaded. Macdonough laid still when the British came around Cumberland Head, and didn't fire on them at first. We had shorter 18-pounders than they did. They might just as well as not have anchored at a distance and fired on us outside our range, but they bore right down on us."

Just now a brass band is playing on the street. The men's mouths must be cold. Now an outsider strikes in with a shrill whistle and whistles the tune the band is playing. The bell of the First Presbyterian Church now chimes, the heavy Witherill House coach passes at the same time, so there is a combination of sound.

DEC. 31—Helen had a whist party last night at the house, which I entirely disapprove of. It is a senseless, useless way of spending time and for which one does not get any valuable equivalent.

Tonight the French people get drunk. All the whiskey used tonight would pay a large portion of our taxes, and yet we are taxed so this whiskey can be sold.

Notes on 1886

1. From Robert Burns' "Tam O'Shanter."

2. Smith M. Weed, wealthy Plattsburgh businessman, political leader and U.S. Commissioner for the Northern District of New York. Caroline Standish Weed was a descendant of Miles Standish.

3. Peter Esprit Radisson (1620?–1710). *Voyages of Peter Esprit Radisson* is an account of his travels and experiences among the North American Indians between 1652 and 1684.

4. This military site, named for its famous commander, the western explorer Zebulon Pike, was about a mile and a half up the Saranac River. It was burned during Murray's Raid in 1813 and never rebuilt. The illness and numerous deaths resulted from a lack of shelter until Christmas, 1812.

5. James M. Hadden (d. 1817), *Hadden's Journal and Orderly Books*, is the account by a member of the British Royal Artillery of his military service in Canada, the battle of Valcour and Burgoyne's campaign during 1776 and 1777.

6. In the battle of Valcour Island and the subsequent pursuit, Benedict Arnold lost

nearly his entire fleet, but by challenging the British for control of Lake Champlain,
postponed a British campaign in the valley during 1776.

7. Hawthorne discovered this epitaph in a Leamington churchyard and recorded it in *Our Old Home.*

8. The Clinton Powder Works was located near the Saranac River about two miles from the center of town.

9. Dr. Kellogg was one of the three Board of Examining Surgeons who examined Civil War veterans from a wide area and certified that their disabilities merited pensions.

10. Louis Joseph Papineau (1786–1871), a Canadian politician and a leader in 1837 of the abortive rebellion against British rule. French Canadians referred to it as the "Papineau War" although it involved English leaders and the English parts of Canada as well.

11. Used by Carlyle in his *French Revolution.* He found "king of terrors" in Job XVIII, 14.

12. Professor of Geology and for many years Dean of the College of Arts and Science at the University of Vermont.

13. This refers to the University of Vermont, of which the Doctor was an alumnus of 1870 and 1873 (medical).

14. Kalm is undoubtedly correct. The French, who usually placed "Saint" before their place names, built Fort St. Frederic in 1731 during their rivalry with the British for control of North America. They destroyed it upon the approach of General Jeffrey Amherst in 1759. Fort Amherst was partially destroyed by fire in 1773.

15. The five-man committee twice visited Plattsburgh, and recommended it to the state legislature as the site of the asylum. However, the legislature overruled the committee and voted for Ogdensburg in the spring of 1887.

16. The fort figured prominently in the campaigns of the American Revolution. In 1775 it held out for 45 days against General Richard Montgomery.

17. Fort Chambly National Historic Park, Quebec, now contains the partially restored fort. A fort has stood on the spot since 1665. The walls of the present structure date from about 1710. Burned by the Americans in 1776, it was repaired in the following year by Sir Guy Carleton, and served the British during the rest of the Revolution and the War of 1812.

18. General John Thomas was sent by Washington to take command of the American army that had been besieging Quebec during the winter of 1775–76. British reinforcements caused his retreat, his army contracted smallpox, and he died during the retreat. His grave has since been marked by the Daughters of the American Revolution.

19. Rev. Francis B. Hall (1822–1903) was a winner of the Congressional Medal of Honor in the Civil War. Marrying the only descendant of Henri Delord, Frances Webb, he lived in the home now known as the Kent-Delord house in Plattsburgh. In 1864 he helped organize the Peristrome Presbyterian church, a splinter group from the First Presbyterian, to which it was reunited at the end of Mr. Hall's pastorate in 1903.

20. Small pieces of ice which, in quantity, could clog the machinery used for producing electricity.

21. Dr. Kellogg eventually collected many muskets, sabers, powder horns and cannon balls from various wars. After the death of Mrs. Kellogg his son loaned them to the Plattsburgh Normal School, where they were lost when the school burned in 1929.

1887

Plattsburgh's volatile dynamite factory blows up again, and the Doctor races to the scene, only to have to retreat because of possible further explosions. The company moved away from Plattsburgh, to the great relief of local residents. Fires, too, especially a fatal one at the Cumberland House, introduce tense drama into his crowded days. He worries as much as any non-medical father would when "loving little boy Nelson" comes down with scarlet fever. But the year brings the Doctor thoroughly happy meetings of his literary club, at one of which the members read aloud the various roles of Julius Caesar. *He goes to New York City for a meeting of the American Association for the Advancement of Science, but can't stay long enough to read his scheduled paper. Back home, his scientific curiosity prompts him to weigh his horse, Fly, before and after drinking, and report with interest that thirsty Fly gulped down twenty-five pounds of water.*

The Doctor makes a rhyming translation of Goethe's The King in Thule *with which to entertain the children at Thanksgiving. At the end of the year, as the family whispers Christmas secrets, he counts up contentedly and records the fact that he has brought sixty-seven babies into the world and collected just over twenty-five hundred dollars from "a large practice."*

JAN. 8—This is the time of year when bills come and go. I hope more will go than come, and I think there will.

A small literary club is to meet at Reverend Mr. Gamble's next Monday evening to consider what to read and when to read it.

JAN. 12—Yesterday was another explosion of the dynamite factory here in town. It exploded February 24, 1886, but had been rebuilt in nearly the

26

same place, only a little farther to the south. That made it a little farther around the hill and so, safer for the village. It was a louder and more severe explosion than the one last February.

This explosion took place a little before 9 o'clock in the morning. I was sitting in my sleigh on Brinkerhoff Street, talking with John Martin. We drove rapidly and were the second sleigh to get on to the ice of the river near the scene of the explosion. We saw some men at the pulp mill who told us that nobody was hurt, that the building had gotten on fire and the men had left it for a place of safety, knowing that there would be an explosion. We drove onto the ice and towards the debris, but were told that there might be another explosion, and soon we retreated. I saw the large crater where the dynamite was. After we turned to come back we met a large crowd of men and horses on the ice and on the shore. We told them of the danger and most of them came back.

When we got back to the village we looked to see what damage was done here. Much glass was broken. At our house, the stovepipe from the kitchen stove to the kitchen chimney was pushed out of the chimney, but no damage was done. Many people describe their impressions to have been that the explosion was in their own cellar.[1]

Yesterday also was the annual meeting of the Clinton County Medical Society. I read abridged accounts of Dr. Nathan Carver and Dr. Silas Goodrich, the first physicians in Chazy and Peru respectively. The meeting was well attended and the exercises were very interesting. Between twenty and twenty-five physicians were present.

JAN. 17—The chimney in Joseph Bird's building, two stores south of my office, has just burned out. The fire blazed and roared like a furnace. I put three bags of fine salt into as many different pipe holes. Others put salt into the stoves and other pipe holes. Water was also poured into the top of the chimney and also into some of the pipe holes. In about twenty minutes the fire was all out. If those two stores had burned this block might have burned too. There was a large quantity of combustible material in both buildings. I think two winters ago this same chimney burned out.

JAN. 18—Last night our literary club met at our house. This was the first meeting for reading. We read considerable of *Julius Caesar*. Mr. Corbin's rendering of Caesar's part was grand. The regulation refreshments of sandwiches, cake and coffee were served. The club dissolved at ten o'clock. To me it was an exceedingly enjoyable evening.

JAN. 28—Mr. William S. Ketchum of the Plattsburgh Dock Company tells me that last summer an English man and woman, evidently recently married, were waiting at the Dock here for a steamboat. In conversation with Mr. Ketchum about the various points of interest around Plattsburgh, Mr. K. told them that "the battle of Plattsburgh was fought out there," pointing out toward the actual site of the battle. "Indeed," said the Englishman, "*I had no idea the Confederates got so far north as that.*" The man was really in earnest and Mr. Ketchum did not try to enlighten him.

FEB. 8—Bessie has been having a severe attack of sore throat, like a tonsillitis. She has been sicker than I have ever known her to be before, but is better this morning.

MAR. 2—On Monday of this week our loving little boy Nelson was taken with scarlet fever. He had no sore throat and no rash on Monday, but only vomited a few times, slept and was tired. Yesterday morning his body was covered with an eruption that has become general today. He seems to be doing well, but is tired. His sixth birthday is next Sunday. He was to have had a little party on Saturday and didn't "know whether to go round and ask them or send regrets." He had taken "regrets" for his mother to some places during the winter.

I telegraphed to Mrs. Smith, who came over yesterday. Fortunately she got through in one day. Theo is staying at Gertie Barker's but on Saturday is going to stay at Mr. J. H. Myers'. Francis, Robert and Baby Bessie are at the house. Nello is sick upstairs away from the others, but I expect Robert and Bessie will have this terrible disease. If they live through it and come out whole I shall be thankful.

MAR. 3—The other day I was talking with an elderly Frenchman who, when a boy, lived in Canada. He said that at their funerals they had almost no expense. A few rough boards were nailed together for a coffin. The body was wrapped up in a sheet and put into this rough box and carried to the chapel and left there, if the priest was not present. When the priest did come and had time, the sexton would tell him that there was to be a funeral. Then he (the priest) would perform the religious ceremonies without sending for the relatives and have the sexton dig the grave and bury the body. Often the sexton would call a man who was ploughing in a field near by, or get some one passing to help him carry the body to the grave. "Twenty four coppers would bury a man then," said he, "but now and here it is all changed. They want twenty five dollars for every funeral."

MAR. 4—The dear fellow seems better today, with less fever. Of course in the afternoon his temperature increases. Then we feel more anxious about him. I should like to know what is before us for the next four weeks, if the future is favorable. If not favorable I do not want to know it. Let the "evil day" be as far away as possible both in fact and in knowledge of it. When it comes then it will be hard enough to bear.

MAR. 8—Nello was restless and feverish last night. He breathes loudly and tosses considerably, or did last night. This evening he is breathing much better, is cooler and I hope for a favorable change. There seem to be no more symptoms of meningitis tonight than last night. In fact, I think there are fewer.

This forenoon I drove up to West Plattsburgh. Sunday it snowed and drifted terribly. The plank road was badly drifted. At George Guynup's a big load of mill wood had been upset and at least twelve men from the detained teams behind were helping reload this wood. I had to drive out into the fields to get past them. On my way back one, or perhaps the same one, of these large loads of mill wood had tipped over near John Butler's at the Reservoir, and I had to go around through John's fields and barns to get past.

MAR. 9—A pensioner today, a Frenchman, wanted to speak of an assistant surgeon in the army and called him "a secondhand doctor."

MAR. 13—This morning Nelson had no fever whatever. He had a good night last night and has a good day today. He ate a piece of buttered toast less than two inches square for dinner, which is the first solid food he has swallowed since he was taken sick.

There was an auction sale of seized smuggled goods at the custom house this afternoon. Some oats, horses and sleds were sold. There were several hundred men present at the sale. As usual, the things sold brought more than the regular market price.[2]

MAR. 16—I went out to the County House in Beekmantown yesterday to see an old man, an inmate of the County House. He was once the owner of considerable property. He is over 80 years of age. He paid me three dollars for my visit. It seems hard for one to spend his last days in a cheerless pauper's home. Of course his wants, as far as food and clothes are concerned, are all supplied. But to be away from all relatives and friends, from home and the enjoyments of home, to end one's life in such desolation, make the following seem real:

"Through me is the way into the doleful city; through me the way into the eternal pain; through me the way among the people lost. Justice moved my high Maker; Divine Power made me. Wisdom Supreme, and Primal Love. Before me were no things created, but eternal; and eternal I endure. Leave all hope, ye that enter." *Inferno*, Canto III, 1–9.

MAR. 22—Went to the Island[3] today and last Sunday to see Dr. Charles W. Petty, who is quite sick. Bob went with me. The road was bushed out

1887 [i.e., its location across the ice was marked by the bushes inserted along-side it] and most of the way we could see ahead only three bushes. There are about 75 bushes between Plattsburgh and the Island.

This morning about 5 o'clock I heard a concert of crows. They were evidently near the old fair ground. I presume they were talking about the coming storm which had not then arrived. At any rate, it must have been some important question.

MAR. 24—Theo, who has been at Mr. Myers' and has not been exposed from the house, is sick this morning. I don't know that she has scarlet fever.

MAR. 31—Theo proved to have the mumps. Nelson continues to improve.

APR. 7—Went to the Settlement across the plains today in a wagon. The Salmon River has raised up in the center of its channel its winter burden of ice. It looked as if some long animal were raising himself from his winter bed and coming out of the ground back first. I suppose his head is yet buried in Lake Champlain and his tail, many times bifurcated, is gradually emerging through the streams in Schuyler Falls.

A spring ice-jam on the Saranac River at Plattsburgh. Dynamiting was usually required to avoid damages such as this picture portrays.

APR. 11—This morning the river is much higher than last night. The water is nearly up to the railroad bridge near Mr. Weed's. About noon today they used dynamite to break out the ice below the railroad bridge. The last charge that I saw fired threw up a large column of water and ice and caused a loosening of the gorge and a rapid lessening of the accumulated water.

This morning I saw a little, stubby, fierce old woman, bareheaded, with

30

dress reaching to her ankles, come out of a house on the Maine Mill street and look fiercely and slyly around in different directions. Pretty soon the object sought, a truant pig, came within range of her vision. She went for that pig with a stick in her hand as the traditional woman goes for her boy with a slipper. Her voice was small and thin like a child's, and she was "going to larn you not to go away," "I'll teach ye not to do so," and so on. If his pigship doesn't do better in future it won't be because he hasn't had good instruction.

APR. 16—Our sleighing ended Monday, April 4, making us in all this season 118 days of sleighing, as follows: November, 10 days; December, 14 days; January, 31 days; February, 28 days; March, 31 days; April, 4 days.

APR. 23—Have been rereading *War and Peace*. It is more wonderful than ever to me. I am also translating "Band XIX. Heft 1. Mitteilungen der Antiquarischen Gesellschaft in Zurich." It is very interesting. It is humiliating to me that people know so much more than I do. While I am unable to identify, positively, even a deer's tooth, Herr Merk identified from this cave in Thayngen bones of numerous extinct as well as *extant* animals, even though he found only fragments of some of them.[4]

APR. 28—Last Sunday the pastor of the Peristrome Presbyterian Church engaged in a foot race. It seems that one small boy, Guy Stanley by name, bent up a pin and put it onto the seat for another boy to sit down on. The other boy not sitting down quickly enough was helped by the Stanley boy, who removed his feet from under him quite suddenly. After Sabbath School was over and the Stanley boy had gotten out on to the street, the matter was detailed to Mr. Hall, who, bareheaded, rushed out after the young rascal. This scamp was walking along oblivious of danger, talking with another boy, perhaps on the benefits of Sunday School. Accidentally looking around, he saw his beloved pastor bearing down on him, his coattails and grey hair flying behind him like the sails and streamers of a man-of-war.

At once the Stanley boy's organs of locomotion were set revolving, so that his knickerbockered legs looked like the two side wheels of a tricycle. He whizzed past some ladies with a velocity that would have made lightning blush. But all was in vain. It was down grade and the beloved pastor had already acquired a prodigious momentum that gave him an unfair advantage over the youth. The b.p. whizzed past the ladies on the other side and it was soon evident that Stanley would be beaten. Both put forth their best "licks" but age, experience and momentum won the heat. The boy was seized and returned to the church ignominiously. What was done there I have not been informed. I think, however, there are some boys on our street that could beat the pastor in a straight, fair and open race.

APR. 30—At ten last night I was telephoned for to go to Point au Roche. I got Fly and went. There was a heavy mist falling all the time and right in my face. The lake is very high, much higher than I have ever seen it. The whole of the turnpiked road north of the Creek bridge is under water excepting a strip close to the bridge. Some of the houses at the Creek have had to be abandoned on account of the high water. Cumberland Head is quite an island. The long line of sawdust[5] and sand beach, on Cumberland Bay, is obliterated and a good-sized yacht could sail up into the excavated sand dunes.

MAY 1—At last May has come, clear, not too warm, not too cold. Snow banks can yet be seen in various parts of the town, but after all the sun has been victorious and winter has had to yield. It seems now as though we had had no winter, that we have always had spring. I hope, however, that there never will be so much sameness of the seasons as to make me accustomed to them. I want every spring to be a new one, every summer to be a rarity, every autumn to bring new mellowness, and every winter a keener delight.

MAY 5—The Thursday of May 5, 1870, seventeen years ago, comes to me in all its sadness. I had been at home nights, going down to college in Burlington on horseback. This day in the morning Mother thought there would be a change in 'Biel during the day. I got home about 4 p.m. and it seems he had tried to keep alive and conscious until I got home. He succeeded and knew me and talked with me a little, but soon became unconscious and passed away at twenty minutes to ten in the evening. How the birds did sing during those beautiful May early mornings.[6]

MAY 18—Last Saturday bought a bay horse for one hundred dollars. The horse is said to be five years old this spring. He drew me to West Chazy both yesterday and the day before in good shape. I still keep Fly, the old stand-by and reliable. He took me to West Plattsburgh both days and to Treadwell's Mills last night like any good and faithful quadruped of his genus.

MAY 21—J. W. Tuttle & Co., the leading printers of this town, have hired the corner store on the ground floor of Woodward's Block, northwest corner of Brinkerhoff and Margaret Streets nearly opposite my office.[6] When Mr. J. W. Tuttle was about forty-five years of age, young Walter H. Benedict, then about eighteen years of age, boasted considerably

about his ability to run. Mr. Tuttle then lived just east of Mr. Benedict's
on the plank road. After a time Mr. Tuttle told Walter he could beat him
running. Walter thought it absurd and told him he could not do it. Mr.
Tuttle insisted that he could and that he would choose the course. Walter
accepted the challenge and Mr. Tuttle said they would run to Dead Creek
bridge and back. Walter demurred, but on his opponent's insisting he
finally consented. So one night after work they started. Mr. Tuttle kept
up with him for a time and then went ahead of him and before they had
gone a mile Walter gave it up. Mr. Tuttle had the more wind. When Mr.
Tuttle told this story to me the other day he laughed over it as though
the event had just occurred.

Margaret Street, the shopping center of Plattsburgh, about 1885. The Doctor's office was on the second floor of a building about half way down the block on the left.

MAY 26—On May 24, I went over to Essex Center, Vermont to a close
of the term and of the year, and to a reunion of the pupils of the Academy.
I took my new horse over on the steamer *A. Williams,* leaving Plattsburgh
at seven in the morning, and got to Burlington a little after nine. The

1887 school exercises were in the Baptist Church and there was a beautiful display of plants and flowers on the platform and around it. After a time the church began to fill by twos and threes until it was well filled. I visited a great deal of the time with Dr. L. C. Butler, my old medical preceptor. I could stay only till three o'clock as I must take the boat in Burlington at five.

JUNE 24—Last night Theo was graduated from the Plattsburgh High School. She took the highest mark of any in her class. Theo's essay was "An Ancient Myth," and in my opinion her production was by far the best of them all. She will go to Wellesley College in September. She had magnificent flowers given her—baskets and bouquets, fourteen in all.

Evening. While riding in the country yesterday, I passed a deserted house. The pillars of a piazza in front stood bravely up. The front door was closed and probably locked. The iron knocker hung unchanged on the door. The few window blinds remaining were closed, but mischievous boys had broken almost every pane. Paint still clung to the clapboards. The shingles remained on the roof. The deserted shed held no wood. Doubtless, cobwebs and insects and mice were the only occupants of the house. The grass and caraway were growing luxuriantly outside, leaving only a trace of the former footpaths and wagon roads. The fence in front was continuous with the ordinary fence between the meadow and the road. No barn or other outbuildings were present. Desolation ruled supreme. "The form was there but not the substance."

It was easy in imagination to repeople this house. The builder and first occupant had selected this site after due deliberation. He had builded the house at, for him, much expense. It was his pride and delight. His neighbors had told him what a good house he had. His friends and relatives had congratulated him on the good qualities of this his home. Less prosperous people had envied him because his place was so much finer than theirs. His wife had felt that so far as her house was concerned none could look down on her. After a time happy, noisy boys and girls filled the house with their merriment. Evening parties and the afternoon "visitings" added to the already overflowing happiness. Sorrow came too, and occasionally removed one from the beloved circle even in the earlier years.

After a time the children, grown up, found other homes of their own. Houses, more costly, sprang up in the neighborhood. This no longer was the finest house in that locality. After a longer time the first owner and occupant passed away. His wife soon followed him. A child less capable and less industrious than his father became master of the premises, which now were aging quite perceptibly. After repeated misfortunes this son was obliged to give up the homestead that was the pride and delight of

34

his father's heart. It passed into the hands of others and yet others.

At length a prosperous and thrifty neighbor, who was born in the country from which the snakes and frogs had been banished by the beloved saint, set his heart on adding this house and surroundings to his own already extensive possessions. He bought up the mortgages, settled the judgments, foreclosed, and this once happy home became this foreign-born citizen's tenant house. The family of his hired man lived here so that this hired man could get to his work earlier in the morning and finish his labors later at night. At length the help no longer lived in it.

When I first saw this house, thirteen years ago, it was occupied by a horde of unthrifty, diseased paupers, and a distant town paid my bill for professional services rendered to one of these. These, I think, were its last occupants. The broken panes, the loose or missing blinds, the general presence of decay, all these, the iron knocker seemed to insinuate, would be exhibited in greater vividness to anyone who should venture to make the rooms reverberate with the echoes of its vibrations. As for me, I felt as if a breath from the past, filled with musty odors, had been wafted to me, and I could not remain longer and endure the suffocation it seemed to bring with it. I hurried along to the living.

JULY 4—One day last week I weighed the horse, Fly, just before watering him. He tipped the balance at 850 pounds. I weighed him again immediately after letting him drink all the water he wanted, and his then weight was 875 pounds.

JULY 12—The Clinton County Medical Society today, on the occasion of its semi-annual meeting, took the steamer *Maquam* and went to Maquam.[8] leaving at 11.40 a.m. and getting back to Plattsburgh dock at 7.15 p.m. There were 150 tickets taken up at the dock at the time of our landing. Besides these there must have been as many as twenty children who did not have tickets. We had a good dinner at the Hotel Champlain at Maquam, though so large a number was not expected. Owing to the length of time occupied at the tables, no literary exercises were held.

We got the boat for twenty five cents per ticket and charged fifty cents each for the same. After paying all expenses the society had left $32.80, which has been deposited in the bank. We hope it is a nucleus for a fund with which to build a building for the society.

AUG. 3—Today went to Providence Island on steamer *Reindeer*. The Central Vermont Railroad has fitted up this island this year and their steamer *Reindeer* takes excursions there. The "Pavilion" is on a high and dry place and is very pleasant. On the eastern slope immense quantities of flint are found in nodules throughout the limestone.

The steamer Maquam *on Lake Champlain, pictured in 1881. Dr. Kellogg took numerous excursions on this vessel.*

AUG. 16—Sunday night, August 14 at 7.45, I started for New York to attend the meeting of the American Association for the Advancement of Science (A.A.A.S.). I had a pleasant visit with Verplanck Colvin, superintendent of the Adirondack Survey, who came onto the cars at Saratoga and got off at Albany.[9] I got my ticket to New York for $8.14 and my return ticket for $2.35 on account of being a member of the Association.

The meeting was held in the Columbia College buildings. I went up to the College and registered, my number being 690. There were numerous interesting papers and lively discussions. As my paper could not come off Monday, but was down for Tuesday, I concluded not to wait for it and came home Monday night, getting back to Plattsburgh Tuesday morning at 6.30.

SEPT. 6—Yesterday Bess, I and Dr. George D. Hersey and wife of Providence went to Chambly. We started in the morning and got back in the evening. On our way down to Chambly we enquired out the location of Fort Saint Thérèse. A man pointed out to us where it was across the canal but said that not much was remaining there now. He could remember when there were some small earthworks, but they were plowed over now.[10] Monsieur J. O. Dion was not at the fort, but his brother was. The brother did not know much about the things there.

SEPT. 20—Yesterday morning water was found running into the store under my office through the ceiling, quite copiously. After much tribulation it was found that a rat had bitten a hole into the lead water pipe, through which the water was running freely.

OCT. 4—Today we visited St. Valentin and Isle aux Noix. I took the morning train to Rouses Point and from there drove with Rev. O. M. Boutwell of the M.E. church to St. Valentin. We looked along the shore at St. Valentin and found about 125 stone relics. The Indian village that Radisson mentions in his *Voyages* as the one he stayed at the night before coming to "a large lake six leagues wide" (Lake Champlain) lay along the west side of the Richelieu. The hundreds of stone implements found by me and by others along this shore testify to the fact that this was a large Indian settlement.

About one o'clock we took a rowboat and went over to the island. Here, where so many armies have halted, where so many expeditions have started, where have been so many beginnings and endings of wars, this place I now visited for the first time. Our attention was kept on the tin roofs of some buildings surrounded by a high earthwork. We found this was from 20 to 25 feet high, surrounded by a deep moat at least three rods in width. A wooden bridge with a gate at the outer end and the remains of a drawbridge at the fort end was the only way of getting into the earthwork. At the fort end of the bridge was a covered stone passage over the outer part of which was cut in large letters the single word LENNOX.[11]

I found no other inscription on stone anywhere, but our visit was hurried on account of approaching rain. Once inside, fine cut stone buildings presented themselves on three sides of the fort. There were also numerous dark places in the earthwork covered with stone which were the bombproofs.

We hurried back to our boat. On our way I found a yard enclosed by timbers set into the ground. Little irregularities of earth showed that this was a cemetery. Of the hundreds and probably thousands of soldiers, brave and otherwise, buried here, no sign remains save some little heaps of earth. Carleton's, Haviland's, Burgoyne's expeditions, expeditions from the War of 1812 and from the war of 1665, doubtless all have contributed their quota to this cemetery of Isle aux Noix. Yet no stone, no inscription, no monument remains for one of these, save some little irregularities of earth and a rotten board sacred to the memory of one soldier's daughter. The mother earth enclosing them is the kindest of all to them, and alone perpetuates their memory.

Before we got into our boat it began to rain. We got back to Rouses Point at 6. It had rained all the time during our return until we passed Lacolle.

OCT. 5—Today the Northern New York Medical Association met in the courthouse in Plattsburgh. Nearly thirty five physicians were present. Papers were read by Dr. Alexander Proudfoot of Montreal, by Dr. Major, also of Montreal, and Dr. A. P. Grinnell gave a talk of more than an hour on "Phthisis." Dr. Proudfoot told me he had an uncle, Dr. Thomas Proudfoot, who was a surgeon in the British army in the Rifle Brigade at the Battle of Plattsburgh, September 1814. He was slightly wounded at that battle.

OCT. 7—Today Mr. Peter Noel, son of M. Noel of Lacolle or St. Valentin was in my office. He went on to tell me the following legend, which he seemed to believe:

"There was once a boiler full of money found at Lacolle near the blockhouse. My father and two or three other men took a stick (wand) that showed them where the money was. They dug down for eighteen feet. Every little while they would get most to the money and then it would sink. At last they gave it up, but one of them determined to dig further although they were down nearly as far as they could make the hole. All of a sudden a flame burst out from the bottom of the hole, a large bright flame which went all around the man and almost killed him. He was made blind so that he could not see for three weeks. They tried the rod again and it showed that the money was only three feet to one side of the hole. Afterwards a soldier got the money."

OCT. 19—The other night Nelson was saying his prayers. His mother, thinking he had finished, told Rob to begin his. Nelson, very indignant at the interruption, said: "If you don't let me finish my prayers I will make me an idol and worship it."

OCT. 22—A couple of years ago Nelson went out into the Settlement with me. In order not to suffer from the pangs of hunger, he provided himself with a small lunch which consisted of a small two-quart basket nearly full of apples and bread and butter. While I was in at Amherst Thorne's near Treadwell's Mills bridge, he disposed of most of his small lunch. At Mr. McCloskey's he was given a plate full of cookies and some more apples. He ate nearly all of them and what he didn't eat he took in his hands to eat while riding home. When we got to Mr. James Fitzpatrick's on the corner, he was considerably depressed because I told Mrs. Fitzpatrick that I didn't believe that he had better eat any of the cookies she brought out to him. When we got nearly down to the plains he took the whip out and said he was going to make that horse go home just as fast as he could. He wanted some of *those ducks we were going to have for dinner.*

OCT. 29—I have had to pay 40 cents per bushel for oats this year. I paid for 66 13/32 bushels today.

I have been asked to devote from 7 to 10 minutes of our time at the Monday evening reading club to the early history of Champlain valley. I have already had three papers, viz. (1) "Prehistoric Settlements in the Champlain Valley." (2) "Discovery of the Valley and first fight recorded therein." (3) "Fort St. Anne." Next Monday I am to devote to Chambly. I shall not have the papers read chronologically, but according as I can prepare them the most easily. I enjoy it much and hope the members of the Club do.

NOV. 9—Yesterday was election day. Considerable money was used, but not so much as one year ago. Today is pension day and only two men to examine.

NOV. 24—Thanksgiving day. The dinner was good. Bob and Nello each spoke a piece. Baby Bessie spoke too. I wrote and read to the children about Thanksgiving thirty years ago. I also made a translation of Goethe's "The King in Thule" which rhymes, I believe. I presume I used considerable of the so-called poetical license in the translation.

DEC. 1—Today Dr. J. H. LaRocque and I were assisting Dr. E. M. Lyon at an operation on George Place, a man employed at the railroad depot. Just as we were finishing at Mr. Place's an alarm of fire sounded. The west wing of the Cumberland House was on fire and a great smoke was pouring forth. After it had been burning for a while the roofs were covered with freezing water, there was a murmur of horror from the crowd. The first thing I saw was a man in a rubber coat, on his face with arms extended, slipping down the roof of the wing. He came very near a ladder that was up against the eaves but missed it by a few inches. Instantly he pitched over head first and fell to the sidewalk, a distance of at least thirty feet. He struck with a sickening thud.

It was John L. Fagan, son of the baker and partner in the firm of L. Fagan and Son. He was a fine young man, handsome and muscular, about 23 or 24 years of age, the pride of his mother and father and one of the main spokes in their business. He was instantly taken to his father's on River Street but died in about two hours. In half an hour after he fell I heard people laughing on the street as if nothing had happened. 'Twas not thoughtlessness either, but so little do the affairs of one person affect another!

DEC. 10—I am still reading *The United Netherlands,* having just completed the third volume. Motley seems to think the question of freedom of religious thought and action was decided in the Netherlands. I do not like to think I have had such interesting and valuable histories as *The United Netherlands* for nearly a year without reading them. I am ashamed to have books I have not read.

1887 DEC. 22—Helen has received an invitation to teach school in Spring Valley, Minnesota, and expects to start west a little after New Year's. We shall miss her very much. Theo and Helen are perfectly wrapped up in each other. It seems too bad that their lives should have to begin to run in different directions.

How much the children are looking forward to Christmas. There are so many mysteries, so many private conversations, so many secret understandings. They all can keep secrets except Baby Bessie. She has to reveal her intentions. She told Theo she was going to give her a tablet and pencil, and showed them to her.

DEC. 31—1887 is on its last legs. In a few hours more 1888 will be here and take 87's place. But it is no more one year's place than another's.

I have had a good year in many ways. The family health has been remarkably good excepting Nello's scarlet fever and Bessie's attack of sore throat. I have had a large practice and have collected twenty five hundred eighty four dollars and eighty cents. I have been present at the arrival of sixty seven children into this external world, quite a host in themselves. I have laid aside only a very little money, but have had my fortieth birthday. I aim in the next ten years to have five thousand dollars invested, which is a modest ambition. I think with my present health and strength it can be realized. So the record for 1887 closes.

Notes on 1887

1. After its first explosion in 1886, the local citizens grumbled about the dynamite factory's being too near the village. After the explosion of January 11, 1887, the complaints became more vocal. Reorganized as the Clinton Dynamite Company, the firm planned to move downstairs, but a third major explosion on April 10th intervened. The company settled in Haverstraw, New York, where in 1891 it blew up again, killing five people.

2. The ten-cent duty on wool and oats led to considerable smuggling from Canada. A large quantity of oats was seized in February and stored in the hall of the customhouse pending the auction, giving an appearance and odor "like an agricultural institution."

3. Grand Isle, a part of Vermont. It was about four miles across the ice from Plattsburgh, half that distance by way of Cumberland Head.

4. Merk published his article in Vol. 19, Number 1, *Communications of the Antiquarian Society in Zurich*.

5. During the years of the great lumber mills on the Saranac River, the sawdust was discharged into the river and thus into Plattsburgh Bay, where it formed a thick coating on water and beaches, and even formed a new reef on which the steamer *Vermont* grounded.

6. The death of his older brother Abiel affected David for the rest of his life. Abiel

had chosen to stay at home and help with the farm so that David could get an education. He died of tuberculosis as a young man.

7. The Tuttle Publishing Company is now located in Rutland, Vermont and is known for its fine editions and its Japanese publishing connections.

8. Maquam was a small resort on Lake Champlain near Swanton, Vermont.

9. Verplanck Colvin (1847–1920) published a series of famous Adirondack surveys in the 1880's and 1890's.

10. One of the early French forts along the Richelieu River, dating from the 1660's and the French-Indian wars against the Iroquois.

11. Fort Lennox on Ile-aux-Noix (Nut Island) was constructed in its present form between 1812 and 1826. It had been a heavily fortified place since 1759. In the War of 1812 it was the shipbuilding center for the British navy on Lake Champlain.

1888

"Much to do but little cash," wryly comments Dr. Kellogg as a new year opens. January ushers in the first of two historic "blizzards of '88," both of which isolate the town. In the famous March storm, the Doctor is called out before midnight, and he and Fly battle their way three miles to a difficult case through a gale "blowing fearfully" and drifts as high as Fly's back. The most shocking event of the year is a particularly brutal murder on a street near his home.

Dr. Kellogg takes a memorable trip to the Midwest—his first. At home, he lectures to the appreciative members of a GAR post on an incident of the War of 1812, and offers prizes to the local young people for their best historical essays. He is appointed Post Surgeon at the Barracks, cheerfully officiating at 6:30 a.m. sick calls.

A third son, David, enters the family, weighing in at about eight pounds. In the fall, Plattsburgh citizens are swept up in the close Presidential election between Cleveland and Harrison, and Dr. Kellogg's ardent Republicanism is deeply gratified by the result. He welcomes an impromptu torchlight parade at 3:30 a.m.

JAN. 3—We are now writing the three eights for the first time in a thousand years.

Helen started for Spring Valley, Minnesota, where Mother now lives with my sister Mary. Her ticket, which included the omnibus transfer in Chicago but no sleeping car fares, was $28.88.

This afternoon I was called to see Mr. Gideon Rugar on Rugar street. He was born in 1806. He gave me a bayonet which his father, John Rugar, with others took from a British prisoner whom they captured in the old Rugar house on Rugar street. There were four of our men, two of them Vermont militiamen, who took a British sergeant and a British corporal prisoners in this house. This bayonet belonged to one of these non-

42

commissioned officers. It is in a wonderfully good state of preservation.
Mr. Rugar said they used to use it in shelling corn, but that for a great
many years it had been stuck into a timber upstairs in the old house.

JAN. 7—Mr. Darius W. Marsh of Beekmantown gave me an old flintlock gun this morning that came through his wife's family, the Heatons.
I don't know its history.

JAN. 10—Today was the annual meeting of the Medical Society of
Clinton County. I was elected delegate to the State Medical Society which
meets in Albany in February. Dr. James A. Nichols was the opposition
candidate. He had five votes and I had nine.

JAN. 19—I have been very busy the last three days, much to do but
little cash.

JAN. 26—A letter Saturday from Mary said that Helen had pneumonia.
I telegraphed at once and heard she was better. A card has come nearly
every day from her attending physician, Dr. Moore, telling how she is.

JAN. 27—Friday evening. There has been no mail from the south
since Wednesday night, unless one has just come in now. The snow that
fell yesterday has blown ever since. The wind has been terrific. The
thermometer has been below zero most of the time.[1]
I sent by express today, as a loan to the Albany Art and Historical
Society, some Indian relics and some relics of the War of 1812 and 1759.
They are to be returned in four months in good condition. I disliked very
much to do so but I could not reasonably decline. This world was not
made for one person.

FEB. 4—I am just reading a notice in the *Nation* of February 2, 1888
of Professor Asa Gray of Harvard College who died this week. I remember,
when at the meeting of the American Association for the Advancement of
Science at Cambridge in 1882, that my friend Professor George F. Wright
of Oberlin introduced me to Professor Gray. In the first part of Mr.
Wright's introduction Professor Gray had put out his hand in rather a
mechanical way, but when Mr. Wright said "*my friend*, Dr. Kellogg," a
look of cordial, hearty friendship flashed from his eyes which made me
feel at once that here was a man whom one could love unreservedly because of his genuine good feeling for the human family. The whole
interview probably did not last more than one minute, yet I never hear
Professor Gray's name mentioned without recalling that look from those
handsome eyes.[2]

FEB. 9—On Monday of this week, in company with Dr. C. B. Vaughan
of Morrisonville, I went to Albany to attend the meeting of the New York

1888   State Medical Society. I went as the delegate of the Medical Society of the County of Clinton. We reached Albany at 2.30 p.m. and went to the Globe Hotel. The hotels were all crowded because of the Masonic meeting, the legislature and the Medical meeting.

I went to Joel Munsell's Sons book establishment. It was upstairs on the first floor, a dingy, unswept and unwarmed den. But the histories that were on the shelves made me envious of the place. I purchased the memoirs of Madame Riedesel and also Arnold's Expedition against Quebec (Henry's). Then I went to Macdonough's bookstore. I enquired for Thoreau's "Winter." The clerk said if he knew the name of the author he could tell. He would order it for me. They had a large store in New York and were doing an immense business, and so on. Much like the woman's experience in *The Gilded Age* in getting Taine's *English Literature*.[3]

After getting to our hotel we went to bed. A knotted rope in the room attached to an iron ring was a fire escape, which in a printed notice we were requested not to handle unless actually needed. We got up about seven in the morning and had breakfast. We then strolled up to the City Hall where the meeting was to be held. The medical and surgical agents were present with their wares displayed. In the room where the society met was a dignified, intelligent and courteous assembly of physicians. A large German from Brooklyn read a paper on Alcohol in Certain Forms of Fever. A youngish man read a paper on localizing the action of medicine by applying it quite near to the spinal cord.

Dr. Fordyce Barker, suffering from chronic laryngitis, spoke in the afternoon. I could not understand him to any extent, but the audience through sympathy, good feeling and respect, cheered him heartily. After supper I got some candy for the children. Then we went back to the meeting and partly made arrangements to purchase a chair for use in our offices, called the "Harvard," for fifty five dollars each. We are to send word to the agent if we finally conclude to take them.

We took our train precisely at 11.30. At Saratoga the conductor got word that the night express from Montreal was four hours late, and orders to go on to Whitehall. We were late at Whitehall, but got orders there to go to Ticonderoga. A little north of Dresden our train, which was a long one, came to a stop. I stood on the steps of a car and heard the engineer say he could not budge her an inch either way. This was at 4.15 a.m. After nearly three hours of waiting, the engine was repaired and we moved on slowly to Ti. There we met the freight that had delayed the Montreal Express and the Express itself. This was about 7 a.m., the time this express should have been in New York. A brakeman on the freight danced about and shouted, "We was the ones that made you wait," a notoriety

he seemed proud of. In the smoker of our car was a prisoner on his way
to Dannemora for life. He had committed a murder and seemed to delight
in telling about it. They gave him a good many cigars and often something
to drink from a bottle.

Well, we got to Plattsburgh at 10.30 a.m., five hours late. I telephoned
to the house and found that all were well and went directly to Dr. Lyon's
office to examine pensioners, thirteen of whom we had that day.

FEB. 11—This morning died my esteemed friend, Joseph Willard Tuttle
of the firm J. W. Tuttle & Co. I have known him for fourteen years, ever
since I first came to Plattsburgh. Though nearly blind all the time I have
known him, having had granular lids and too strong astringents applied,
he was always cheerful, though inclined to lament over the foolishness
of people.

He was much interested in local history and also in the history of certain
parts of New England. He told me that two thirds of the property of the
city of New Haven, Connecticut, was in possession of descendants of the
Tuttle family. He also told me that Dr. Samuel Beaumont, formerly of
Plattsburgh, when a printer in his younger days, was in the same office
with and worked beside Samuel Woodworth, the author of "The Old
Oaken Bucket."[4] It seems lonesome to have the curtains drawn in the
corner store opposite, because he who has been in the printing business
since 1842 and at the head of his firm during these 46 years has finished
his partnership today.

FEB. 21—Last night I was present at the arrival into this external world
of a small female infant. She had the misfortune to persist in coming feet
first. And as a result her life was ended before it could reasonably be
said to have begun. She never breathed, but her heart beat perceptibly
and unmistakably for twenty five minutes by my watch. All my efforts to
make respiration begin were unavailing.

FEB. 29—In examining pensioners today, the usual question, "What
is your disability?" was asked one. The reply came promptly, "I'm a
Democrat." I imagine this is as serious a disability as an applicant often
has.

MAR. 13—The storm continued through yesterday and increased last
night. About eleven p.m. a man came for me to go out to the old Moffitt
Place on Moffitt Road, a distance of about three miles. It was blowing
fearfully, but he came in a buggy because the going, in spite of the drifts,
was better for a wagon than for a sleigh. I harnessed Fly to the open
buggy and started after him. The northwest wind was pitiless. Often I
could not see his buggy, even when he was only three or four rods ahead

of me. The snow was well up on to the horse's flank, but was very light. My lantern, fastened underneath the wagon box, ploughed its way through the light snow and was burning well when I reached my destination. One drift, just where I turned to enter the lane leading to the house, was as high as the top of Fly's back. I did not get through and home until nearly seven this morning. What made it still worse was that the case was so difficult that I asked for a consultation and sent and got Dr. J. H. LaRocque.

The last night's mail from the south, reported two hours late at Addison Junction, reached here this afternoon about 20 hours late. The Montreal Express of last night was abandoned and so have all through trains today, except as above mentioned.[5]

MAR. 14—No south trains today or tonight. A little while ago, as I was coming to my office, I heard the whistle of the Montreal Express on time, which is the first train from Montreal since Sunday night. I hope we shall get a New York mail in the morning.

APR. 1—Last night a horrible murder was committed on Brinkerhoff Street near the corner of Wells, north side. A man, Charles Harrison, who eight years ago was a soldier at the Barracks here, killed his wife. He was jealous of her. He found her walking with another man and her sister. He rushed up to her and said, "I've caught you now and I'll fix you," or nearly those words, and with his arm somewhat around her neck cut her throat twice with a razor. He put her into the gutter and went immediately to the nearest house, in which lived a gardener, and told him he had just killed his wife. Soper, the man who was with him, ran for a policeman, who came at once and took the murderer to jail. The sister ran away, but both she and Soper were lodged in jail as witnesses. Crowds visited the place that night and all day today. The blood on the snow oozed up red in spite of all efforts to cover it up with ashes and earth. The murderer made no denial of his deed and gave himself up peaceably. He told the officer who arrested him that he need not puff so, he should make no attempt to get away.

APR. 11—Last week a high board fence that has surrounded the ball ground on Court Street above us was taken down and drawn away. A few weeks ago the toboggan slide was taken down. The large roller skating rink on Clinton Street has been converted into a wagon store.

So these three "crazes" have passed. The furor that each caused in its day was remarkable. The toboggan slide, when in running order, drew large crowds. As it was too far for many to walk, the livery man got out large sleighs and made money carrying people there. The ball craze raged for two or three summers. I don't think this is dead yet. The roller skating had two rinks, yes three, for Norton's Hall was used for a short time as a rink. The band was hired for one or the other, night after night. Fancy skaters were imported from other places and the whole thing was boomed until it was doomed. The Catholic priests, thinking rightly that it was proving morally injurious for their church people to attend these skatings, forbade them to go there. Mothers found their daughters were being injured physically and the thing soon collapsed. Roller skates are now looked at with curious eyes, as belonging to the distant past. *Omnia mutantus.*

The Salvation Army is here. Just this instant I can hear them singing on the street. They have not very large numbers, but are enthusiastic and energetic. A Mr. P. A. Burdick, a lawyer by profession, is holding a series of temperance lectures in Music Hall, with good success.[6]

MAY 6—Yesterday died Mrs. Rebecca Laflin Leeke, aged 93 years, 6 months, 4 days. Mrs. Leeke had taught school before 1815. She was married to David Leeke in 1820. He died in 1856, I believe, she having survived him 32 years, more than a single generation. Her children had all been dead for some years. Today a funeral procession winded its way to Pt. au Roche carrying the body there to moulder back to the dust of the earth. Indeed if it were not for the hope of a future life, the longest life here would be a matter of small moment.

MAY 7—This evening was the first Historical Prize Contest. I privately, through the Teachers' Association of Clinton County, offered a prize of seven dollars to the one who would have the best essay on any historical event in the Champlain Valley, and three dollars for the second best. This offer was made through the papers in the county to any pupil of any school in the county. Judge Peter S. Palmer, the historian of this valley, Judge W. C. Watson, son of W. C. Watson, the author of *History of Essex County*, and myself were appointed judges. Seven essays in all were prepared, each under a fictitious name. We looked them over carefully and separately came to the same decision, viz., that the one, "Engagements at Valcour and Split Rock" by "Joan" was entitled to the first prize; that the essay, "The First Settler in Ausable" by "Carrie A. Bruce" was entitled to the second prize; that the essays "Lake Champlain as an Important Factor in the Revolution" by "Historian" and "Ticonderoga" by "Candor" were equally entitled to honorable mention.

The contest was in Academy Hall before the County Teachers' Association, which had a meeting tonight. These four essays were read by the writers and were well received. They were prepared by the writers without assistance and were read without correction. It seems to me that the contest was a success in all respects.

MAY 26—I went to Cumberland Head this morning. The new tele-

1888 graph poles are up along the beach and over on to the Head and the wire is strung also. I believe the cable is laid from the Head across to the Island. This new line, the Commercial Union, extends to Burlington and elsewhere. This is the first *direct* telegraph communication between Plattsburgh and Burlington. I hope there will be telephonic communication soon.

MAY 30—The parade of fire companies and school boys on foot, and soldiers from the Garrison, also on foot, and the G.A.R.'s in wagons was unusually good. Volleys were fired by the soldiers at each of the three cemeteries. At the Barracks cemetery a monument was unveiled to the memory of soldiers unknown whose remains were unearthed years ago in making a railroad near the Barracks.

At this point in time, Doctor Kellogg took the first of several extended out-of-state journeys that were to refresh his mind and give him badly needed rest at infrequent intervals throughout the remainder of his life. He never brought the Journal along on those trips, however; he wrote about them at length after returning home. Most of his accounts are too long, or too crowded with personal details to be included here. Instead, the Doctor's descriptions of his trips are usually summarized in brief, as the following one is. The only exceptions are to be found among the Journal entries for 1893, when he took his eldest son with him on a sentimental journey to his own boyhood home in Vermont, and later to the Columbian Exposition in Chicago; and 1905, when he made his first trip to California. Those accounts have special appeal or historic interest, and are reproduced nearly in full.

Between June 6th and 18th in 1888, Dr. Kellogg made a trip to Spring Valley, Minnesota, to visit his mother and his sister and her husband, Mary and Henry Griffin. He traveled by way of Chicago and Milwaukee. The pleasure he had from observing human nature, meeting new people and seeing a new part of the country appears in every line of the Journal.

He missed his train from Chicago by five minutes and had all day to wait for the next one. He found Chicago "immense in its buildings, dirt and smoke." Spring Valley was a pleasant country town, where he met many fine people. The village had well-kept houses and the streets were in good condition. He commented on its sidewalks, which were all plank. He found the season about ten days behind Plattsburgh's, "though they are more than 100 miles south of us."

His hosts took him for rides into the countryside, where he saw many water snakes. On one trip they saw what the Doctor was sure were Indian mounds. They borrowed a broad grain shovel with which to dig. Regretfully, he recorded: "As it was warm and late and the shovel not suitable to dig through the hard clayey muck, we had to give it up."

48

He found his mother blind in both eyes from cataracts. After his return
he learned that one cataract was removed in a moderately successful
operation. He brought his niece Helen back with him. They arrived home
early on the morning of June 18th, "safe, sound, sweaty and sooty. We
almost feared we had injured the railroad grades on account of the amount
of dirt we took with us." He found that the entire trip cost him $115. "I
presume it was well invested" was his concluding Journal entry.

JULY 5—I began to attend at the Barracks as Post Surgeon. This is
in place of Dr. W. A. Owen, who has been ordered to Fort Leavenworth,
I believe. I go every morning and am present at sick call at 6.30. I am
to have $2.50 per visit and $2.00 for every second visit necessary to be
made in any one day.

JULY 10—Went on the third annual excursion of the Medical Society
of Clinton County today. The society chartered the steamer *A. Williams,*
and we went down the Richelieu as far as Isle aux Noix. We did not land
on account of the absence of a suitable landing place. I have written a
detailed account of the excursion in the annals of the society.

JULY 26—Today I took my horse and buggy on board the steamer
Maquam and went to Adams' Landing in the town of Grand Isle. I drove
from there to Mr. Daniel Sampson's, who has quite a number of good
Indian relics. He told me that he had a blue pitcher that had a picture of
the battle of Plattsburgh on it. When I got there he could not find it, but
would make further search for it and give it to me.
I did see one pitcher, however, at the Rev. Dr. Fay's, a short distance
from Mr. Sampson's. It has two pictures of the battle, one on each side,
very much like my battle of Plattsburgh plate and saucer so far as the
picture itself is concerned. My affection for Mrs. Fay would have been
heightened had she given me the pitcher. Had I been in her place I would
not have given it away.

AUG. 2—Today I inspected the sanitary condition of the Barracks. I
went around with Captain O. B. Read of Company F, 11th U.S. Infantry,
the commanding officer of this company stationed here. Everything was in
capital condition. We took breakfast in the room next to the men's dining
room. Our breakfast, the same as the men's. It was hash, coffee, bread, all
well-cooked and good enough for anybody. The men all seemed to think
Capt. Read was perfect.

AUG. 7—Went to St. Johns on steamer *Reindeer* with a French excursion, the St. John Baptiste Society. There were between five and six
hundred persons present. Some of the party imbibed the Canadian whiskey

49

NATIONAL CITY PUBLIC LIBRARY

quite freely and a little fight was indulged in, on the street in front of Monette's Hotel just before leaving for home. No one was injured and the conflict was short, but one amusing incident I noticed which was worth the whole price of the excursion. Napoleon Paro, a slater from Plattsburgh, when he saw the fight in progress thought he would have a hand in it. He had not drunk anything to speak of, but evidently had imbibed a little. So he sailed in with a shout and prepared to fight. Suddenly his wife, who is larger than he and probably stronger, stepped into the crowd, seized him by the collar, dragged him out and away from the crowd, told him he did not come there to fight and that he must behave himself. He cowed down at once after trying to make a slight resistance, but his wife was too much for him. She stayed with him all the way home and when he landed he was perfectly sober.

A Mrs. Senecal does our washing and supports her family by her work. Her husband is a dude Frenchman over 70 years old, but just as able to work as his wife. A year or two ago, like a faithful spouse she picked blueberries and sold them to a lady for a secondhand suit of clothes, which she gave as a present to her dude husband. The clothes were excellent ones but somewhat threadbare, but on account of their shade, a shade of blue, Mr. Senecal would not wear them because this color did not look well on him. Recently the lady found out that the clothes had not been used so she offered to pay Mrs. Senecal the money for the berries and take the clothes back. "No," Mrs. Senecal said, "I'll keep 'em. *They'll do to lay him out in.*"

AUG. 20—Last Saturday Forepaugh's great circus was in town and exhibited on the athletic grounds just above us. There were perhaps seven thousand people at the afternoon exhibition. The three boys, Francis, Robert, Nelson, were the only members of our family that attended. It is probable that at least ten thousand dollars were carried away from this county by the circus managers as proceeds from their two exhibitions here. Just think how much that money would have done had it been used for a public library here. But worse than all is to know that such a large number of people here consider a circus their highest enjoyment.

I have purchased recently Kinglake's *Crimean War* and am nearly through the first volume. It is exceedingly interesting. Kinglake unconsciously illustrates the theory of Tolstoi that no one man causes a war, but rather the spirit of the people. Because the English people were anxious for war with Russia, even after the Russians had evacuated the provinces and virtually yielded all that was demanded, *war had to be.*

AUG. 28—Went to Crown Point on an excursion and visited Fort St. Frederick, Amherst's fort, and redoubts and other places of interest. Where once were life, active scientific investigation and observation, the drilling of men and roar of artillery, now only are ruins.

SEPT. 1—Today at 5.45 a.m., in the bedroom west off the dining room downstairs was born my third son and fourth child, David Sherwood Kellogg, Jr. He weighs about eight pounds. Elizabeth Kellogg was born in the same room October 26, 1883. Nelson Kellogg was born in the room over my office, where we then kept house, March 6, 1881. Robert Douglas Kellogg was born in the same room January 31, 1879.

Elizabeth, now a baby no longer, is proud of her new brother and holds him a great deal. She was quite indignant because she had supposed she was to be the mother of the expected baby.

The Kellogg home at 64 Court Street, Plattsburgh; now 100 Court.

SEPT. 4—Today Robert goes to the public school for the first time. He has been in school one year in our house with Gertie Barker as teacher.

SEPT. 11—Went to Ellenburg Depot today and gave an address on "Incidents Connected with the September Invasion of 1814" before the McGregor Post No. 463, G.A.R. I took up several relics of the invasion and showed them. The audience paid good attention and seemed interested. The exercises were in a grove about a mile from the Depot.

1888   SEPT. 12—Francis Kellogg Kyle, my nephew, left this afternoon on steamer *Chateaugay* for the University of Vermont at Burlington, where he has been admitted as a freshman, conditionally. He was seventeen years old July 29, 1888. He was born in Westerly, Rhode Island. He is strong, active, capable and is naturally a good scholar.

SEPT. 28—David is growing, having gained two pounds the first three weeks of his existence. He is very busy all the time doing one or two of three things, viz. sleeping, eating, grunting.

A monstrous hotel is just begun at Bluff Point.[7]

OCT. 6—I have a little girl, Florence Turner, sick with typhoid fever. She is six years old and very sick. I visited her twice daily but day and night while awake she is constantly in my mind. Every step on the stairs to my office, every ring of the telephone bell or door bell startles me. I think word is coming that she is worse and that I am wanted immediately.

OCT. 13—Yesterday afternoon I went to Burlington with Capt. O. B. Read, a member of the Sigma Phi Society, and returned this noon. Francis Kellogg Kyle was initiated into the Society of the Sigma Phi last night. He wears his father's badge today. It would have been a proud day for his father had he been living.

I walked up to the college a little before dark last night. I went over to the expensive Billings Library. The building itself is said to be beautiful. It certainly looks as if it cost a great deal of money but it is not beautiful to me.[8] After my return to the main college building I stood in an east door and looked over the campus and the Vermont hills. Almost everything was changed. I felt glad that I had not the whole thing to go over again. I am not a day too old or too young.

NOV. 8—Election has come and gone. Benjamin Harrison is to be our next President. The excitement on Tuesday, election day, was quiet but intense. Both parties worked with all their powers, among which money was of the most consequence. The Democrats were *perfectly sure* that Grover Cleveland would be re-elected. One man, Mr. Hull of the Customs House, is reported to have said that one might as well talk of the Saranac River flowing back up the valley as to talk of Harrison being elected. I went in the evening to the Music Hall to hear the returns. I stayed until ten and heard from outside that Connecticut had gone Democratic and also Indiana.

I started for home and on the way up two Democrats overtook me and said that New York was Democratic by 17,000, that Indiana, New Jersey and Connecticut were Democratic, and possibly Illinois. It did not seem to me possible that the American people could do so foolish a thing, but

I feared that so overwhelming news must have some foundation. On getting home I told Bessie that Cleveland was elected and to bed I went in disgust.

About 3.30 in the morning I was waked up by the sound of a drum. I told Bess the Democrats were having a procession. On going to the door the crowd and torches and red lights could be distinctly seen. I put the lamp as much out of sight as possible so that no light could be seen in the house. The drum kept coming nearer and nearer. Just before they got to Mr. Myers', in the shouting I heard hurrahs for Harrison. I thought they meant Cleveland, supposing the crowd was so drunk they did not know what they were saying.

As soon as they reached Mr. Myers' house there were three cheers given for John Henry Myers. A window was raised. Mr. Myers' voice said: "What is the latest news?" The answer was, "A clean sweep. Every Northern state for Harrison excepting Jersey. Twenty five Republican majority in Congress." You may believe I let my light shine then. I went on to the piazza with my lamp in hand. There were hurrahs for Dr. Kellogg.

Bob, Elizabeth and Nello were awake and downstairs by this time, and there was no more sleep in the house for any of us that night. This crowd of about 30 went all over town. They had brooms, torches, red lights and drum corps. A little before eight, headed by Charles Ransom they went into the post office and swept it out, an act of retributive justice. Four years ago the Democrats did the same thing, rather maliciously, too, it was then thought. Harry S. Ransom, the then postmaster, felt badly about it. His son, Charles, then head clerk but now of Omaha, came last week from Omaha largely to do this very sweeping should Harrison be elected. He had his revenge.

About nine in the morning this crowd broke up. All day long there was only confirmation of the good news. There was, therefore, a grand torchlight parade and illumination planned for the evening. Hundreds of houses were illuminated. At our house the south rooms were all illuminated with candles, 14 in each window with bright lights inside. I had Roman candles and red lights in the yard as the procession passed. Bob and Nello helped fire the candles. There were cheering and shouting and hurrahing and the drums and band made all the noise they could. The procession must have marched six miles. It is said that Plattsburgh was never so brilliant.

In the evening procession there were several quite funny things. Mr. J. J. Drown, who I believe voted for the grandfather of Benjamin Harrison in 1840, was in his yard firing off Roman candles while the procession was passing. He held his candles in front of himself, horizontally, so that he fired right into the crowd. They could not make him understand what he was doing.

1888   Tonight, in a pouring rain, about half a dozen drunken men are marching around shouting "Hill, Hill, Hill. He's all right." The Democrats and
liquor sellers have got their governor for New York. Well, let them have
him. The Prohibitionists elected him by throwing away their votes on
Fisk.[9]

NOV. 25—I made my last visit at the Barracks this morning, having
been on duty there 144 days. I began July 5, 1888. Dr. J. H. Bartholf is
my successor. He is major.

NOV. 29—Thanksgiving Day. We had a big turkey today and chicken
pie to match. This evening Bob and Nello have gone to Music Hall to an
entertainment given by the kindergarten children. Bessie wanted to go but
she was too tired and too little. Just think of having a family of four fine
children and the best wife in the world. They are real "sweetness and
light."

DEC. 7—A little child of Dr. J. H. LaRocque has whooping cough. She
also wanted a finger ring. Her father put one on to her finger while she
was asleep. After waking and seeing the ring she was greatly delighted and
wondered how it got there. Her mother said that as she had been a good
girl lately, perhaps the little Jesus put it there. The child, delighted with
this idea, went to sleep again. In the morning when her larger brothers
came down she showed them the ring and said that neither her papa nor
her mama gave it to her, but, "the little Jesus put it on her finger."
"Humph," one of her brothers said, "the little Jesus *with a long beard*."
(Dr. LaRocque had a long, heavy beard.)

DEC. 17—A letter received today from Mary says that Mother gradually sees better and that her health is good. She cannot see to read.

DEC. 22—Last Sunday evening Bob read with his mother and me a
considerable part of *Macbeth*. He read with considerable emphasis and
appreciation and enjoyment. His average standing in school for the fall
term in all his studies was 83.5. His spelling brought down his average,
having stood only 63 in that. Of course his quite long sickness also during
the term brought down his marks, but we feel he has done well.

DEC. 25—Christmas. Well the children *did* have a fine time. I think
Nello did not sleep after three. So with him his wish to have Christmas a
long day was gratified. The piles of presents they had were as much as a
good many hundred children received when I was their age. *Then*, two
sticks of candy was a good deal, and a twenty-cent knife and a "tippet"
were enormous. Yet it was worth the while to see them so happy.

Only, tonight Harry Barnard, a bright little boy in Bobbie's school and class, was drowned. At this time his body has not been found. I do not know the particulars and do not want to. To think, the cold water of the river and lake and the darkness of night should surround him. His warm bed is vacant. His only brother saw him fall in and tried to get him out but could not. Is it possible so terrible a calamity could come to any human and loving family!!

Notes on 1888

1. This was the first of the great blizzards of this winter. The trains were several hours late on January 24; the next night a southbound train was derailed when it ran into snowdrifts. All movement stopped and drifts completely filled the tracks.

2. Asa Gray (1810–1888) was the country's leading botanist in the nineteenth century.

3. Mark Twain and Charles Dudley Warner in *The Gilded Age* gave Laura Van Brunt a difficult time when she tried to purchase Taine's *Notes on England* from an unlettered clerk in Washington.

4. Both Beaumont and Woodworth worked for a time on the *Plattsburgh Republican*. Woodworth developed a talent for writing patriotic and sentimental songs and poems, as well as popular plays. "The Old Oaken Bucket" was written in 1818.

5. This was the famous blizzard of '88 which completely immobilized New York City and southern New England. After the storm the first telegraphic communication between Boston and New York was by way of cable to London and back.

6. Sponsored by the W.C.T.U., Mr. Burdick's lectures attracted overflow audiences. Without repeating himself, he delivered 21 lectures in two weeks, for which he received $600. Fifteen hundred people signed the temperance pledge. The *Republican* commented ironically that "Satan's kingdom trembles in Plattsburgh this week, with the temperance crusade and the Salvation Army, both laboring to 'rescue the perishing.'"

7. The D&H railroad budgeted $150,000 for its construction if citizens of Plattsburgh would purchase $25,000 in stock. In consequence a five-story, 372-foot structure was erected. As the Hotel Champlain it was a popular summer resort until it burned. Rebuilt, it served as a hotel for many years more.

8. This Henry H. Richardson structure is an excellent example of his Romanesque Style. It was built between 1883 and 1886 at a cost of $150,000.

9. Although New York voted for Harrison, the Democrat David Hill was re-elected Governor by a close vote. The Prohibition party's 30,500 votes undoubtedly cut into the normal Republican strength.

1889

Doctor Kellogg receives two stunning shocks this year: a good friend and former patient is senselessly murdered, and another commits suicide without warning. He is startled to discover many insane and idiot inmates housed in the County Home. After being suddenly and inexplicably dropped from his strenuous but lucrative post on the Pension Board, he is reappointed a few months later, to family rejoicing.

In pursuit of a favorite hobby, he one day borrows a manuscript orderly book of a New York militia company of 1812 and proceeds to make a handwritten copy of all one hundred and fifteen pages of it.

The wide prevalence of sickness in town twice during the year weighs heavily on his compassionate mind. "It seems to me I could not bear the strain of so much anxiety a great while without injuring me," he comments on the first occasion. At a later day he declares, "I believe it is much easier to endure the real troubles than the constant worrying about them."

As Christmas of a more lucrative year than last approaches, the Doctor wistfully confesses that he wishes someone would give him a thousand dollars to spend on nothing but books.

JAN. 2—Since Christmas Rob has read through *Little Men, Little Lord Fauntleroy,* a small life of Daniel Boone and also a life of Gen. Sherman. He gets up into an armchair, curls his feet under him and reads.

JAN. 4—A letter from Mary last night says that Mother, with the aid of her glasses and a stereoscope, had read the Bible.

Today Bob got out of patience because I would not let him go on the ice skating, and made his will as follows:

Robert Douglas Kellogg

Give my skates to the first boy that comes past our house. Give all my knifes and cups and spoons to my brother Nelson Kellogg. Give my bow to my sister Bessie. Give my stud butens to Francis

K. Kyle. Give all my money to Dr. D. S. Kellogg. Give all my cloves to Nelson Kellogg. Give all my hankerffs to my mother. Give my sled to David S. Kellogg. Give all my books to the Y.M.C.A.

Robert Douglas Kellogg

JAN. 14—A few days ago I got from Mr. John D. Fitzpatrick, who lives on a McCreedy place on the Beekmantown road just north of Smith's Corners, a five-pound cannon ball that had just recently been picked up on his place. Now Maj. John E. Wool, at the time of the advance of the British, located his battery at Smith's Corners and fired at the oncoming British. I think this ball was one fired at that time by him.

JAN. 18—For a long time I have been struggling for a new bookcase for the back sitting room. Last spring I got some good ash lumber of Mr. I. E. Tabor and had this put up in the woodshed chamber, where it remained all summer. It could not have been better seasoned. One week ago today a man began to work at it and now it is nearly done. The case reaches nearly to the ceiling. It may not be very ornamental but it will be useful.

JAN. 22—Sunday evening about half past five the new Methodist church was found to be on fire. The church was full of smoke and yet but little damage was done. The fire was under the organ and pulpit. From what I learn, perhaps a hundred dollars will repair the damages. It was a narrow escape from a serious disaster.[1]

JAN. 26—On Thursday of this week I got my pay from the United States for attendance at the Barracks from July 5, 1888 to November 25, 1888. I attended sick call daily at $2.50 per visit. My whole bill was $360.00.

JAN. 31—On Monday evening about 4.30 Mr. I. E. Tabor was murdered on the highway a little east of his home on the Miller Road, three miles from Plattsburgh. A neighbor, Joseph Chapleau, killed him with a sled stake most cruelly.[2] If he had shot him or poisoned him or even stabbed him, the affair would not have been so merciless. But to run after a man wholly unarmed and unawares and pound him in the face until he is dead is more like the action of a beast than of a human being. Mr. Tabor was a very honorable and honest man. I have known him for nine years and have been his family physician for much of that time. In all my dealings with him he has been just and upright.

His body lay in the snow for two hours and then was carried up to his house on a wood sled. 'Twas horrible to see his blood on the door casing of his own house, from which he had gone out a few hours before, well, strong and happy. His wife, an invalid, bore up bravely. His two daughters and one baby were not at home. The body was brought to Plattsburgh that same night for a thorough post-mortem examination. The inquest was concluded today and Chapleau is held for murder.

FEB. 1—Today began the first free United States mail delivery that Plattsburgh has ever had. The corporation is divided into three districts, each with a carrier of its own. All are uniformed with a greyish-colored suit, with cape and cap if necessary. An iron letter-box is on the old gas lamp post that stands on the street near the eastern corner of our lot. However, we have not yet decided to have the mail brought to our house. I keep my post office box yet.

FEB. 6—On Monday evening of this week, in company with Dr. T. B. Nichols of Plattsburgh, I went to Albany to attend the meeting of the State Medical Society. We got to Albany at 3.25 Tuesday morning, our train having been considerably late.

Very interesting papers were read by different physicians. In the evening Dr. Piffard of New York gave us some views of diseases of the skin by means of a stereopticon. Before this, however, he showed us how he took photographs at night by flash. He had the room darkened and by means of a little contrivance threw some magnesium on to an alcohol flame, which produced instantaneously a blinding flash.

For a short time I stole out during the forenoon and went to the State Library in the Capitol building. The books from the historical part were being removed but a man showed me the books I wanted to see. I then went into the Assembly chamber and called on our member, General Stephen Moffitt.[3] After dinner I went into Munsell's and afterwards to a bookstore on Main Street, where I was economical and bought only one book, Tolstoi's *The Invaders,* for a dollar.

FEB. 18—On Wednesday of last week I received a postal from Francis stating that he was in the Mary Fletcher Hospital. He had written me the previous week that he was sick and I wrote him at once to see Dr. Grinnell. He did so and on Monday Grinnell advised him to go to the hospital. I telegraphed Grinnell and had that day and next three answers—he was not very sick, that I need not come over, and so on. However, Friday I thought it best to go over and see what was the trouble. The day was fine and with the horse "No. 2" I drove over in just three hours.

I found Francis in the male free ward. He had been there and in bed since Monday. I wanted to take him home, and on calling on Dr. Grinnell he thought because the day was fine I had better bring him that afternoon. I accordingly got a covered sleigh to take him to the Island, and telegraphed

H. B. Ransom to meet me at the Island. We put on a plenty of warm clothes; I gave him a small dose of morphine and he endured the journey well. At the Island we changed sleighs and I had a shoe set on No. 2, where he had pulled one off on the slushy ice. We got to the house about 5.30, having been only a little more than three hours on the road. Francis stood it well and in fact felt better after reaching Plattsburgh than when he left the hospital. He was only a little cold.

FEB. 22—Today I borrowed a manuscript orderly book of "Capt. John Straight's Company of the 7th Regt. New York Detach'd Militia Rendezvous'd at Salem July 7th, 1812." This company was raised at Salem, marched to Whitehall, embarked there and came to Plattsburgh. This book contains numerous muster rolls, monthly returns, provision returns, orders, morning reports, weekly returns, items of interest. In fact, it is the complete record of the doings of a militia company from the time of entering until the time of leaving the service, between 6 and 7 months. I shall make a complete copy of it, 115 pages in all.

MAR. 1—Nello and Elizabeth have chicken pox, the latter thoroughly covered with pustules. Bob had it about two weeks ago. David will have it next, probably.

MAR. 11—I went all over my copy of Capt. Straight's Orderly Book, Bessie reading the original and I comparing. I found a very few slight mistakes which I corrected, so now I have a real duplicate, accurate and exact.

MAR. 18—Bob, Nello, David, Francis have hard colds and cough dreadfully, especially David and Francis. Francis' cold has been so bad he could not go back to Burlington.

MAR. 22—The mischievous English sparrows, I think, keep the other birds away. They have stayed in our barn all winter without improving the wagons or barn furniture. They chirrup often so much like respectable birds that I often look to see if a robin, a blue jay or a ground bird has come. Well, the other birds will be here in force soon.

MAR. 23—Clear and perfect. I saw and heard a robin this morning. The whole air is full of spring sounds. The carpenters' hammers shut out everything for an instant, then wagons predominate, then the sparrows prevail. Soon the whistle of the small boy over-sounds everything. Dust begins to rise on the streets, though there is often snow at the sides and mud a foot deep in places. The amber Saranac is breaking out through its winter covering, after absorbing the water from its thousands of little feeders.

APR. 6—During the last week a great many have been sick here, although no epidemic prevails. It seems to me I could not bear the strain of so much anxiety a great while without injuring me. The physical effort is comparatively nothing.

APR. 14—Last night a little before 11 o'clock occurred a terrible affair. My friend Capt. Ogden B. Read committed suicide by shooting himself. He had been in town in the evening, got back to the Barracks about twenty minutes past ten and went into his house. His wife had gone to bed, spoke to him from the head of the stairs and he replied, cheerfully as usual. It seems then that he ate his usual lunch of crackers and milk, took off all his clothes excepting undershirt, drawers and stockings, went to his private closet, got his revolver, lay down on the lounge in his back parlor, put the end of the pistol in his mouth and fired. The ball went up through the roof of his mouth and projected out through the scalp on the top of his head, from which place I picked it out with my fingers. His wife and three children were in the house and came down immediately and saw the bleeding corpse.

Capt. Read was a genial, intelligent gentlman. His one failing was not great enough to prevent his doing his duty. Poor man. He at last found the burden of life so heavy he could not carry it any longer, so he concluded to lay it down. While grieving over his sad end we may indeed not be certain that a like fate may not be ours.[4]

APR. 16—Today was Capt. Read's funeral. His company, the battalion of high school boys that Capt. Read drilled, and Walter Benedict Post of G.A.R. escorted the remains to the dock. All went over to Burlington except the G.A.R. on the steamer *Chateaugay*. There was some doubt about the company going to Burlington. This could only be done by an order from Division headquarters or from Washington. Monday forenoon First Sergeant Brooks came into my office with tears in his eyes and said how much the men wanted to go. He thought if Gen. Peck of Burlington knew about it some arrangement might be made. I went immediately to the telegraph office and sent the following message:

"Gen. T. S. Peck, Burlington, Vermont.

Please ask Secretary of War to authorize and order F Company 11 United States Infantry to escort remains of Capt. O. B. Read to Burlington tomorrow. D. S. Kellogg. Private."

The result of this was that today at noon an order came signed "R. Proctor, Secretary of War" that sent the company to Burlington.

Last week was the trial of Harrison, the wife-murderer. Two hundred and thirty jurors were called before a panel was obtained. The defense was insanity. A strong effort was made. The jury found him guilty of murder in the second degree. This sends him to prison for life. It seems to me this was a compromise. He either should have been executed or acquitted.

APR. 29—Today began the tearing down of the courthouse. A new one is to be built where this one now stands. I tried to get the bronzed eagle on the top of it but failed. It is too bad for this house which has stood for 55 years to be torn down.

JUNE 13—Bob has his first tennis racket. This morning he and Nello and Lispeth had a set-to, before they came downstairs. Bob was defending Lispeth and Nello was against the two. Bob explained that he was Wilfred of Ivanhoe. Lispeth was Rebecca and Nello was Bois Guilbert.

JUNE 15—Last evening Mother and Mary reached Plattsburgh from Spring Valley, Minnesota. Mother has glasses and can see by daylight pretty well. She can see the children distinctly and this pleases her. Like all grandmothers she thinks there never were any children like her grandchildren. Mother, who is 81 years of age, endured the journey well.

JUNE 27—Yesterday we had fourteen pensioners to examine, a large number and hard work. I had yesterday and the day before the most terrific headache I have had for a long time.

JUNE 28—This forenoon I attended the graduation exercises of the Plattsburgh High School. They did well, but their essays were bookish and artificial. They were not allowed to show any individuality, or at least they did not show any. That such things should be done in the name of education!

JULY 10—Today was the picnic of the Peristrome Presbyterian Church Sabbath School. Lispeth was very anxious to go, so last night when she had finished her usual prayers she added, "don't let it rain tomorrow." Then turning to her mother she said, "I made that up myself." She was so much pleased with her success in making a new prayer that she continued, *"Don't let any member of this family drink or smoke."*

JULY 23—Last Saturday morning Robert had the misfortune to fall into the river. I do not know how it happened, but he was riding on a log and in some way fell in. He got out alone, but his clothes were wet up to his shoulder blades. He was not hurt any. In the afternoon he was at a party at Mr. C. E. M. Edwards' and he had the further misfortune to fall and cut his knee open. Dr. Lyon, right across the street, came over and dressed the wound and brought him home.

SEPT. 9—Today Nello and Lispeth begin their school. They go to Stella

Sherman; she has four scholars who are under her care from nine to twelve only. They both feel quite proud of the undertaking. Lispeth had to leave the table at dinner to go upstairs to "ftudy." We soon heard the sewing machine running and her singing.

The original Normal School in Plattsburgh, being built in 1889 two blocks above the Doctor's house. The school burned in 1929.

SEPT. 16—The work on the Normal School building commenced to-day.[5] The building is to stand directly across Court Street about two blocks above our house. I went up the street there this afternoon and the digging of the cellar had begun. Some men were nailing up a rough boarded building, which I presume is for a toolhouse.

SEPT. 18—I received notice tonight that my services as United States Examiner for Pensions are hereby dispensed with. I have held this place since May 1883.

SEPT. 27—On Tuesday evening of this week I started for Sorel, Canada. After breakfast I went over to see Father Dupre but he was sick and in hospital, so I could not see him. I then went to the priest's house to see Father Senecal, but he was at a funeral.

I met a gentleman on the street who said he was treasurer of the place. I told him I was trying to find any record of Madame and Baron Riedesel,[6] and especially of their little daughter, Canada Riedesel, who was born and

died in Sorel after a five months' existence. He directed me to a notary,
J. G. Crebassa, as one who could tell me about this. He thought he had
some reference to the Riedesels but on looking could not find it.

I then called on Mr. Windsor, whom I found to be a pleasant gentleman
of perhaps 35 years. He showed me his church records which began in
1784, just one year too late for the record of Canada Riedesel. From
there I went to the office of the county clerk, if that is his title. He showed
me the records for both the English and Catholic churches for 1784 (the
former) and for 1783, the latter. I found nothing here or anywhere else.
I was leaving the beautiful Sorel without indeed having found any record
of the Riedesels, but I hope another year to search again and expect to
be more successful.

OCT. 1—Today with Dr. R. E. Hyde of Beekmantown I examined all
of the insane and all of the idiots at the County House in Beekmantown.
This was done by order of the State Board of Lunacy. There are ninety
four inmates of the County House. Of these thirty five are insane and nineteen are idiots. Just think of that![7] Many were apparently rational enough
until they were touched on their peculiar delusions. One man attended the
boiler of the steam-heating apparatus. He was faithful from morning until
night, always in the boiler room, but ask him what he met on the road
and he would go on and give a long conversation between himself and some
animal he had met.

OCT. 14—A letter came from Francis this morning rejoicing over his
class's victory over the Freshmen last Saturday at Burlington. Francis told
Bess last week that the Freshmen had put him under the pump or into the
water, that in the operation he pulled one big Freshman into the water
and ducked him. As a result the Freshman ducked him again. I presume it
will do Francis good.

NOV. 1—Last night I went over to Burlington to see Francis. He rooms
at No. 2, North Hall in the College. His second cousin, George C. Martin,
is his roommate. I took tea with Francis at the "hash house," where we had
a good enough supper. I stayed with the boys that night, sleeping in their
north bedroom.

In the morning before breakfast Prof. Perkins came over for me to take
breakfast with him, which I did and also dinner. I made enquiries of different ones in regard to Francis. Prof. Perkins said "he heard only good
of him." Prof. Emerson said "he was one of our good boys." Prof. Goodrich said he might study more, but he seemed to think well of him.

NOV. 8—I want some new books to read and must have them.

NOV. 9—I have had a good many sick ones today, none of them, I hope, dangerously so. I believe it much easier to endure the real troubles than the constant worrying about them. There is theoretically no need of shaking hands with the devil until you meet him. However, with a doctor it is almost daily life or death. The beginning of life, the end of life. What are they?

The world is full of things to delight us. The very fact of living is a luxury. A man told me the other day if he knew he could be as happy in the other life as he had been in this when his wife was alive, he would not care to live five minutes. After all, it is not to be wondered at that men do get desperate and discontented, yet what good does it do?

NOV. 16—They have ten electric lamps around the Normal School building in order to enable the men to make out full days' work. It looks very pretty to see that dark place so well lighted up to half past six at night.

NOV. 30—On Wednesday evening died a patient of mine whom I first saw on Monday. She was about 30 years of age, an orphan. Whatever her life may have been, her end was very pathetic. She seemed to me very quiet and sad during her illness. She impressed me as one who would have been highly respected and beloved had she had any chance for her life. Death was rather welcome to her than otherwise. It was a solution of the sad problem of her life.

DEC. 11—I wish some one would give me one thousand dollars on the condition that I spend it all for books before the beginning of the year 1890. I would complete my set of *The Nation*, I would complete my set of the Prince Society's publications. I would have Ponchot's *Memoirs of the Late War*, and Justin Winsor's *Narrative and Critical History*, also Charlevoix's *History of France*. These would take at least 225 dollars. I could easily make up the balance. Like Traddles and his list of girls looking into the shop windows and pointing out what things they would buy if they had the money, I must look through the book catalogues and long to buy these volumes which I some day, even as it is, intend to have for my own.

DEC. 21—Thursday morning Francis came home on the steamer *Chateaugay*. Thursday evening Theo came home via Albany, reaching Plattsburgh at 7.20. Friday night Helen came home from Clifton Springs. All three of them are well and happy.

On the 22nd Dr. Kellogg received from Washington a formal letter of reappointment to the Board of Examining Surgeons, whose chief work for years had been to examine Civil War veterans for pensions. When he get things charged just as we did before."

DEC. 25—Christmas. What a happy day for the children. All four were awake before three in the morning but did not come downstairs until after five. A good many children came to the house to wish us a Merry Christmas and get a present.

DEC. 28—Today the new Board of Examining Surgeons for Pensions was organized in my office. It is as follows: President, Dr. Romeo E. Hyde; Treasurer, Dr. George D. Dunham; Secretary, Dr. D. S. Kellogg.

DEC. 31—The last day of the year. This has been a good year for me pecuniarily. I have collected thirty five hundred nineteen dollars and twenty five cents and have been present at the arrival of eighty two children into this cold world.

Notes on 1889

1. The Methodist church had been dedicated in 1885. It escaped destruction in 1889, but burned to the ground in 1956.

2. Chapleau was apparently obsessed with the conviction that Mr. Tabor had poisoned his cow, although this had been completely disproved at the time; she had been found to have two nails working outward through the walls of the stomach.

3. During the Civil War Moffitt rose to the rank of brigadier general. He lost a leg at Five Oaks and spent some time in the notorious Libby Prison.

4. Captain Read served in the Civil War and the Indian wars in the West. The coroner's jury decided he took his life "while laboring under a fit of temporary insanity," but friends thought it might have resulted from financial difficulties.

5. In June Governor Hill signed the legislature's bill authorizing $60,000 for a Normal School. The County Board of Supervisors contributed $3,000 for the site and with remarkable speed, work was started in September.

6. Major General the Baron Friederich von Riedesel (1738–1800) commanded the German troops in Burgoyne's campaign to Saratoga. His wife Friedericka (1746–1808) and her three children shared his fate on the campaign and as a prisoner of war. He was exchanged in 1779 and rejoined the British forces for the remainder of the war.

7. This care of the insane was not unusual. In May the legislature defeated a bill to remove the indigent insane from the country poorhouses. Nevertheless, the State Care Act of 1890 forbade such confinement of the insane and made them wards of the state. At the time the state assumed their care, 2,200 were in county institutions.

1890

In one of the year's most anxious moments, the Doctor's horse No. 2 falls through the ice on Lake Champlain while hauling him and his daughter in a sleigh. Luckily, all three escape with no lasting ill effects.

By all odds the most memorable experience of 1890 for Doctor Kellogg, so admiring of literary personages, is that of becoming acquainted with William Dean Howells and his family. This is a chance event that appears to have been equally gratifying to the latter. The Doctor writes at length and enthusiastically of their various meetings during the Howells' vacation in town.

During the year, Doctor Kellogg becomes a permanent member of the New York Medical Society, is increasingly in demand as a speaker on non-medical subjects, and pursues a new interest: the geology of the Ice Age.

Admiring the splendor of his assembled Indian relics in a large case he has had built for them, the Doctor exclaims, "One is not aware what enjoyment there is in a hobby, well ridden, unless he has experienced one."

JAN. 11—Yesterday thermometer was 8° below 0 all day. Early this morning it was thirteen° below. About 10 a.m. it began to snow heavy, large and firm flakes. Thermometer below 0 all day but rising. At 5 p.m. it was at 0, at 7 p.m. it was 30° above, a most remarkable change.

JAN. 13—Nelson has the mumps—on one side only, the left side. He had it in 1885 but I don't know whether on both sides. He is not sick at all but complains because he cannot get enough to eat. His appetite has not diminished in the least.

We are having quite a remarkable epidemic called the "Grip," influenza, or some other name. I have seen upwards of one hundred sick with it within the last two weeks.[1]

JAN. 20—This is court week and Joseph Chapleau, who murdered J. E. Tabor, is to be tried for his life. I suppose I shall have to go as a witness and I dread it. This is the first case in the first court in the new courthouse.

JAN. 22—The trial of Chapleau lasted two days. The jury after a short session found him guilty of murder in the first degree. He is to receive his sentence next Tuesday.

Today I have had a few minutes to myself. I have hardly ever been so busy during the same length of time as during the last three weeks. Still, I have hardly had a patient dangerously ill.

FEB. 1—Joseph Chapleau received his death sentence on Wednesday. He was to be taken to Dannemora, kept in solitary confinement until March 3, 1890, then during the week following that date he is to be executed by having a current of electricity passed through his body until he is dead. I believe he will be the first person to be executed by electricity under the new state law. This is a doubtful honor.[2]

During the week, while coming up Bridge Street I met a funeral procession. There were six or eight open sleighs and cutters followed by a one-horse buggy containing one man. There was no hearse, but an open two-horse sled held the little coffin covered with a blanket. The horses were poor and looked as if they had never been groomed. The harnesses were shabby and tied together by pieces of strings. The whole procession looked like starvation itself. Yet it was a feeling for humanity that brought these poor people to follow the remains of one of their friends to the grave. I do not doubt there was more real grief in this one abject procession than in many others where the display would attract the attention of everybody.

FEB. 4—This morning when Rob came downstairs he had the mumps. So far the right side only is swelled. He is quite feverish this evening.

FEB. 8—At the meeting of the New York State Medical Society held in Albany I was elected a permanent member of that society. I had been delegate from the Medical Society of Clinton County for two successive years and had attended the state society meetings for these two years. At the third meeting I was eligible to membership of the state society whether I attended or not, so by resigning at the last county society meeting I could give another man a chance to gain one year on his time for becoming a member of the state society. This I did, and Dr. T. B. Nichols was elected delegate and attended the state society meeting at Albany this week.

FEB. 10—Yesterday I had a singular experience. I started for the Head with Lispeth in the cutter. I had horse No. 2. In the north part of the village I met Mr. George H. Anderson. I asked him if the ice were good and he said yes, it was good there and everywhere. So I felt safe and drove on at the lowest beach.

The ice looked all right. I soon came to a crack which was closed and apparently solid. The horse had no sooner got on to this than he began to sink, and down he went. I hurried Lispeth out of the sleigh and told her to run back where it was safe. I managed without any difficulty to unfasten the tugs and unsnap the holdbacks. Then with one hand I shoved

67

the sleigh clear back out of the way. I happened to think of a strong strap neck halter that was in the cutter. I got this immediately and by good luck managed to get this buckled around the neck and put the strap through the bit ring. I shouted to Lispeth to run over to the houses, about 100 rods away, and have the men come to help me. Meantime two or three teams passed along the road, but with all my shouting and gesticulating and whistling I could not attract their attention. When the horse was quiet it was not hard to hold him, but when he floundered it took all my strength to keep his head above water. Occasionally his shoulders would come up out of water, but nearly all the time his head only was up.

Pretty soon I saw a man running whom Bessie had routed out. I found afterwards that she had gone to one house, but the man was so deaf he could not understand her. Then she went to another. The first man soon got to me and I asked him to hold the halter while I ran for a rail from a fence about 40 rods away. By the time I got back more men had come with a chain which they proceeded to fasten around the neck with the idea of choking him so he would come to the top of the water. Then one of them put the rail under his shoulders and by pulling on the halter and chain we got him so his right foreleg was on the ice. Then by getting the rail down so as to crowd his left foreleg from under the ice and by all pulling the halter and chain that could get hold, we instantly had him on top of the ice and at a safe distance from the opening. Immediately the men had him up and fastened on to the sleigh.

I had four dollars in my jacket which I told them to divide among themselves. They did not want to take it, but I insisted and they took it. One of them got in to drive for me, I was so out of breath, and in less than two minutes from the time the horse was out of the water we were off. Arriving at Mr. Calkins', the horse was put into a warm stall and had three blankets put on to him. Although he had shivered from the time of getting him out of the water, he was soon warm and went immediately to eating. I put one blanket on him under the harness before starting home. The horse had broken the check rein and was a little scratched behind his left knee. Otherwise he seems all right, eating and drinking well. After getting him out of the water and up, he looked around with a look that was almost human, as if grateful.

While I was gone after the rail the horse floundered so the man lost his hold of the halter. I thought certainly the horse would get under the ice, but the man finally got hold of the halter again. This same man came up to the house before one o'clock to tell me what a mean fellow the one was that I handed the money to. He had sent him only a quarter, while some had 75 cents and others 50 cents. I gave him a quarter more, which seemed to satisfy him. The horse was in the water at least 20 minutes.

68

Had it not been for Lispeth he would have been chilled through and died before I could obtain help. This afternoon I took Bob, Nello and David down to see the place of our adventure. We measured the depth of the water and found it to be 8 feet. It was about 125 paces from the ridge of sawdust next to the shore.

FEB. 21—I have just finished Mr. Wright's *The Ice Age in North America*. It is a valuable book. I must say I cannot yet believe in the theory of upheavals and depressions. I think the movements of the large glacier will yet be accounted for in other and more satisfactory ways. Why may not the rotation of the earth have had something to do with it? If there is a tendency of the earth to accumulate at the equator and to "flatten" at the poles, may not this rotation have been a factor in the southward ice movement? Of course modified by existing mountain ranges and valleys? Perhaps when I learn more of the reasons for thinking there were upheavals and depressions I may the more believe in them.[3]

I am trying to get more numbers of *The Nation*. I have sent a list of my wants and duplicates to the Fletcher Library at Burlington where I learn they have some duplicates they would like to exchange.

FEB. 22—An old and poor Frenchwoman has for years come into my office to have me remove her ingrowing eye lashes. She is always very polite and invariably asks "Wifey well?" "Yes," I say. "Baby too?" "Yes." "Good." As only once in a while does she have any money and then only a quarter of a dollar, she thinks a little flattery will help me. She always says, "Ah, bon garcon for me. Ah, me sick, sick, poor, poor, poor. No money. Me die pretty soon. Tank ee, tank ee. Me mori. Bon soir."

FEB. 24—A woman cut her throat in town yesterday. The gash was about four inches long, but never very deep. Her daughter is insane and her son is a nervous drunkard. She was taken to Poughkeepsie last night by the County Superintendent of the Poor.

FEB. 28—I am having a large case made for relics in the little room at the end of the hall.

MAR. 9—This morning I drove over to the Island to see a patient with Dr. Petty. We got back about noon. In the afternoon Col. Palmer met me with a note from his sister wanting me to go to West Chazy to see her daughter. I drove out and got home about 9 p.m. Of course I was tired, but the 15 dollars received for the two visits eased my weariness.

MAR. 12—The ice-men are working hard and piling up immense quantities of ice. I hope they will sell as much in New York as they can put up here. The ice famine on the Hudson will be a good thing for us.[4]

1890   MAR. 13—I am getting my new case filled with relics. I have taken up all the Big and Little Chazy find. That is much more enormous than I was aware of. It will look well, spread out. One is not aware what enjoyment there is in a hobby, well ridden, unless he has experienced one. I would not give the enjoyment I have had in finding and gathering relics for any pecuniary consideration I can think of. To think of the times I have gotten up in the night to drive out to the Big Chazy so as to be on hand early in the morning. I have visited so many places to look for, and to get, relics. I can truthfully say I have looked the whole lake shore over from Rouses Point to Port Kent. I do not think there are many rods in that whole distance I have not travelled over.

MAR. 21—Francis brought over 153 numbers of *The Nation* for me from the Fletcher Library. I am to pay 10 cents per number for all before Volume VIII, and 5 cents for all later. Cheap, cheap.

APR. 8—Last evening was the last session of our Monday Evening Club for this season. Miss Helen D. Woodward had her fifth talk on architecture. These talks have been during the winter, interspersed with evenings in which some of Shakespeare was read. Frank Palmer had a pretty story, the scene of which was laid at Winchester Cathedral. Here he found the remains of Sir George Prevost, who had "gloriously" conducted a campaign in America in 1814.[5]

APR. 12—This week we examined 30 men for pensions. It is very hard work indeed, still it pays pretty well.[6]

APR. 17—Poor Nello has the mumps again, on right side only. This morning he came downstairs complaining his face hurt him. It was already swelling in front of the ear. He is feverish and uncomfortable. This is the third time he has had the mumps, on one side only each time.

MAY 17—Mrs. Smith came from Burlington yesterday forenoon to stay while Bessie and I make our trip to Boscawen, Boston, Wellesley and Providence. This is a journey we have been looking forward to for some months. I presume we have spent more time and brains talking about it and planning for it than many people do in taking a trip to Europe. It has required more time than brains, I imagine.

Between May 21 and May 26 the Kelloggs made a whirlwind trip into southern New England. Whether Mrs. Kellogg enjoyed this kind of travel is not recorded, but the Doctor's pleasure is manifest. Examination of museums and private collections of artifacts, visits to bookstores and exploration of the countryside with his new eye for geologic formations gave zest to his trip. They made two brief visits to his niece Theo at

Wellesley, and tracked down the old haunts of his late brother-in-law,
Osceola Kyle, in Westerly, Rhode Island. Concerning the return home he wrote, "Of all the beautiful scenery we had met with in all of our wanderings, there was none equal to that we saw on our way from Burlington to Plattsburgh. No wonder people sing the praises of Lake Champlain."

JUNE 23—Today Lispeth is all broken out with the measles. She began to break out yesterday. She is coughing much and is very uncomfortable.

Dr. LaRocque and Dr. Dunham are both sick. Dr. T.B. Nichols is in Chicago, so we that are on our feet have much to do. I attended a postmortem examination today. Some weeks ago I had made a positive diagnosis of cancer on the posterior wall of the stomach. Dr. A.W. Fairbank, unknown to me, had previously made the same diagnosis. Drs. D'Avignon, Low, McKinney and Nichols were unable to make a diagnosis. Well, in the presence of all the above-mentioned physicians excepting Dr. Nichols, Dr. Fairbank's and my own diagnosis was fully and completely substantiated.

JUNE 25—I went to Burlington to attend the Sigma Phi reunion last night. I had the Oration. We adjourned to supper from the Hall a little after 12 m. at the Van Ness. I spoke on Thoreau. We got up from the table at 3.45 a.m. I returned by boat this morning on account of pension day.

JULY 8—Today was the fifth semiannual excursion of the Medical Society of the county of Clinton. We went to Highgate Springs per steamer *Reindeer* and train. A few more than 400 persons formed the party. Our way back a terrible wind overtook us. We were between Swanton and Alburg. Rain came, too. We went through this storm and when we got to the *Reindeer* only a little rain was falling. We got on to the boat all right. When a few miles from the point of the Head, we saw a heavy gale and sea in front of us. This soon met us and we it. The waves were at least 15 feet high. Under the good management of the captain and pilot we went along all right and got in to Plattsburgh, a safe and quiet harbor, at five minutes past seven.

Here a different scene met us. Our hard wind on the train had been a cyclone, almost, at Plattsburgh. Trees had blown down on the streets and all around. The elm in front of our house, that had suffered so much from horses and winds, had its top broken right off about 18 feet from the ground. The pines near the garrison were blown over to the number of a hundred. Bluff Point Hotel was considerably injured. Barns in the country were blown down. Roofs were blown off and chimneys were toppled over. However, our excursion party had escaped all this.

AUG. 4—Yesterday afternoon I had the pleasure of spending the time two until five with William D. Howells, the author. He, with his wife and daughter, are spending a few days at Witherill House. Mr. J.H. Myers introduced me to them. We two went down to the hotel and sent up our cards. We found them on the middle piazza. Mrs. Howells was quite thin and spare, dressed in a black silk. The daughter Mildred, apparently about 16, had a beautiful mouth and teeth and was very pleasant. My good fortune was to be near Mr. Howells.

I spoke to him about the historic and prehistoric matters of interest here, and after a few minutes' conversation asked him if he would like to see my collections and also take a little ride around town. He seemed glad of the opportunity and heartily wanted to go. Nello had been holding the horse below. A little boy got between the wheel and wagon. I called out, "Nello, don't let the little boy stay there." Mrs. Howells at once spoke of the name Nello and said it was in George Eliot's *Romola*. I told her I was afraid it came from there, although it was a nickname for Nelson.

Mr. Howells had on a light shortcoat and vest of the same material. He put on a havelock hat and we started. I drove at once to the house. It began to rain a little. I asked him if he would mind my driving around into the barn. He did not at all so rode around and into the barn with me.

We went into the hall and he was much interested in the guns, swords, bayonets and other relics of the War of 1812. Then he went into the little room with me where were the cases of Indian relics which he seemed to enjoy much. He stood up in a chair to see the two jars of pottery from the Creek which are on the top shelf. He pulled out from among others a modern red stone pipe and asked if that were not modern. I showed him the reference in Radisson's voyages to the occupation at the Creek and on the Richelieu in 1651–52. Then we started out again for a drive. He went out to the barn and got into the wagon with me in the barn. He remarked that he thought Kinglake gave the best description of a battle that he knew of. I told him I thought we should except Tolstoi in *War and Peace*.

"Yes," he said, "we must always except Tolstoi. I think him the greatest, by far the greatest novelist that I know of."

He asked me if in my experience with death I did not find that Tolstoi's descriptions were accurate, such as, for instance, Andre's thoughts while facing the swath behind the battery and his men. I told him that my actual experience of death was comparatively small, that I well remembered holding a man's pulse while life was going out. The pulse stopped, surprised, began again, stopped again as if surprised, began again, then finally gave it up and went out. He referred again to the scene when Anatole K. has his leg taken off. He spoke of the death of Ivan Ilitch as

most powerful, as also Sebastopol. I then further told him how I read and
re-read *War and Peace* and how Tolstoi awed me and how I admired him.

He remarked, "I am very glad to hear you say so."

In reference to *Kreutzer Sonata* he said as a work of art it was very fine, but that Tolstoi made a mistake in adding his views of marriage. He then told me of a dream he had after his oldest daughter died. She had quite an active mind and overdid, had nervous prostration. He took her to Dr. Weir Mitchell and after a time she had to go to a private retreat, where she died. This dream was that her spirit came back to him and he was helping her up a hill. He questioned her about her present state. She said she was "lonesome at first and cried but had not weeped since." He asked if she were happy now. She replied cheerfully, "Oh, yes." He said he was brought up a Swedenborgian.

I drove down past the Boynton place and showed him the well where Mr. Lowell is said to have hidden the British gold at the time of the invasion in 1814.[7] He was interested in the story, but was more interested in the old Boynton house itself. He looked back at it, turning around in the buggy saying, "What beautiful elms, what a beautiful place. How I should like to live there."

We drove around the Point and to my office. He held the horse a few minutes while I was in the office. I picked out a pretty arrow point and gave him. Then we went around and saw the old earthworks on the government grounds—Forts Scott, Moreau, Brown.[8] At 5 p.m. we reached the hotel where he was staying.

AUG. 6—Yesterday forenoon I met Mrs. Howells on the street near the post office. She recognized me before I did her. She wanted to know about the grave of Lucretia Maria Davidson.[9] They had been all through the cemetery the previous day but could not find it. I took her in the buggy with Nello, David and myself and went up to the cemetery. She was much pleased to find it. She read the inscription on the north side of it, but thought it was not good and could hardly believe it was from Bryant. I drove on and around the Point and showed her the house where Lucretia lived and died. She thought it was a charming place and that she would like to live there herself. After she went back to the hotel Bess called on her and asked her and hers up to the house to tea that evening, which was accepted. At 6.15 Nello drove down with the horse and brought up Mrs. Howells, while Mr. Howells and daughter walked. At the table I let Mrs. Howells eat off the Battle-of-Plattsburgh plate, a thing not done before. We had a delightful evening. All talked. Often I could not make Bessie hear me across the table, so many were talking.

After tea I showed them the manuscript book of L.M.D.'s poems, transcribed mostly by her mother, but some by Lucretia herself. I also showed them several advertisements in the old newspapers of Oliver Davidson, Lucretia's father. After a time I went in to the front sitting room and talked with Mr. Howells himself. I remarked to him that I disliked the word "class" as applied to people. He said he did too, very much. He could not bear the expressions "upper class" and "lower class" as often used. Another word he disliked much was servant. He said, "They are not our servants, they are our helpers."

At ten they started. Francis carried Mrs. Howells. I walked with Mr. Howells and daughter. On account of the wet sidewalks Bessie insisted on the daughter's taking and wearing some rubbers of Theo. After some hurrying the rubbers were produced and Mr. Howells remarked that Millie had not had so much attention shown her feet for some time. We had a pleasant talk on the way down. I told Mr. Howells how much I enjoyed his acquaintance, or rather seeing him. He said to me he felt as if he "had met an old friend in me and hoped that we should meet many, many times again." I must say I felt complimented.

Mrs. Howells told me of a letter her husband had once received from Robert Louis Stevenson. They had been in England and had seen many of the younger authors, such as Andrew Lang. These wanted the Howells to meet Mr. Stevenson, but he was away. Some time afterwards, while in Italy, Mr. Howells received a letter from Mr. Stevenson stating that his wife had been divorced from Mr. (naming the man) in order to marry him, and that he could not receive under his roof anybody who was too good to associate with her.

AUG. 7—This morning I took Mr. Howells out for a drive to Fredenburgh Falls and Treadwell's Mills. His father and brother live on a farm or in a farming region in southern Ohio. He thought it strange that so little money passed among farmers. His brother had told him that among some farmers hardly fifty dollars were circulated during the year. He also told me of an experience he once had in Washington of things that had better not been said. One evening he was introduced to a lady, perhaps 25 years of age, who was very tall. Her first remark to him was, "Mr. Howells, I have read your books ever since I was so high," making a gesture with her hand to indicate *how* high. To his own utter surprise, unmeaningly and before he was aware of what he had said, he replied, "Am I so old as that?" He said he spent nearly the whole evening trying to apologize for that.

While coming down Rugar Street I called his attention to the Green Mountains and to the Adirondacks. He said, "Do you know, this level plain really attracts me more than the mountains. It is more like the land where I was born and spent my childhood. One really makes his

The "Singing Sands" beach at the Hotel Champlain in 1890.

companions in life by the conditions of his childhood." At Fredenburgh Falls I tried to start a log over the falls, but did not succeed. I did not think specially about it but I saw him at once try to push it off at the expense of getting his feet wet. I immediately took off my shoes and stockings, waded in and got the log off. He watched it go down through the rapids until it was out of sight.

Quite a number of years ago Mr. Howells, when a young author, went over to see Hawthorne. While there Hawthorne gave him a letter or card of introduction to Emerson. When he called on Emerson and presented him his letter, Emerson looked it over and said, "Yes, Hawthorne is a good neighbor, but that last book of his is all bosh." Mrs. Howells told me that her husband only went to school two years in his life, but he now could speak fluently in five languages.

AUG. 8—Mr. Howells called at the office in the forenoon but I was not in. He left two books which he gave me. About 5 p.m. he called at the house. I was at the office, but Lispeth drove down for me. He was just as cordial and friendly and agreeable as ever. He told Bess that he could not leave town without coming to see me again, that he had been to the office twice during the day but I was not in.

I spoke to him about John Burroughs, telling him how much I admired him, but that I thought he was out of his element when he wrote about other things than nature, and instanced his paper on Thoreau. "Yes," he said, "John Burroughs is not a good critic."

AUG. 13—Philo came over last Saturday evening. He and I went out to Peru yesterday to a farmer's picnic in Smith Grove. There was a large number present of comfortable-appearing people, both men and women and children. Speeches were made and I think a farmer's alliance was formed.[10]

AUG. 19—Helen started for Shelbyville, Kentucky yesterday, where she is to teach.

AUG. 30—On Wednesday I went to Crown Point on the 1.10 train and returned on the evening train. There had been a landslide about 2 miles this side of Crown Point and a freight train had sunk down with the track. About 2 acres of ground had slid towards the lake. A passenger train had held back at Crown Point for this train to get ahead and onto a switch. The passengers scolded about it a good deal, but had they gone ahead of this freight, hardly a man would have been left alive. The cars piled in one on top of another, three deep, and some of them were covered up in the mud. Hardly a man was hurt.

Today I have been over to the house of the late Judge Peter S. Palmer to look over some books and papers with the view of buying them. It was sad to see the rows and rows of books and magazines and papers piled up in his upstairs rooms and in his attic, which he had accumulated with so much pains and expense, now held in no esteem by his sons and only prized by them for their money value. I wonder if my collections of Indian relics and of books will be as little valued by my sons and family!

SEPT. 2—Today Bob and Nello went to school, the beginning of the new school year. Bob enters the Grammar School, Nello the Intermediate. Lispeth does not go to school unless she recites to her mother. David is the only one now who would prefer to be with his mother or me; in other words, the others are beginning to grow away from their parents and become individuals. 'Tis better so, in fact it is the only true way, yet it sometimes seems rather hard.

SEPT. 11—I went to Crown Point Center and about four miles beyond to examine a pensioner. I left at 10.30 and got home at 8 p.m. or later. The government pays my expenses and allows me the enormous sum of two dollars!

OCT. 16—This morning I found pinned on to my office door a note of which the following is a copy: "please Doctor cone up to Lause Ashline we nead you afol dade cane rite strat off aas you gate this noat." On the back was "Prue streat Lause Ashley." Not recalling who Lause Ashley, or Ashline, was or where he or she lived, I did not respond then but did later. Typhoid fever.

NOV. 4—Voted this morning for the first time under the new law. Each man has to be registered beforehand. A little wooden house twenty or more feet square has been built here for a voting place. A railing extends nearly across the one room, within which are the election officers and polling place. Two officers sit near the entrance through the railing with five piles of papers in front of them. These papers have stubs and are the tickets.

One ticket is the regular Republican, one the Democratic, one has two names, I believe—the Prohibition, one has one, a Socialist, and one is blank. The five are given to a single voter, who goes into a little enclosed space by himself where is a shelf for a desk, a lead pencil and a pen and ink. Here he closes the door and selects the ticket he wants to vote. He can take pasters in and put them on over any name he does not want to vote for, substituting his preference. He can write all the names he wants to vote on the blank ticket. When done he comes out with the ticket he wants to vote in one hand and the other four in the other. He gives his name, age, street and number, and hands his ticket to one man and his unused tickets to another. No man is allowed to do any electioneering whatever within 150 feet of the polling place. The whole arrangement so far seems to please everybody. It certainly makes one feel that there is a dignity in voting.[11]

NOV. 7—Tonight Rob and Nello's little dancing club met at the house. After the dancers were gone and after supper we played authors, all excepting David. Then the mother played on the piano and all sang, even David. "The Campbells are coming" and "Rig a jig jig, way we go" are his favorites. To see the children all marching and singing and shouting was as pretty and agreeable entertainment as one ever need have.

NOV. 18—Today I got Sir Walter Scott's *Journal*, also Howells' *A Boy's Town*. I am anticipating both very much. I have not yet succeeded in completing my files of *The Nation*. A.S. Clark of New York offers to complete my set for $90, which is far beyond me.

NOV. 25—Our reading club met at H.W. Cady's last evening and read the latter portion of *Henry VIII*. Next week the club is appointed to meet at our house and work up the preliminaries of *King John*.

I am reading the second volume of Sir Walter's *Journal*. The courage and hard work of that wonderful man are something marvelous. His *Journal* reveals him as he was—a human being, great-hearted, energetic, modest, of wonderful brain power, such a man as one feels he would like to have known personally and intimately.

NOV. 26—Francis came home from college today for Thanksgiving. He says the students had a rejoicing last night over the defeat in the Senate of the Vermont legislature of the bill to remove the State Agricultural College from Burlington to Rutland. About a hundred of them put on their uniforms with their nightshirts outside, got the Sherman band and a drum corps, and marched through town. They also went around to the houses of several of the professors whom they called out to make speeches.

DEC. 12—Have finished Sir Walter Scott's *Journal* and have loaned it to several different persons. It is charming, exquisite. Have also finished Howells' *Boy's Town*, which I like very much. Am reading Wm. B. Weeden's *Economic and Social History of New England*. This is a valuable work.

DEC. 16—Last Sunday George cut Lispeth's and Nello's hair. Bessie told Lispeth that David's must not be cut, but she understood her to have it cut. So when the two were completed, off came David's curls. When the mother came home from church at noon she cried very hard. This is the first time David's hair had ever been cut excepting a little in front.

DEC. 20—Have finished the first volume of Weeden's. I like it much. I wish I were able to write a good book, one that people would enjoy reading.

I began to attend at the Barracks yesterday in the absence of Dr. J.H. Bartholf on his wedding tour. The bride is less than 27 years of age. He is considerably over 60. But they say he has money. Poor things.

DEC. 22—I started to drive to Lapham's Mills but met Dr. Kinsley two miles this side of that place, who told me the patient was dead.

The whole range of the Green Mountains was snow-covered and purple. It reminded me of the winter schoolteaching when I was in college, in Panton, Vermont, just south of Vergennes. I taught three winters during my college course. The white schoolhouse on the hill gave us a fine view of the hills and mountains east and west. The brilliant sunset and sunrises, the hills and valleys, and the kind people come before me like a picture. The marvelous kindness of every one, whether scholar or parent, convinces me of the actual goodness of the human family.

I remember, during my first term, that Mr. C.S. Harris, the committee-man, visited the school and stayed during the afternoon. He wrote in the register on the page for "Remarks of Visitors": "Good order—good deportment—good school." I don't know that I have felt prouder of anything in my life.

I boarded around, staying two or three weeks in some places. The best of everything was given to me at every place, and every member of the family was uniformly kind and polite. During the first part of my first term I lay awake until 3 or 4 o'clock in the morning, fearing that I could not explain satisfactorily the next day some reasons for some of the processes in fractions.

DEC. 25—Christmas. Last evening there was a tree at Peristrome Church. The children had beautiful things there. Then they came home and after many secret whisperings and consultations and journeys they went to bed. Theo, the mother and I, and later, Francis, arranged the presents. Rob and Nello each fastened a stocking onto an end of the sofa in the front sitting room, and Lispeth put one in the middle. There was a basketful of presents for the children alone, the basket holding at least a bushel.

After we had gone to bed and been asleep what seemed only a short time Nello appeared and said it was after 6. It was very bright moonlight. The mother got up, lighted a match, and with Nello stood on tiptoes in the corner of the dining room to see the time by the clock. It was half past two. So all went back to bed. However, at 6 the three children came down and examined what they had. Everyone seems unusually happy. It really pays to give them all so much pleasure.

DEC. 31—This has been a wonderfully good year for me. While my collections have not been quite so large as last year, this is due not to less

1890 business but to more extra collections last year. I have this year collected $3,373.92 and have been present at the arrival into this outside world of eighty nine newcomers.

Notes for 1890

1. It was known at the time as Russian influenza. One publicized treatment was hot lemonade and raw onions.

2. Chapleau's case was unsuccessfully appealed for a new trial on the grounds that a confession was insufficient evidence of guilt. He was resentenced to be electrocuted in July, but Governor Hill commuted the sentence to life imprisonment. Meanwhile, the new electrocution law of the state had been appealed to the Court of Appeals on the grounds that it was unconstitutional because it took the killing of convicts out of the hands of sheriffs and placed it with the wardens. The Court ruled it constitutional. The U.S. Supreme Court, where it was next appealed, on May 23 found the law "unusual" but not cruel in the context of the federal constitution. The first electrocution took place at Auburn in August.

3. Dr. Kellogg's reaction to Wright's book reveals a bold and questioning mind. Modern knowledge of the movement of glaciers provides explanations that neither Wright nor Kellogg thought of.

4. Five thousand men were engaged in the ice harvest on the lake. The ice sold for an average price of $1.25 a ton, producing a clear profit of 75 cents. Freight costs to New York City were $2 a ton, to Philadelphia $2.50.

5. Sir George Prevost was the Governor General of Canada and leader of the British forces at the battle of Plattsburgh in 1814.

6. Dr. Kellogg's pension work was stepped up considerably in 1890 as a result of the Morrill Service Pension Bill. It greatly liberalized pensions to Civil War veterans regardless of the origin of their disability, put all 90-day veterans on pensions at age 60, and liberalized pensions for widows.

7. Samuel Lowell lived in this house, which still stands at 98 Boynton Avenue, at the time of the British occupation. It was the brigade headquarters of British Major General Brisbane. Lowell is supposed to have secreted a keg of British gold in the well.

8. These three forts were built for the defense of Plattsburgh in 1814. Only the earthen depression of Fort Brown survives. Forts Moreau and Scott were levelled in the creation of a parade ground at the Barracks.

9. One of two sisters, highly regarded as poets in their day. Lucretia was born in Plattsburgh in 1808 and she died of consumption before her seventeenth birthday.

10. This was the heyday of the Farmers' Alliances in the Midwest and South. In the Northeast it was the National Farmers' League. It was nonpartisan but prompted the professional and political welfare of farmers. At Peru three town Leagues were formed as branches of the State Farmers' League, and in October a County League was formed.

11. The Saxton Ballot Bill was the culmination of years of effort by the reformers. It for the first time required registration to end the frauds of unauthorized voting; the printing of ballots at public expense; and more careful watch at the polling places. It provided privacy in the voting booth but not yet a secret ballot.

1891

Doctor Kellogg's intellectual horizons are widened this year with his delighted discovery of the poetry of Emily Dickinson and the histories of John Fiske. His geographical horizons are expanded by trips to Washington, D.C., and historic Quebec City. He yearns to write a book "that would interest people and that would do them good," but feels the lack of "something to say, some good point to make."

When permitted a brief time to pursue one of his hobbies, he makes an exciting find for his collection of old blue dishes. In the course of his professional duties, he is amused to report one pension applicant who claims sixteen disabilities, though failing to mention the only one the Doctor finds worthy of serious attention.

Doctor Kellogg's professional standing is recognized with his election to the presidency of the Medical Association of Northern New York. He notes the bare fact in his Journal, but what appears to have impressed him most that day is his first reading of Emily Dickinson's poems. "These seem to stir up a field in my mind that needs cultivating," he writes.

JAN. 1—I wish I were worth as much as there has been spent for whiskey in town during the last 48 hours. Why is it that Frenchmen *will* get drunk New Year's! The enjoyment they get out of it is a mystery to me. I presume they would tell me it was because I have never been drunk.

I have for years had a great desire to write a book. Still, I do not know that I have either. It would be humiliating to me to write one that would fall flat and be of no value. One has just come out by Mrs. Veeder, who used to live in this vicinity. I should not like to write such a book as that. Much rather would I go down to the grave "unsung." I should like to write one that would interest people and that would do them good. But one not accustomed cannot sit down and write by mere force of will. If he does so his effort will amount to nothing. He must have something to say, some good point to make.

Let us see. We have in this locality the story of the lead mine, known to the Indians and revealed to one white man alone, who died before he made the place known to other white men. This has been located at Trembleau mountain near Port Kent, also near Gouverneur, also back from Malone.

Then there is the story of British gold, brought here by the British at the time of the invasion in September 1814, and rolled into the well by Mr. Lowell on the present Boynton place.[1]

Then there is the story of the lost Prince, the Rev. Mr. Williams, who was a scout here at the time of the invasion.[2] Over in Essex, Vermont, is a place called "The Lost Nation." Something might be worked out from that.

There was also the incident of Dr. Aubrey, who was married just before the Revolutionary War in Essex, and who went off to the war and was reportedly killed by the Indians. After many years he returned to find his wife married to Mr. Castle.[3] Some good stories might be made out of these.

JAN. 10—I am preparing a lecture on "The Ice Age and Some of Its Indications in the Champlain Valley" for a lecture course in the High School, to get books for the High School library.

JAN. 13—The Medical Society of the County of Clinton held its annual meeting today and adopted a new constitution and by-laws unanimously. I was elected Corresponding Secretary and also Librarian. These two offices are new.

JAN. 31—I have had letters in response to some I have written in regard to the Ice Age from Prof. Sir J. Wm. Dawson of McGill College, also from his son, G.M. Dawson of Ottawa, of the Canadian Geological Survey. Also from Prof. George F. Wright of Oberlin, Ohio. I have found the subject to be even more interesting than I had supposed.

FEB. 5—Both boys went to a dancing party at Johnny Witherill's last evening. Nello came home with quite a list of dances in which he had danced and had had partners. Bob, poor fellow, was too timid and did not dance at all. He was afraid he should make mistakes.

FEB. 14—I may have to go to Albany tomorrow night to be present the next morning at an operation on a patient of mine. I would much rather remain at home.

FEB. 21—I made my trip to Albany last Sunday. On my return I saw clearly that the outlet of glacial Lake Champlain was south to Fort Edward.[4] At Fort Edward the valley is about two miles wide, gradually narrowing north toward Fort Ann and Whitehall.

The lecture of Royal Corbin at Academy Hall last evening was well attended. His subject was "The Progress of Humanity." He made state- ments that doubtless have provoked much discussion today. I think he is an agnostic. My lecture comes off next Friday evening. This subject, The Ice Age, is a much larger one than I at first supposed. It almost seems to me now that the whole world has individually written a pamphlet on it.

FEB. 28—I delivered my lecture last evening in Academy Hall. Geo. H. Hudson and his mother had copied it with a typewriter and so the reading of it was easier for me. I had a fine audience and they paid good attention and seemed much interested. There have been numerous pleasant things said to me today.

MAR. 8—Last evening from 9 – 12 a banquet was given at the Witherill House to honor our ex-Congressman, John H. Moffitt, whose term of office in Congress was finished the fourth inst. Mr. Moffitt had been the sole means of getting two hundred thousand dollars appropriated by Congress for regimental headquarters in Plattsburgh.[5]

MAR. 18—In the evening Monday went to Sciota and returned by cars from West Chazy yesterday forenoon. In the afternoon went, in consultation with Dr. Frank Cole, to Lapham's. Had a hard headache all the time. Today we had 17 pensioners to examine. Bessie has copied the 17 certificates, we have verified them and they are now in a sealed envelope ready to be mailed. It has required some "hustling" to do all this work. I feel like going to bed and to sleep tonight. Hope I shall not be called out.

MAR. 28—Dr. J.H. Bartholf, Major and Post Surgeon at the Barracks, has been ordered away to Detroit for temporary duty. I have been engaged to attend daily at the Barracks if anyone is sick. I get $2.50 per visit for 5 men or less, and 50 cents additional for every man more than 5, and $2 for each daily visit after the first one.

APR. 25—The other day Lispeth taught David to say "God is love." After he could say it well she said to her mother, "I don't want David to die, but if he should die he knows *one* verse from the Bible."

MAY 5—Yesterday went to Peru and then about 5 miles west to see a patient with Dr. Morehouse. At Peru village I went with Dr. Morehouse into the store of F. Elmore. This store was in existence in 1814 at the time of the British invasion and owned and managed by some Elmore. A good many years ago at the time of Mr. Elmore's death, the store was closed to the public. Mrs. Elmore, the new widow, had money enough and thought she would not have an auction and sell off the things, but would let them remain just as they were. If anyone wanted anything from the store they could have it by paying the original price for it.

An Indian jar as reconstructed by Dr. Kellogg from fragments he discovered at an ancient pottery-making site in Plattsburgh Bay.

So there are now things there that were purchased for sale not less than 15 years ago and perhaps 50 years ago. I was in search of some old blue dishes and purchased a dozen light blue tea plates, three pickle dishes, three cream pitchers and one beautiful gravy dish consisting of a bottom platform like the dish proper with top and ladle, all perfect and beautiful. I paid $2 for the whole 22 pieces.

MAY 15—The other day in moving my office table a cannon ball rolled off from it onto the floor and smashed a spittoon all to pieces. That was not so hard a blow as this same ball once struck.

MAY 20—I got 17 more plates from the Elmore store tonight, all there were.

MAY 30—I have had a photograph taken of one of my jars of Indian pottery. Have sent one to the Peabody Museum, the Smithsonian, the State Museum at Albany, the College Museum at Burlington and to various individuals.

JUNE 25—Theo was graduated Tuesday from Wellesley with the degree of A.B.

Today an examination of applicants for appointment to West Point was had in the Norman School building. Mr. Fox Holden and self from Platts-

burgh, Mr. McCleary from Malone, Mr. Neal from Crown Point and Hon.
F.A. Johnson of Glens Falls were the board of examiners. Merch Bradt
Stewart was the successful applicant, taking the highest mark in the written examinations as well as being as good as the best physically. He is
from Glens Falls.[6]

JULY 10—On Tuesday of this week Prof. George H. Perkins came over
from Burlington and stayed until yesterday afternoon. We took the 7 a.m.
train yesterday for West Chazy. Then with a horse and buggy we went
west to the Turnpike. We drove around towards Cold Spring. This is in a
gorge and is simply a magnificent spring of very cold water. This is the
home of the berry pickers. A store with a pavilion in front furnishes
goods for the pickers, who come from various parts in berry times. There
are 40 wooden shanties, like small fish houses arranged in rows, in which
the men, women, and children live. They pick berries in the daytime and
dance in the pavilion in the evening. They seem to lead a Bohemian life
during the huckleberry season. They sell their berries to the storekeeper. I
suppose they pick hundreds of bushels every year.

AUG. 3—Helen and I drove to Dannemora. I had to examine a convict
for pension. He was in a Vermont regiment. He was drafted at Middlebury,
he said. He was in prison for 8 years and had about 2 years to serve. He
said his wife put up a job on him and got him into prison. He remarked,
"I'll fix her when I get out of here."

I heard the prison band play, twenty eight pieces. It seemed strange to
hear fine music in a prison. The band marched for us and played, a drum
major heading them. After some one or two had played, the rest clapped
their hands in appreciation, like any audience. They have new instruments,
the former ones having been burned by the fire.[7] There were white and
black and young and old men in the band. The drum major claimed to
have been a West Pointer.

AUG. 14—Yesterday Nelson and I went to Montreal with a Grand Army
excursion. We left about 7 a.m. and got home about 9.30 p.m. We went
down to the dock and on board the French frigate *Bisson*. The sailors were
fine-looking men; some of them were jet-black Negroes. They were said to
have been from the French portion of Africa. The color caste evidently
did not touch them. We also visited an old bookstore where I saw a fine old
blue platter which I would like to own.

AUG. 18—I am planning to go to Washington tomorrow or next day
to attend the annual meeting of the American Association for the Advancement of Science (A.A.A.S.). I attended the Boston, Montreal, Philadelphia
and New York meetings when they were held.

Between the evening of August 19th and the early morning of August 23rd, Dr. Kellogg went to Washington on one of his flying trips. As usual, he sat up all night on the train both ways. He stayed the first night at a hotel and thereafter with military friends at Washington Barracks whom he had known when they were stationed at Plattsburgh. At their quarters he found that "It was so warm that even a sheet over me made the sweat roll off of me. Then I would uncover & give the mosquitoes a chance. I killed as many as I could, so many that the bed was somewhat black with them. But in the morning I must have had at least half a hundred bites which have hardly decreased in virulence in spite of carbolic acid & corrosive sublimate."

He attended only one session of the A.A.A.S. and the room of his section was so full he could not stay in it because of the heat. Instead, his scientific education was more happily advanced when he sought out the people with whom he had corresponded at the Army Medical Museum, the National Museum, the Smithsonian Institution and the Pension Office and under expert guidance examined their departments. He saw the place where the conspirators in the death of Lincoln had been confined, and also the spot in the Union Station where Garfield was shot—"I wanted to take off my hat." He and Mr. Hudson of the Normal School faculty reached Plattsburgh "well pleased with our visit."

Dr. and Mrs. Kellogg joined a party of ten for a trip to Quebec City. They left on the evening of September 16th, and he returned ahead of the others, arriving in Plattsburgh on the evening of the 18th.

The Doctor had made the arrangements for the excursion. Once in Quebec members of the group went their own way and met for meals. Predictably, the Doctor's path led him to bookstores, the Citadel, the Plains of Abraham and Wolfe's Cove, where he saw for the first time the famous places he had read so much about. He and his wife went to Montmorency Falls in a calash. He admired the Falls but was principally interested in figuring out the geology of the area.

AUG. 31—I have just read *Chance Acquaintance* by W. D. Howells. I like it very much. Also *He Couldn't Say No* by John Habberton. He pictures a complete vagabond as vividly as I ever read one. I also have just read *The Adventures of Huckleberry Finn!!*

SEPT. 9—Pension day. Eleven examined. One man claimed pension on "gunshot wound, left hand and right hip, and results; lung and bilious fevers and results; disease of heart, lungs, liver, kidneys, piles, rheumatism, nervous prostration, general debility." Sixteen different claims. His worst disability was his varicose veins which he did not know he had.

The band at Clinton Prison, Dannemora, in 1890. Dr. Kellogg and his niece admired their music on August 3, 1891.

1891   SEPT. 30—Helen catalogued our library while at home this summer. There were a few more than 800 books in all.

I have just obtained John Fiske's *Critical Period* and also his *Beginnings of New England*. Also Sarah Orne Jewett's *Tales of New England*. I also have sent for Emily Dickinson's poems. I am ashamed to say that my first conscious knowledge of her was last night when I read the article concerning her in the October *Atlantic* by Col. T. W. Higginson. I hope to enjoy them.

OCT. 7—Went to Malone last evening and read a paper there before the Northern New York Medical Association on "Puerperal Eclampsia with Reports of Cases." I was elected president of this Association and also delegate to the Vermont State Medical Society.

I went into a bookstore in Malone yesterday and found and purchased a copy of Emily Dickinson's poems which I have revelled in ever since. These seem to stir up a field in my mind that needs cultivating. I read them on the cars coming home in the presence of a gorgeous sunset.

OCT. 8—Today Bess and I drove into a field at the Creek which had been recently plowed, in search of arrowheads and pottery. We drove to a house from which an elderly man came out, and in response to the question if he had found any arrowheads he said he didn't know any such place and never heard of it. A youngerly female tried to tell him what I said and partly succeeded. He said, "Some French folks that lived here before we did used to find *putry* in the field and take it into the village and sell it for medicine. They sometimes dug over half an acre of ground to find it." This is now the myth. It arose from the circumstance that the French people at the Creek when I first began to collect Indian pottery (putry) used to ask me if I ground it up and made medicine of it.

OCT. 20—This afternoon by boat Bessie went to Burlington. Tomorrow she expects to start for Hartford, Connecticut to attend a reunion of Mr. T.W.T. Curtis' scholars. She went to this school in 1867, I believe. Mrs. Roland Mather, her uncle's wife, has given her a cordial invitation to stay at their house.

On the 22nd, Dr. Kellogg followed his wife to Hartford. There he stayed with her at the Mathers'. They visited the hospital for the first time since his internship in 1873–74. After further sightseeing and visiting on the 23rd, they went to a performance of Iolanthe, "prettily produced." On returning late to the Mather house, they discovered their night key would not work, nor could they rouse anyone. They spent the night at a hotel.

Next day, leaving Mrs. Kellogg in Hartford, the Doctor went to New

NOV. 6—This afternoon I read some of my "Stories" (or perhaps "Sketches" would be a better name for them) to Mr. H. S. Johnson. He advised me sincerely, I think and believe, to continue writing them with an idea of publishing them.[8] I really wish there were something in them that "would bring a message" to someone, using an expression of Mr. Howells. By the way, I am just reading Mr. Howells' *Criticism and Fiction.* He tells a wonderful amount of truth in that book.

NOV. 10—Some queer stories are reported about last week's election. It seems that a young fellow named Coles in the employ of Smith M. Weed one day last week collected about 225 dollars for the Democrats to celebrate with. He hired the band and got some fireworks for about 50 or 60 dollars and saved the balance himself. Saturday he wanted a train to go to Lyon Mountain. It was offered to him for 50 cents a person, with a guarantee of 200 persons. The train was ready, having backed down to the station. The band and a few hoodlums marched down in fine style. They had secured for the expenses only 23 dollars. So the train did not go. They all marched back, not in order, receiving the gibes of the outsiders all the way.

Nov. 18—Examined 14 pensioners yesterday. An interesting case has been in court this week. Dr. Willis T. Honsinger of West Chazy has been sued by a man named Pike for malpractice. Over three years ago Pike broke his kneepan, or rather ruptured its ligament. He got the ordinary ligamentous union and a serviceable limb. He was probably induced to sue, thinking he might get some money out of the doctor, perhaps without a trial. Drs. A. M. Phelps of New York, A. P. Grinnell of Burlington, Drs. Madden and Schuyler of Plattsburgh testified as to the proper treatment that Dr. Honsinger had given.

Dr. Irwin of Malone was the expert for the prosecution. He made a pitiful appearance, not knowing what he was talking about. After the testimony was in, the Court directed the jury to bring in a verdict of no cause for action. By the plaintiff's own testimony and by the testimony of his expert it was shown that the plaintiff's ligamentous kneepan was in no manner due to the defendant's neglect or want of skill. It was also shown that the defendant was unusually attentive and that the result was the average.

DEC. 5—Another public funeral occurred this afternoon, that of Joseph A. Baker (little Jo Baker, as he is called.) He was an old soldier and a member of the G.A.R. The G.A.R. Post of this town out in uniform and swords. Their number is growing constantly smaller. One by one they are dropping away.

DEC. 25—For a week or more it has been announced in the papers by Brown the caterer that he was authorized to give free Christmas dinner to anybody who would go to Armstrong's Hall. If anyone was sick and could not come he would send a dinner to the house, provided they would tell him where to send it. This certainly was a generous and good Christmas celebration. I don't know who the generous person was. I learn that 1,000 dinners were thus given away.

DEC. 26—The number of dinners given yesterday is said to have been over *3,000*.[9]

DEC. 31—We have all had a good year. Theo has graduated from Wellesley. The whole family has been well. The children are all growing and doing well.

I have collected $3,894, which is more than three hundred dollars more than any year before. I have helped into this world ninety two infants, some of which have been a heavy load. I wonder what 1892 will bring.

Notes for 1891

1. On this British gold, see entry for August 4, 1890 and footnote.

2. During the War of 1812 Eleazer Williams was the head of a group of spies called the Corps of Observation, based at Plattsburgh. Later he was identified by many as the lost son of Louis XVI, who presumably died in prison in Paris. Historians still occasionally debate his identity, but the weight of evidence, including that of his mother, is against his being the Lost Prince.

3. For the story of the Aubreys and the Castles, see the entry for March 11, 1886.

4. At one time Lake Champlain emptied southward into the Hudson River. The ice age tilted the earth and made the lake flow northward into the St. Lawrence, as it does today.

5. The appropriation was contingent upon a gift of the necessary land. Since every added company presumably would spend $12,000 a year locally, money was quickly subscribed to buy 500 acres of land for the expansion.

6. Stewart became a major general in the U.S. Army.

7. On New Year's Eve much of Clinton Prison was destroyed by fire. The state spent $150,000 on its reconstruction.

8. Dr. Kellogg left 85 stories and sketches. Many of them were written for his children, and concerned his boyhood in Vermont and the trips and adventures of his later life.

9. It was later learned that Smith M. Weed, the local business and political leader, financed these Christmas dinners. A total of 1,800 meals were provided in Armstrong's, 532 at the Town Hall and 764 sent to the homes of those unable to come for them.

1892

The Doctor comfortably faces the blasts of winter with a new coat of buffalo skin and a new heating system for his home. He anxiously brings his son David through a severe attack of scarlet fever.

In the course of the year, though having to spend much time behind his horse, visiting widely scattered patients, this nature-loving physician finds many compensations in the moods of the elements. Roused by an emergency call at 3 a.m., he declares the discomfort worthwhile when he gets caught in a spectacular thunderstorm, whose violence he relishes. Later he extols the beauties of midnight rides.

He takes busman's holidays whenever he can get away, and on his trips he nicely balances his quest for new medical knowledge with the pursuit of his several hobbies. After earlier sputtering over his nephew Francis's wide-ranging excursions with the University of Vermont baseball team, he is pleased to report in June that Francis has become the third member of his family to graduate from college.

In the early fall, the Doctor, his wife, and David are victims of an alarming carriage accident precipitated by a drunken driver. In the national election campaign, the Doctor hears President Benjamin Harrison speak. This is the first President he has ever seen, but despite his instinctive ardor for Republican candidates, in this case he finds the office more impressive than the man. Still, Doctor Kellogg is morose at Cleveland's subsequent victory and its probable damaging effect on part of his practice, the Pension Board work.

JAN. 15—I am asked by the Alpha Gamma Delta Society of the Normal School to be one of the judges tomorrow night in a contest in which one side presents *Kenilworth* and the other *The Tale of Two Cities*. I suppose I am to help decide which side makes the better presentation. I have never read *Kenilworth* but once, over 20 years ago. The death of Amy Robsart was so terrible to me I felt I never wanted to read it again. But I am obliged to read it now.

91

1892   JAN. 21—We are having a new heating apparatus put into the house, an arrangement for steam or hot water. We can use whichever we like, changing from one to the other in about ten minutes. I am to pay $467 for the entire thing. We expect to do away with our heating stoves. Then we shall have much more room and less coal dust, and the house will be heated more uniformly. Smith, the head man for Mr. Mooers, would not begin the work tomorrow because it is Friday and he thought a job begun on that day would not be lucky.

JAN. 26—I have a new buffalo skin coat. I got it at McGregor and Marsh's. They had a fine buffalo skin brought them for sale the other day and I bought it for $30. It is the best skin I have seen since the decline of the buffalo.

FEB. 6—I have been having an attack of bronchitis, confining me to the house for a few days. I have been out more or less for the last five days. It seems as though I had been away for some time.

Theo began her work as teacher of history and rhetoric at the Normal School on Wednesday. One day in December we heard that Miss Lyon had resigned, to take effect February 1. I went immediately to the teacher's committee of the Normal School Board and offered Theo's name as a candidate. I got Mr. Myers to do the same to some of the committee. I put everything to work that could be utilized. The report of this committee was unanimous in her favor. Then the full board met in a few days and unanimously ratified the nomination.

I drove out onto the Beekmantown Road this afternoon. I wish I could

The kindergarten class of the model school at the Plattsburgh Normal School in 1897. It was here that niece Theo had her first teaching position.

92

describe what I saw. The sleighing was good. The side snow was lined by a load of hay that had dragged its hanging straws, the hills and mountains were blue. The smoke from a moving train of cars grew whiter and larger as the train went up grade. The white snow covered everything. It was beautiful in every detail. One must feel and see such a scene in order to realize what it is. How much southern people lose who have never seen one of our beautiful northern winter days.

FEB. 29—It will be four years before this date can be written again. The other day I received a note in lead pencil:

I like to get some medicen—my head ack and my stomick ack and I am aful sick with my head. I think I am billious. I want some thing to make me trow up.

MAR. 3—Theo got her first pay today for teaching in the Normal School. It was seventy dollars, for the month February. I think she has done splendidly. There is hardly a girl in her college class that has really so good a place. One girl has $800 per year in Providence, but hardly another one had $700.

MAR. 11—Went to West Chazy this morning to examine a man who is insane. He had been drawing a pension and his pension had been cut off for some reason unknown to me. He had been drawing seventy two dollars per month.

I am reading *Uncle Tom's Cabin*, which I am ashamed to say I have never read before, probably never shall read again. I was in a sense brought up on it.

MAR. 14—Our steam goes splendidly. This morning we did not know that the thermometer was near 0. We thought it was much warmer outside.

Among recent orders received for examinations for pensions one applicant claims to have the following disabilities: "Piles, disease of liver, rheumatism, colic, tonsillitis, pharyngitis, inflammation of liver, epilepsy, constipation, acute bronchitis, foecal obstruction, transinar colon, recurring hepatitis, obstruction of bile ducts, haemorrhoids, chronic hepatitis and bilious colic." These are only seventeen. One applicant a few weeks ago claimed twenty disabilities. Yet they are still alive.

MAR. 22—A letter from Francis today states that he is on the baseball team and that March 29th the team starts for a tour to New York, Philadelphia, Baltimore, Washington, and Charlottesville, Virginia. It seems to me they ought to have included Jerusalem and Madagascar in their trip. I wonder if it is a good investment to send a boy to college to teach him to play ball.

1892   MAR. 24—Yesterday about 2 p.m. David began to vomit. He kept it up tremendously until evening. He slept fairly well last night, but this morning the rash of scarlet fever began to come on his body and face.

MAR. 27—David has slept much today, though his fever has nearly all left him and the rash is much less. He breathes only 27 times per minute to 33 yesterday. His neck is swelling under both ears. Inside, his throat is dark purple. His right ear is discharging, owing to abscess. He hears the watch in this ear, however. A few days more will decide. The chances now seem against him.

MAR. 28—Evening. It is hard to say what is the condition of the dear little fellow tonight. He sleeps most all the time. At times when he is roused for a few minutes his eyes are perfectly natural. Drs. Lyon and LaRocque saw him this afternoon. They both think he will get well. I am giving him the tincture of iron alternating with the peroxide of hydrogen.

MAR. 30—It really seems as if David were better. He has no fever and is awake more. Nelson is quite sick at his grandmother's with tonsillitis— we hope nothing worse. The mother has a severe tonsillitis also, which developed yesterday.

APR. 4—David has hardly seemed so well. His other ear is discharging and he sleeps and is uncomfortable.

APR. 9—David hears better. Dr. Schuyler says he will have his hearing. Dr. Schuyler inflates his Eustachian tubes with a politzer. Dr. Lyon lanced an abscess behind his right ear yesterday. This discharges quite freely. There is not much discharge from either ear.

APR. 20—Today for the first time in four weeks David has had his clothes put on. His left ear has not discharged for several days. His right ear keeps running, but much less. The abscess behind is also less. Still, he is hearing better.

APR. 27—Yesterday Elpeth and I drove to Dannemora. I heard of a woman who had some blue dishes. I stopped at her house and she sold them to me. There were about 45 pieces in all. I gave her her price, ten dollars. She had had them a good many years, had washed them herself so as not to have them get broken. She wanted to sell them but almost cried when she did so.

MAY 20—The other day I received a letter from a woman who wanted me to see her brother, who seems to be out of health. I quote from this letter:

> he cant eat one mouthful of solled food he has a tirable pain
> acroust his kiddnes I think he has got brites desese worse than
> eney man ever had it in the world. his bowels are bloted– he has

94

bin blotting since February 1 but he lyes down– he gets worse through the day towards night— you know the law is now if a Dr is not colled to see a sick person that they have no right to give a bairal surtifickett untill the case is Investagated

I suppose all that is necessary is to make one's meaning understood, and this woman certainly did that.

JUNE 3—Today was Field Day for the High and Normal Schools. Robert ran in a hundred-yard dash for boys under fifteen. I do not know how he came out, but he did not take a prize. I hope he will not try to be an athlete.

JUNE 7—Yesterday Bess and I drove to Dannemora. We came back a new route. However, I did see that the glacier had passed along over the valley and that the Saranac Hollow was once a lake ten miles long, two miles wide and more than 50 feet deep. Where is now the "Seven Mile Run" was the bottom of this lowest Saranac Lake at the close of the glacial times. I had supposed this to have been the case for years. Now I saw that it was correct.

JUNE 20—Last Saturday Rob, Nello and I went to Fort Ticonderoga with the high school cadets on their annual excursion. We had a pleasant time. I came back on the cars, reaching Plattsburgh at 6.50. The *Reindeer* did not get to the dock until about 9.20.

On a board nailed onto quite a high post is the following notice:

These Ruins Are Private Property and Visitors are Earnestly Requested Not to deface or damage them in order that they may be preserved.

Estate of Mary Pell.

The ruins of Fort Ticonderoga in Dr. Kellogg's day. Near here he made extensive Indian finds. The fort has since been entirely reconstructed.

So if "visitors deface or damage" it must be for some other reason than the preservation of the "Ruins."

JUNE 30—Yesterday Francis was graduated from the University of Vermont with the degree of A.B. So now Helen, Theo, Francis each has the degree of Bachelor of Arts. As it was pension day with prospect of a large number (sixteen actually were examined) I could not be in Burlington, though I went to the Sig supper Tuesday night. Francis had nearly all the family there some of the time.

This week, in fact for several weeks past, there has been an immense amount of rain. For the first time water has stood in our cellar so as to necessitate opening the plug into the sewer and letting the water out.

JULY 11—Saturday afternoon the water in the Saranac began to rise. I don't know how many feet it came up, but several. It was a turbulent, angry flood. The bridge at the sewing machine factory cannot be crossed on account of washing out at the east approach. The south bridge at Treadwell's Mills has gone downstream, so the road there is impassable. It is said that one or two dams have given out above Redford.[1]

Mr. John H. Myers told me the following story last evening. He said that years ago up the river at Redford their store was burglarized and a large quantity of shelf goods was taken. Sam Newcomb told him to go up to Chateaugay and consult Old Mother Foster, a fortuneteller. He finally did so on the sly, not letting anyone know where he went.

The old woman said at once that Mr. Myers was from Plattsburgh. She told him how many brothers he had—two older, correctly; that his own mother was sick but would recover and live a good many years, which also proved true She described his store, told him that the man he suspected was innocent, told him where the goods were but that he did not come soon enough because some of them had crossed water twice, and she could not trace them farther. She would only take 25 cents for her pay. He went back and found the goods—part of them, a large part, too—just where she said, but he never found the thief.

JULY 22—Yesterday myself, Mrs. Kellogg, Robert, Nelson, Theo and Laura Batt went to St. John's on an excursion of the Harmony Band. We left on steamer *Reindeer* at 7.50 a.m. and reached the Plattsburgh dock about 9 p.m. in the evening. I got a willowware blue platter from a woman in St. John's for which I paid a dollar.

JULY 29—Went yesterday to Middlebury, Vermont to a Fireman's Muster. We took the steamer *Reindeer* at 5 a.m. Went to Burlington and thence by cars to Middlebury. We found in a three-story building what is incorporated as "Sheldons' Museum."

Mr. H. L. Sheldon was born August 15, 1821, was never married and is a little deaf, but he has made and is making a marvelous collection of things pertaining to Middlebury, to Vermont and also to other places. He told us that in 1875 he bought a Roman coin. From this single thing was started his enthusiasm for what in recent years has taken his whole time and probably money. Mr. Sheldon is a direct descendant from John Alden through his mother.

AUG. 11—The thunder and lightning the past two or three days and nights has been grand. I had to drive a little distance about 3 a.m. yesterday. A flash of lightning, followed immediately by a tremendous crash, was worth all the discomfort I had in getting out and wet in the night.

On August 17th Dr. and Mrs. Kellogg departed on a five-day trip to Rochester, New York for the meetings of the American Association for the Advancement of Science. Gamely, Mrs. Kellogg registered as a member for the meeting. The famous California geologist, Joseph LaConte, was president of the Association.

Although registered for the anthropology section of the convention, they spent much of their time at the geological sessions, where they heard a great deal about the glacial period. They saw "an interesting glacial work" in the Pinnacle Hills near Rochester, and went on conference excursions to the Genesee gorge, and to Niagara Falls on observation cars. They also attended a reception in the Powers art gallery, where Susan B. Anthony was in the receiving line.

In a Rochester bookstore the Doctor saw a manuscript orderly book of Captain Ichabod Norton's Revolutionary service in the Champlain Valley. He subsequently wrote the owner, borrowed it for ten days and, as he had done with other long manuscripts, made a verbatim copy.

AUG. 26—Yesterday Robert and I took the trip down the St. Lawrence rapids from Valleyfield to Montreal. It rained from early in the morning every minute until long in the night after we reached home. On the St. Lawrence the wind blew from the north a gale. This added to the height of the waves caused by the rapids. We went through Coteau, Cedar and Cascade Rapids. Owing to the wind and rain and fog it was not thought safe to go through the Lachine Rapids, so we took the Canal instead.

SEPT. 3—I heard President Benjamin Harrison speak today from the second piazza of the Fouquet House. He came in on the 12.30 p.m. train and I suppose went to Loon Lake at 1.30 p.m.[2] A very large crowd was out, also the band. He is the first President I ever saw. His speech was a good one and he made a good appearance. After all, the thing seen was

President Harrison campaigning at Saranac Lake in September 1892. Dr. Kellogg heard and admired him in Plattsburgh a few days previously.

not so mighty as the thing heard. To hear about the President, to see his name attached to proclamations and to official documents, to think of him as the highest authority in all this large country, to know that he is the head of this nation, seem more marvelous than a sight of the man. We feel that some of these things should show in him and be a prominent part of him, but like any other man he stood up portly, dignified, and talked pleasantly and grammatically. After the speech there was a handshaking, but I did not know of this so did not shake.

President Harrison is more a man of the people than was President Cleveland. Harrison, like Garfield, one feels drawn towards. Cleveland I never should care to see. Indeed, when he has been in town and people have been invited to see him, I have never gone.

SEPT. 5—The other day a young woman 18 years old consulted me in my office. She now weighs 87 pounds. Her greatest weight has been 105 pounds. She apparently is in the beginning of consumption. She has been married two years. I asked her why in the world her mother let her get married so young. "Oh," she said, "she herself got married when she was 13 years old."

SEPT. 16—Last Saturday, Mrs. Kellogg, David and I were driving up Brinkerhoff Street in the open Concord buggy. While crossing Oak Street near the Academy, I saw a horse coming along Oak on a full gallop, urged on by a drunken driver. He was so near us we had no time to stop or go along. His horse made a plunge to go over Fly's back, crushed him right down, broke or twisted every spoke out of the near front wheel, crushing our wagon down.

Bessie was on her face in the center of the street, David was a little beyond her. The Frenchman's horse was on the ground holding Fly down by lying on his head, while the Frenchman was over beyond his horse. I have the recollection of trying to avoid stepping on Bess. She and David went into Mr. Scribner's store on the corner. She had severe bruises about the knees, right hand and shoulder. The skin was off her face a little in one spot. David's left arm was somewhat injured. My right foot was considerably sprained. However, we are recovering. The man, Frank Rivers, was put into jail. Today his people paid me the cost of having my wagon fixed and I presume he was let out of jail today.[3]

The week of October 10th was probably the most strenuous the Doctor had ever experienced. At 5 a.m. on Monday he started for Ogdensburg for the meetings of the Northern New York Medical Association, of which he was president. During a stopover in Chateaugay he obtained from Mrs. Edna Roberts the story of the stolen children, which follows.

1892 *The sessions next day were held at the State Asylum, where Dr. Kellogg delivered an inaugural address. The Superintendent, Dr. P. M. Wise, gave a talk on paresis illustrated by cases in all stages, and also demonstrated a method of nasal feeding of a patient with complete dementia.*

On Wednesday at 6 a.m. the Doctor left for Plattsburgh. There he had eleven pensioners to examine and much other business to look after, "so I managed to get to bed that night with a terrific headache." Nevertheless, the next morning he started for Montpelier, Vermont as a delegate to the meetings of the Vermont Medical Society.

In Montpelier he toured the state capital and attended afternoon and evening sessions of the Society, where he was called on for a short talk. He left a late banquet in time to catch the Boston train at 1 a.m. Next day in Boston he "skirmished around in several bookstores," the sole purpose of the trip. Intending to buy several books, he bought instead 47 bound volumes of the Atlantic Monthly for $25, "all thet money I could spend." He returned to Plattsburgh by way of Albany, arriving home at 5 a.m. on Saturday.

OCT. 19—Jonas Maurice was asked today about the political situation. "Well," he said, "I go to all the speeches on both sides. I want to see how much a man can lie without dying on the spot."

OCT. 25—The following is in substance the story of the two stolen children, as told me by Mrs. Edna E. Edwards Roberts two weeks yesterday at Chateaugay:

"There are now living in this town John Smith and his sister, Mrs. Maria Smith Fitzgerald. When these two were children—the boy an infant and the girl two or three years old—they began to live with their Grandfather and Grandmother Smith in the town of Chateaugay, New York. When they were about 18 and 20 years old their grandmother said to them one day, 'Don't you ever want to know about your father and mother?' They said they never thought about them.

" 'Well', she said, 'your father brought you here when John was a baby and Maria was 2 or 3 years old. He stayed here about two weeks, went away, and we have never heard a word from him since. Your mother's name was Maria Blake, daughter of John Blake of Remsen, Massachusetts, where your father married your mother. Now, if you want to go to see your mother and find out about her and your grandfather, I will give you the money to go with.'

"After considering the matter, these two children decided to look up their mother. So one day they started on the cars for Massachusetts. There they saw a lady driving who asked them if they wanted work. No, they were looking for their grandfather, John Blake. Are you Maria Blake's children? Yes, they said. This lady said, 'I was teaching school in your neighborhood when your father carried you off. Your mother is yet living, has remarried and is very feeble.' So they were taken to their grandfather's.

"Their mother lived a few miles away and was so much of an invalid (she had heart disease) they thought it best not to go to see her that night. The grandfather was much overcome, but was greatly delighted to see these children. Early the following morning John was taken over to see his mother. She was in bed. The attendant took her up a cup of tea and some toast and she saw that there was something unusual occurring. The mother said, 'Have you got any news? Have you heard from my children?'

"All were much overcome. The mother told them how she married their father. He seemed to be to some extent a wandering person. After the daughter Maria was born the father went away and was gone a year without the mother's hearing from him. She supposed she was a forsaken wife. When he came back he told how sick his own father had been, and that there was no regular mail, and gave various other reasons for his absence. So they got a house, moved into it, and stayed until after the boy was born.

"Then after a time the husband wanted to go elsewhere and keep house by themselves. Then the father, John Blake, who all the time had supported his daughter and her children, told her that he would take care of her where she was, but that if she went off and lived with that man he would have no more to do with her. So she delayed the new departure.

"One afternoon, towards evening in haying time, the little boy was in his cradle and the little girl was playing on the floor with a doll. The father came and told his wife he wanted her to get him some water from the well back of the house. She went out and got it. When she came in she saw her husband getting into a wagon with a child under each arm. She screamed, ran out and caught hold of the baby boy and pulled until she was afraid she would kill him, and then let go. The husband drove off with the two children. The mother shouted to the men in the field, who came immediately. Two of them got on horseback and followed, but could get no trace of the stolen ones.

"They searched for six weeks, watching at the corners and everywhere, but to no purpose. They advertised, followed up clues, but never could get a trace of them. She never heard a word from her husband from that time. She had given him and the children up for dead, but always had hope she might sometime see the children and always had them in her mind.

"The grandfather offered to educate and clothe the children and do anything for them if they would stay with their mother. They did stay for a few weeks. They found their mother's ways were different from theirs. The mother was a Protestant, they were Catholics; the mother was an invalid and married again. So, they decided it was best for them to return to their home in Chateaugay, which they did.

"They corresponded and visited back and forth, but the mother lived only 4 or 5 years longer. After a number of years Maria Smith married John Fitzgerald, a widower with four children. He was a good man but uneducated, and Maria taught him to read after they were married. She has had four children and her husband has been dead some years. She owns a large farm which she manages herself. The brother John is a prosperous Irish farmer living a few miles from Chateaugay village on the farm which was formerly his Grandfather Smith's."

The previous pages are substantially what Mrs. Roberts told me. The story is strange and probably more or less true. I have been unable to find any town Remsen in Massachusetts.[4]

NOV. 8—This is election day. It looks as if the whole Democratic ticket were elected by an enormous majority. That is certainly the condition in this town. The Republican money gave out early and the Democratic money yet holds on. They had more than we did.

NOV. 10—The whole country has gone Democratic. This will of course throw me out of the Board of Examining Surgeons for Pensions.[5]

NOV. 11—One of the most amusing incidents of the recent election is this. Capt. Pond, who has charge of building the new Barracks, is a Democrat and has no legal right to vote. However, he registered and in the afternoon voted. He went over to his house where his man was putting up some curtains in the parlor. He mentioned the fact of his voting. His man dropped his work and said, "That settles it. I'm going over to vote against that vote." And he did. They could not stop him. He was a Republican and was the last man to vote in his district that day.

NOV. 21—One month from today is the shortest day and the longest night of the year. Then the days begin to lengthen and the weather to strengthen. Then spring, then summer, hurrying away into fall again, all too short, yet each day full. It is a wearying thing to regard seasons mathematically, watching them come and go, over and over again. But what is the use of this constant thinking, thinking, thinking, thinking? We cannot make things much different even by taking abundant thought for the morrow. Of what avail is it for a man to calculate that at the age of 45 he has perhaps 25 years more of usefulness, and 10 or 15 of helplessness? Such is life.

DEC. 13—One week ago tonight and also last night I had to drive out onto the Miller Road about midnight. It seems strange to me that people do not get up parties at midnight and drive out to see how beautiful things are. The moon was high in the heavens and the grandeur was marvellous.

DEC. 17—I went to the County House yesterday and saw a case of varioloid [a mild form of smallpox]. The woman's story is peculiar. She came from Ireland three weeks ago in a steamer of the White Star Line, the name of which she does not know. She landed in New York and came direct to Plattsburgh where she was to meet her lover, who was to come on the next steamer. She wandered about in Plattsburgh staying at some place in the suburbs. She finally gave up the idea of her lover coming, thinking he had deserted her. Then she got out to the County House on Monday of this week—how, I do not know. On Tuesday she was taken sick. She also expects to be a mother in 4½ months.

DEC. 26—I have just finished "Hell and Purgatory," translated by Prof. Charles Eliot Norton. I have "Paradise" yet to read. It seems to me that in "Purgatory" are some of the most beautiful descriptions I ever saw.

I have also just finished *The Bondman* and *The Deemster* by Hall Caine. The latter is the better, but why the reading people of England or of any other country should be so much stirred up over these I cannot see. They are a return to the old style of blood and thunder impossibilities. He seems, especially in *The Deemster*, to kill off the women in childbirth. The wonder to me is that he did not have his heroine Mona get married and die in a confinement at the end of nine months and two days. Still there is a certain power in both books.

DEC. 31—So end the week, the month and the year—a good one all through.

Notes for 1892

1. All records were broken in June with a rainfall of 7.62 inches; Lake Champlain rose four inches. On July 11 the Saranac River rose five feet. Bridges and factories along the river and its tributaries were washed out, with the heaviest damage in the town of Saranac.

2. The Harrisons first went to Loon Lake early in July. Mrs. Harrison, who was in poor health, spent the summer there and the President made several trips there. Mrs. Harrison died of tuberculosis shortly after returning to Washington in the fall.

3. During this year a local campaign was started to "bell your horses. It makes it safer for pedestrians and adds to the music."

4. There never was a town in Massachusetts called Remsen. Probably through oral transmission the name was incorrectly understood. Perhaps it was Monson.

5. Grover Cleveland won 277 of the electoral votes to Harrison's 145 and Weaver's 22. Dr. Kellogg does not mention the *Democratic* celebration in Plattsburgh, consisting of a parade, house illuminations and fireworks.

1893

This year brings the Doctor's eighteenth wedding anniversary, the death of his much-loved mother-in-law, and two memorable trips. The first journey is a sentimental one; he takes Bob and Nello to Essex, Vermont, to show them the scenes of his childhood. The second is to the Columbian exposition at Chicago, a special treat for Rob, whom he indulgently escorts through four exhausting days of sightseeing. His own chief pleasure derives from seeing Lake Michigan stirred up by a storm. The Doctor goes on to Kentucky to visit his niece Helen at the school where she teaches, while Rob dodges disaster on his separate way home.

Doctor Kellogg relishes the lectures of Plattsburgh's new Catholic Summer School, and particularly the reminiscences of Emily Dickinson and her family that one woman lecturer provided. He and several friends establish the Plattsburgh Institute, "for historical and scientific investigations, especially local."

JAN. 11—Yesterday was the annual meeting of the Medical Society of the County of Clinton. I was elected Corresponding and Recording Secretary.

JAN. 19—Miss Kellas tells of a child who was in a great strait to go to church one Sunday evening. As this was a very unusual circumstance the mother asked why he wanted to go. "Why, to see the fun. The Christians and devils are going to meet together." He had heard there was to be a meeting of the Christian Endeavor Society and this was his hearing of it.

JAN. 25—Last Friday I received from Rev. E. C. Starr of Cornwall, Connecticut, a manuscript copy of a manuscript diary of Ensign Ebenezer Dibble, probably of Cornwall, who was at Ticonderoga and Crown Point in 1759 and 1762. I copied it entire.

FEB. 11—Letters from Spring Valley show that Mother, Mary and Henry are all going to move to Whittier, California, which is near Los

Angeles. Henry is going to buy a fruit orchard there. The climate is said to be delightful. It is a good ways to go.

FEB. 25—Bessie went to Burlington the day before yesterday to see her mother, who has pneumonia. I drove over yesterday and back today. Mrs. Smith is very sick indeed and have not much hope of her recovery.

FEB. 28—I went to Burlington again yesterday and found Mrs. Smith somewhat better. I went via Rouses Point by cars, and back by stage across the ice. The distance to Rouses Point is 24 miles, from there to St. Albans 24 and to Burlington 32 miles. The distance home, as given me, is to Thayer's Bay 6 miles, across the ice to the Island 5 miles, thence to Keeler's Hotel about 2½ miles, then to the west side of the Island 4 miles and to Plattsburgh 5 miles. So it is 80 miles around and about 23 across.

MAR. 8—Old Mrs. Paul Marshall told me this morning of an old woman here many years ago who was required to give evidence in court. When she came to swear she demurred. She said that "she knowed it was true, Judge Platt knowed it was true and God knowed it was true, so there were three good fellers that knowed it was true and what more did they want."

MAR. 9—Francis went to Saranac Lake this morning. I hope he will succeed. He certainly has capacity for newspaper business. The paper of which he is business manager is the *Adirondack Pioneer,* and is published at Saranac Lake.

MAR. 11—I sent by Mrs. Mead to Mr. W. D. Howells, her brother-in-law, a photograph of David with his first pantaloons on. Today I received the following:

40 West 59th St., March 10, 1893.

Dear Dr. Kellogg:

Thank you for the picture of the dear boy, whose gentle and rather pensive little face greatly appeals to me.

Mrs. Mead told us all about you and your family, and brought back our Plattsburgh days, and the best friends in them, most vividly. My wife and daughter join me in love to your whole household.

Yours sincerely,
W. D. Howells.

MAR. 13—Francis came down from Saranac Lake Saturday evening and went back this morning. He is greatly pleased with his prospects. He is to have sixty dollars per month for the present. He thinks he can be correspondent for some of the city papers during the summer and make money in that way.

1893   MAR. 15—A telegram has just come from Bessie stating that her mother is much worse. In half an hour one came saying that Mrs. Smith is dead. I go over by cars this afternoon.[1]

MAR. 29—On Monday of this week Robert and Nelson started for Brooklyn, New York to visit their great-uncle, Lewis Francis. Mr. Francis had so cordially invited them it was thought by Bessie and me it would be a part of their education to go.

Last Friday I was quite ill. Had almost a pneumonia. This morning had a slight hemorrhage. Bessie was taken ill Sunday and was very miserable, but is much better today. We may have had the grip.

APR. 6—Last evening was the opening of the Plattsburgh Theatre. Thomas W. Keene played *Merchant of Venice*. The house was filled. The seats *were auctioned off to give Mr. Weed a benefit*.[2]

APR. 17—The ice drifted out of the bay yesterday and the first boat of the season came, the *A. Williams*. Instead of Mrs. Smith's coming, as she often did on the first boat, a portion of her household furniture came.

APR. 21—The new Democratic postmaster, John Crowley, entered upon his duties today. There is considerable excitement over his probable appointments. For some reason or other unless made before tomorrow the applicants would have to go through a civil service examination.[3]

APR. 29—I purchased the Frank Holland collection of Indian relics for twenty-five dollars. It was made largely in Peru in the early eighties. I intend to "take an inventory" of them soon. Later: I have counted them and find a little more than five hundred, some of which are very good.[4]

MAY 15—One day last week, Ascension Day, the Masons gave the children of the Home a banquet in their hall. They had the Plattsburgh band out heading the procession, and marched from the Home in fine style. Robert said it was like blowing the trumpet in the market place before one said his prayers.[5]

MAY 25—The night before last I went to hear the opera "Robin Hood" in the new Opera House. The play was mediocre all through. I presume I should have enjoyed it more had we not sat too near and had not the space been so narrow I could not stretch out my legs. We could see the paint and lines and colored lashes and eyebrows of the actors, and through these and the stage smiles we could see the sad, natural faces of the actors. Many a time they lapsed back into sadness.

MAY 30—Dr. H. O. Perley, U.S. Army, reached town last night and relieved me from duty as Post Surgeon at the Barracks. I have been attend-

106

ing surgeon there since the latter part of March. I attended at $2.50 per
visit, going whenever anyone was ill. I have been up there daily since
April 14.

On May 29th Dr. Kellogg took his wife up the 2,200-foot Bald Face
Mountain in Essex County. They drove to its base and set out to follow a
sheep path, which they soon lost. The purpose of the trip was accomplished
when he found "conclusive evidence" of the glacier having passed over
the top of the mountain.

The beautiful sunset on the return trip reminded him of Emily Dick-
inson's

> *Night after night her purple traffic*
> *Strews the landing with opal bales.*

JUNE 19—This evening Bessie, Elspeth and David started at 6.30 for
Sloan via Montreal and Chicago. Round trip ticket Chicago $26.50, good
for 30 days.

JUNE 20—This morning at 1.30 a.m. it was perceptibly light in the
east. At 2 a.m. I could tell the time by my watch from this light alone. It
was somewhat difficult but I did it. So last night was only three hours long,
as the evening twilight remains until 10.30 p.m.

JUNE 24—There is a sign in town telling of the "8th Wonder of the
World," an Edison phonograph reproducing songs, band pieces, etc., and
closing with *"Don't Fail to Miss It."*

JULY 3—Theo started this morning for Chicago. There were ten Plattsburgh people besides her going to the same place by the same route.

JULY 7—On Monday of this week was a terrific thunderstorm here.
Lightning burned a barn on Rugar Street. It struck a locust tree in front
of Mrs. Hall's on the point and soon her Fanoline factory, ten rods away.[6]
It burned Mat Howe's barn at Beekmantown Depot and killed a horse in
the barn. Howe was on the piazza near the barn when struck. He rushed
to the barn, which was all on fire. He thought to get the horse, but it was so
near dead he could not and had to hurry out in order to save himself from
the fire. It struck the barn of Cornelius H. Anderson over Wallace Hill,
killed a horse and badly injured Anderson, who was in the barn, and also
injured his hired man.

JULY 24—Last Monday, July 17, began here the first day of the second
session of the Catholic Summer School. I attended several of the lectures.
I was especially pleased with Miss Helena Goessman's and Miss Agnes Sad-
lier's lectures. But Father Zahm's lectures, four of the five I heard on

A game of croquet at the Catholic Summer School, near Plattsburgh. Here Dr. Kellogg made the acquaintance of many men of science and letters.

science and religion, were remarkable. I never expected to hear a clergy-man speak the truth he spoke. He was eloquent without a hand gesture, forcible, sincere, convincing, religious.[7]

JULY 25—After supper last evening I took Miss Goessman for a ride in order to talk with her about Emily Dickinson. Miss G's home is in Amherst, Massachusetts. She knew Emily Dickinson, but knows her sister much better. The sister and one old servant are the only occupants of the Dickinson home in Amherst. The Dickinsons are all eccentric, doing things other people do not do. Some Dickinson children, nephews, I imagine, of Emily, say and do things in such ways that people say that that is a Dickinson way.

The sister has realized about 15 thousand dollars from the sale of Emily's books and this has enabled her to live comfortably and is nearly all she has. Miss Goessman said the last time she saw Emily she was near the gate she was passing. Her voice was strange, though soft and pleasant. She had been shut up so long she was pale and it almost seemed as if a specter had appeared to her.

There *was* a love affair connected with Emily. When about 26 years of age a young man, a graduate of Amherst, was in love with Emily and Emily with him. Unfortunately this man, who was in Emily's father's office, drank. After a time he went to Boston and unfavorable reports came back about him. The father, Mr. Dickinson, a stern man, went to Boston to investigate. He told Emily if he found things all right he would tell her; if not he would not say much about him. Emily picked a large bouquet of roses from her garden and told her father to give them to the young man. When the father returned he told Emily the man was in no condition to receive flowers from a lady. That ended it.[8]

Emily was constantly making dainty dishes to send to the sick. Her jellies and other dainties were famous in Amherst. Often when some person would call on the sister a dish of something would be sent in with Miss Emily's love. She almost never saw any people after she was 26 years old. Two notable exceptions to this were Dr. Holland and Col. Higginson. To the former she once sent some of her verses and asked him to criticize them. He did so and pointed out where they might be changed and in this way there was opened a correspondence between them. Afterwards Dr. Holland was in town and saw her, and thence he saw her quite often. An almost similar thing happened with Col. Higginson.

Emily's sister had no idea of the amount of material that Emily had written. She used to say that Emily was scribbling. After her death nearly 1,000 poems were found. Her acquaintances she communicated with by letters. Some of her intimate friends hardly ever saw her, yet wrote to her and received letters from her frequently. The last 30 years of her life were spent at home in her father's house or in her garden. She attended her own flowers and had an abundance of them. But she even went into her garden at times when people would be the least apt to see her.

JULY 29—This morning the mother, the daughter Elizabeth and the son David came back from their western journey. They left Sloan, Iowa, where Rebe lives, on Thursday of last week, came to Oskaloosa to see my cousins, Nettie Faxon and her sister, Lottie Faxon Everett.

This week Richard Malcolm Johnston has been giving a series of 5 lectures at the Summer School which have been a delight to all. Yesterday afternoon he read two of his dialect stories. He is a Georgian, white-haired, 70 years of age.[9] He knew well and was in college under my great-uncle, Adiel Sherwood, who was a Baptist clergyman in Georgia for many years. I loaned him my copy of Adiel Sherwood's *Memoirs*.[10]

AUG. 7—The Catholic Summer School closed its second annual session and first session here last Friday. The lectures by Father Holpin on Ethics were nearly as remarkable as Father Zahm's. We met quite a number of pleasant people, among them Rose Hawthorne Lathrop, daughter of Nathaniel Hawthorne. She is not very prepossessing at first appearance, but after a little she is more pleasing. Her red hair (auburn), freckled, hirsute face are not thought of after a few moments' conversation.

AUG. 15—As it was a beautiful day those of the family at home drove up to Fredenburgh Falls. As we were coming out of the woods Fly seems to have gotten into a hornet's nest. The angry animals stung him dreadfully. He tore around, got into the bushes, but did no damage. One hornet stung Bessie on the face, but her face is not swelled much today.

SEPT. 5—Last Thursday Rob, Nello and I went to Burlington on steamer *Chateaugay*, taking with us a horse and buggy. We drove to Essex Center and stayed at the hotel there that night. Nello had gotten better [from a mild disorder] but not strong, so we got him to bed after supper and Rob and I went out to call.

Early in the morning I went over to the cemetery and saw my father's, brother's and two sisters' graves, also the headstones of many other Kelloggs. We went over to Norman Bradley's. He has many Indian relics, one fine old clock which he says is 110 years old, also a powder horn on which was the name of a Bradley ancestor who was in the battle of Bennington. Then we went up to see Philo Pierson.

In the afternoon we went up to the Uncle John Sibley place. On the way there, Rob and I got out and walked over the oblong hill by the roadside which as a boy 35 years ago I used to run over with the Sibley boys going to and from school. The path was there, though I imagined it was not so much worn as it used to be. At the Sibley house I tried to find the peculiar ventilator in the ceiling of the kitchen which made the light of Uncle John's candle appear like three new moons on the ceiling of the sleeping room above, but it was not there. The brick oven, iron-topped, was gone. A partition had been put across the room, but one old fireplace was left in the room made by this partition. The well stood behind the house, but the fine old bucket attached to a chain running over a wheel in the well house was gone. I did not want to drink from the degenerate iron chain pump. The man [at the Sibley place] knew nothing of the sheep pond in the brook on the side hill, but I took Rob up and found it. We went on up to the "big pond" where we boys were not often allowed to go in swimming. The rock projected the same as 35 years ago, beyond which it was dangerous for us to venture. I saw that formerly the pond had been acres larger, and that its outlet was making a gorge through the nearly vertical schistose rocks. I also saw that the "Beaver Meadow" in front of the house had formerly been a glacial pond.

I took tea at Jennie Nichols Greene's and Rob stayed there all night. Nello and I stayed at Philo's. In the morning a black cloud in the west began to pour down a heavy shower. The south wind blew hard and it threatened to be a rainy day. However, the sky began to appear and about 9 we started for Aunt Sarah Faxon's in Milton. We went across by the Seymour Parker place and met the Milton road near the Reed Bascomb place. On that terrace north the view was grand. I remember once seeing a heavy, cold storm sweeping up from the west there, and the storm on the marshes in *Great Expectations* always reminds me of that. Aunt Sarah was as glad to see us as we were to see her. She made us stay to dinner and we were very glad to see her a little longer than we had planned, as our time was limited. About 12.30 we started south again.

We went up on top of Brigham Hill. The view was marvellous. Then we went down and around to our old farm. One tree at the turn of the road, a red birch, stood as before. This was at the corner of the Bliss woods. These woods and all of our sugar works had been cut off years ago—20, perhaps—but now have grown up a dense mass of young and small trees, so thick one would have difficulty in going through them. We looked into the window of the brick school house which stood as I always remembered it, but the pine seats and desks around the three sides had given way to a few "modern" patent seats. At our old house, things were changed. Not the house itself so much, but the surroundings. Four of our fine maples remained—there used to be seven. The lilacs and rose bushes and yard fences in front of the house were all gone. The sitting room was the most natural because the least changed. A few only of the trees in the orchard remained, but I found the sweet apple tree by the road, which Philo had told me was all gone, and got some good apples from it. They had the same taste and color as of old, but they were smaller. I found some other new trees which bore apples that were just like some of the old trees, so these were their descendants.

I had told Nelson of an old flax spinning wheel up in the attic which some of my ancestors had used before my time. He was anxious to get it and did. It is to come over here later. The horse barn and lower shed and granary remained, shrunken and dilapidated. The big barn has been replaced by a larger one. The fruit yard is all gone. Young Severance told me they tapped a thousand trees—all below the road in what was a new growth when I left home 27 years ago. One old hitching post stood in front of the house, which Father had put there long before I can remember. But our old view of the mountains and valleys and hills and fields remained. Was there ever a more beautiful spot on earth than old Vermont?

SEPT. 22—Eighteen years ago today we were married. Today the dear Nello, who is much better but not strong yet, took a horse, drove out in the rain to Cook's flower houses, got a fine plant with his own money and put it on the dinner table, a complete surprise to his mother. He planned this some days ago and executed his plan alone.

SEPT. 25—Last Saturday I took advantage of excursion rates and went to Saranac Lake. Francis seems to be doing pretty well. Certainly this is a great discipline for him. It seems too bad that Francis should be so much alone—really without any home—at Saranac Lake.

SEPT. 27—A pensioner examined today said he had neuralgia in the back part of his head. He "*rubs it with kerosene and spirits of turpentine and bakes it in the oven.*"[11]
The other day one of the horses was a little sick, or at least it did not eat well and seemed dumpish. David looked wise and said he "*presumed he had bowel trouble.*"

SEPT. 30—Yesterday afternoon a poor woman had a baby. Her stockings were wet and her feet cold. After the baby was born the woman's sister took off her own stockings and put them on to the feet of the sick one, going stockingless herself and barefooted this morning. There is much real kindness among the very poor.

OCT. 3—I am planning to go to Chicago next week. Mr. James Cavanagh has just been there. He told me he thought more of me while there than of any other person, that I would enjoy seeing the things there more than any other person of his acquaintance. Then he said, "If you will go I will give you 25 dollars, yes 50 dollars, and take my pay in doctoring." Of course I couldn't do that but the offer was made in good faith. Who says there is not friendship in existence?

OCT. 27—Well, on Wednesday evening, Oct. 11th, Rob and I started for Chicago, via Montreal, Grand Trunk Railroad. We stayed at the St. James Hotel [Montreal] Wednesday night and left at 8.30 a.m. We were due to reach Chicago at 8.30 the next morning, but really reached there about 1.30 in the afternoon.
The World's Fair was simply tremendous, great beyond comprehension. It was by far too great. I was thoroughly tired out the first day, Saturday, and would gladly have gone home then or to Shelbyville [Kentucky] to see Helen, but I could not leave Rob and it would not do to have it said that I stayed so short a time. I enjoyed, intensely, the anthropological building and the States buildings and the forestry building and above all the fine, massive billows that, during a storm, rolled in over Lake Michigan. We visited a large number of the various buildings, rode in the lagoons and out on to Lake Michigan in a steam yacht, went around on the Ferris Wheel, visited a street in Cairo [where Little Egypt danced] also a German

The Plattsburgh Shirt Company in 1893. It was humble people such as these that provided Dr. Kellogg with much of his medical practice.

village, and did the proper thing in various other places. We visited the fair Monday, Tuesday, Wednesday and Thursday, leaving the grounds about three on Thursday, in order to get ready for the journeying.

I had secured Rob's sleeping car ticket to Montreal on the 11.30 P.M. train. My train on the Monon Road to Louisville left at 7.40 P.M., both the Grand Trunk and the Monon leaving from the Dearborn Depot on Polk Street. There was a second train leaving for Louisville at 11.25, but the earlier one, if on time, would reach Louisville so early that I could go out to Shelbyville in the morning and not remain in Louisville until 4 P.M. I explained to Rob and told him if he would in the least prefer to have me wait until the second train I would do so. Although he apparently dreaded to remain alone very much, he braced up and *insisted* on my leaving on the earlier train. It was an act of moral courage on his part that required no small effort. The station was crowded and whenever a train backed in to leave, a tremendous jam took place as soon as the gate was open. However, I told him to telegraph me the first chance he had in the morning. So I left him.

I took a sleeper and bowled along through Indiana, reaching Louisville about two hours late, making it necessary to remain in that place until 4 P.M. I telegraphed Helen and asked her if Rob had telegraphed. She answered me at once, telling me to come on the Louisville Southern, but said nothing about Rob. I was at the Galt house and had dinner there. I took a bath in the water of the Ohio, yellow and muddy, so much so as to leave a mould in the bottom of the bath tub. As I was nearly ready to go to the station, I went to the desk and asked the clerk if there was another telegram for me. There was one from Helen worded something as follows: "Rob detained at Durand, Mich. Wreck ahead. Rob all right." I showed the telegram to the clerk, and he handed me out a Louisville paper telling of the dreadful wreck at Battle Creek where 26 were killed and 50 more wounded. I could not help being nervous and anxious.

I left Louisville at 4 P.M. via Louisville and Nashville road and reached Shelbyville at 5.47. Helen and Miss Hettie Hawes were at the station to meet me. We walked up to Dr. Poynter's [where Helen taught] and a cordial greeting was given to me by all to whom I was introduced. I was given the guest chamber, a large, delightful old room with a grate in it in which a soft-coal fire was blazing. The bedstead was large, massive, mahogany-veneered, a treasure which I told Mrs. Poynter I wanted to carry home in my pocket. As it was five feet eight inches wide and long in proportion, there was not much danger of its being spirited away. The house itself was of brick, surrounding a covered, stone-paved court. There were 70 young lady boarders in the house and the day pupils increased the number daily up to nearly two hundred. It was quite interesting to be told that such a pupil was the daughter of the Rebel General So and So, that such a young lady's father was the leader in Morgan's raid into Ohio. That another one was a daughter of a rebel officer whose mother was with her husband during the whole of his campaigns.

There are no crossroads here. One has to return by the same route he goes out on, unless he is on horseback, then he can go across farms. But the country is God's own. Here for miles and miles the land is irregularly sloping down to the creek bottoms and covered with the *greenest* of *blue* grass. The forests are large trees, now just beginning to take on their autumn coloring, with the turf as fresh and vigorous as our best of pasturing—close up to their very trunks, not a particle of underbrush—but green grass, abundant and luxuriant. The two days I was there were clear and autumny, a haze filled the air, and at night the clear moon made light and shadow.

On Sunday Dr. Poynter drove out to Waddy, eleven miles, to preach, and I went with him. We met people on horseback—men, women, children; black, white, large, small. As Dr. Poynter was going to preach, he had no toll to pay, though he passed two or three tollhouses on the way. At Waddy the church was a new wood building, well-filled with an audience of respectable people. The singing was congregational. A small boy who sat by me and looked in the same hymn book sang loud enough to have supplied alone the whole requirements of song. The sermon was capital, one of the very best I have ever heard. After service was communion. The bread was unleavened. A piece was put on to a plate and passed around and each one broke off a little and ate it. The church was Campbellite.

After services we went to dinner. Here was a splendid feast of hoecake, sweet potatoes, new corn, cold boiled ham, chicken, tea, coffee, milk, butter, bread and pie and some other things which I have forgotten. It was well cooked, abundant, excellent. A little darkey boy with a long white apron, barefooted, waited on the table. My host showed me sweet potato vines—he had dug the potatoes themselves. I mean to try to have the boys grow some next year.

During all our ride I looked in vain for one rounded stone or pebble or cobblestone or boulder. There were absolutely none there. This was beyond the limit of the glacier. But it showed me the probable condition of our own country before the glacier passed over it. All of these hollows were doubtless eroded out during the long ages by the water and air disintegration. Now should a glacier pass over, the soft material would be passed along and then silted down in places. The rocks themselves would be broken off, ground up and made into cobblestones and boulders. These eroded valleys would be filled up and new ones would have to form or old ones be eroded out.

In the evening at 6.20 I left Shelbyville for Chicago. I got a round trip ticket for $5.60—a straight, *single* fare was about $7.93. My ticket was good for 6 days. I sold the stub in Chicago for two dollars. As my train on the Monon was late, I got off at Maynard, 25 miles from Chicago, hoping to catch a Grand Trunk. I found this was not feasible, so had to take another train into Chicago. I left Chicago at 3 P.M., had an upper berth secured in a sleeper, and reached Montreal at 12.30 A.M. Wednesday and Plattsburgh at 11.15 A.M. Seven pensioners were waiting for examination and were examined, and I did much other work in spite of my being so tired that I called myself dead for 2 or 3 days.

NOV. 11—The election of this week Tuesday is as overwhelmingly Republican as it was Democratic last year.[12]

Yesterday I notified several gentlemen and this afternoon at 4, pursuant to that notice, they met in my office to form an organization for historical and scientific investigations, especially local. The first meeting is to be held in the High School building on November 20. I was elected president and Mr. Walworth secretary. A committee of three was appointed to name the organization.

NOV. 21—Last evening our organization held our first meeting. The committee reported for a name "The Plattsburgh Institute," so that is our name. Seventeen gentlemen were present. I read a paper on "Some Old Letters." H. Walworth read half of a paper on coins, a very interesting paper.

NOV. 30—For the past two or three weeks I have been having a place made in the dining room to put some of my blue dishes in. It extends from floor to ceiling and has 8 shelves. I have put in it platters, pitchers, plates, teacups, saucers, sauce plates, bowls, pickle dishes, gravy bowls, salad dishes, teapots, sugar bowls, and some other things.

DEC. 13—All of the invalids in the house are better now except one new one, Nelson. He claims to have a sore throat. David is convalescent again. Bessie was out of school only one day. The mother and Theo have fully recovered, but Nello seems to have more evidence of illness this morning than during the last three days he has been claiming it.

DEC. 14—At 3.30 this a.m. the mercury was 18° below zero. I was called out at that time and drove to Luther Hagar's, a little more than two miles out. In spite of cold or heat, rain or shine, children are born into the world. It was a boy this morning.

DEC. 16—Last night at the table most of the family were joking. Nelson said, "Papa and Mamma had an engagement of five years at the beginning of a twenty years' war."

DEC. 25—The children have all been very happy today. They had a handsome spruce tree. This was placed in the middle of the front sitting room, trimmed with colored papers and strings of popped corn, lighted by 18 candles, and it all looked very pretty.

DEC. 28—There is now in town what is called "The Hagey Institute" which is for curing of drunkards.[13] I suppose it is like the so-called Keeley cures.[14] At any rate, it is expensive. One poor woman had saved a little money by working out before she was married. Her husband lost his position on the railroad on account of drinking, and would not try to work. A young fellow, under pretense that some rich man had offered to pay his expenses at the Hagey concern, got the husband to begin treatment and then went to the wife and told her she must pay the bill, as it was only a ruse to get him to go for treatment. So the woman, in order to help her husband, grasping at the last straw, decided to pay the bill.

116

1. The beloved Mrs. Smith died in her 68th year. Her husband died of consumption in 1858. Her two daughters were Mrs. Kellogg and Mrs. Rebekah (Rebe) Gallaher of Sloan, Iowa.

2. The Plattsburgh Theatre and Opera House was built by Smith M. Weed. The advance auction of 275 tickets brought $1,700, seats selling from $100 to $2. The theater consisted of an orchestra and two balconies, with seats for 1,500 people.

3. Shortly before he left office in March, President Harrison extended the merit system to cover 7,000 additional positions, including the clerical force of free-delivery postoffices, effective in April.

4. Dr. Kellogg already had about 15,000 artifacts, and newspaper editors began to talk of an Indian museum in Plattsburgh.

5. At the "Home for the Friendless" about 40 children were cared for and educated until they could be adopted. It was non-sectarian and maintained by voluntary contributions of money and food. Robert's comment is probably based upon Matthew 23, where the Pharisees are denounced for their hypocritical good works.

6. Fanoline, a popular product named for its originator, Mrs. Frances ("Fanny") Hall, was advertised as useful for chapped hands and lips and for dressings. Mrs. Hall, the last descendant of Henry Delord, had her own pharmacy and made Fanoline in her home, the Kent-Delord house. The lightning struck a small shed on the property.

7. In 1892 the first session of the Catholic Summer School was held in New London, Connecticut. The following January the church acquired a 450-acre farm at Cliff Haven, on the lake just south of Plattsburgh. During its 1893 season in Plattsburgh, the meetings were held in the new theatre. Father Zahm came from Notre Dame University, where he had formerly been vice president.

8. This is only one of the speculations engaged in by the people of Amherst even before the death of Emily Dickinson (1830–86). Interest was intensified with the publication of her poems, beginning in 1890, but the truth remains a mystery.

9. Johnston (1822–98) was an author and educator. He was a professor of literature at the University of Georgia, served as a colonel in the Confederate army, and established a boys' school which he moved to Baltimore in 1867.

10. Adiel Sherwood (1791–1871) published a Gazetteer of Georgia.

11. New pension rules were formulated by the Pension Bureau under the Democrats. To lessen the number of fraudulent claims under the easy law of 1890, pensioners must now submit a certificate, signed by a reputable physician and two witnesses, stating that he could not work because of disabilities "not the result of his own vicious practises."

12. Republicans carried both state and local contests. The price of votes seems to have averaged two dollars in the county.

13. Dr. W. H. Hagey of Norfolk, Nebraska had devised a treatment using bichloride of gold. Plattsburgh had one of the 60 branches in 22 states. Four injections a day for 21 days, with a tonic, constituted the treatment, which was guaranteed to abolish the appetite for alcohol. For morphine, cocaine and opium the injections continued for four to five weeks.

14. Dr. Keeley of Dwight, Illinois operated sanatoriums in 33 cities. He claimed to have treated 50,000 patients for the use of alcohol, drugs and tobacco. He also used bichloride of gold.

1894

This is a year of lingering economic ills throughout the nation, and Doctor Kellogg, harassed by spotty collections, quite naturally places the blame on the Democrats. His winter rounds are marked by one accident, in which his sleigh overturns when a runner breaks, and his horse drags him for some distance on his back. The Doctor is not hurt, however, and before spring returns he has a particularly agreeable experience to relate. He meets and entertains another author, George W. Cable, who reads delightfully from his books and later properly enthuses over the Doctor's various collections. By summer, still another literarily inclined Southerner, Richard Malcolm Johnston, a whiskey-savoring colonel who lectures on poets, is treated to the Kellogg hospitality and slightly tempered hero worship.

The Doctor touchingly describes the death of the family dog, Jove, and the children's funeral ceremony for him. In September, he welcomes his fourth son, Francis Fellows, a truly bouncing boy, and when December closes he can look back contentedly and declare that "in many respects it has been the pleasantest year of my life."

JAN. 4—The bills are coming in thick, heavy, large. Collections are slow, tedious, unsatisfactory. This is the Democratic good times promised us before Cleveland's last election and of which now all are tired.

JAN. 9—Last evening was the fourth meeting of the Plattsburgh Institute. Mr. Hiram Walworth showed a flintlock, breech-loading rifle of his father, given to him and the company of boys who served gloriously at the battle of Plattsburgh.[1]

JAN. 11—The work of sending out bills and of collecting them goes on, though Bessie makes out all of mine and sends them. Collections are fair and business pretty good.

118

JAN. 13—Have just read two essays by Austin Dobson, one on Charlotte
Corday, the other on Madame Roland.[2] What kind of an immortality have
both these women! Both characters are foreign to Puritan New England,
yet both are in many ways admirable. Charlotte Corday thought the death
of Marat would bring *peace*, and yet how mistaken she was. Madame
Roland thought the Republic was the one thing needful and yet how
mistaken *she* was. Still, both have an immortality that makes them seem
to be yet living. They impress themselves on us now as though they were
in the next room, where we had just been amazed at them and at their
conversation.

JAN. 18—One day this week a pathetic incident came under my notice.
A poor vagabond who was in the war tried a few years ago to get a
pension under the old law. His disabilities were not such as were incurred
in the service, so he failed of getting a pension. However, consumption set
in and he applied under the new law, "Act of June 27, 1890." His case
was made special and this week he got a full pension. This gave him about
one hundred dollars back pay and will give him 12 dollars per month so
long as he lives.

His half sister, an elderly widow of rather shady reputation, had hired
or purchased an old house and has taken care of him for some months.
The fellow sent for me on Tuesday. I found him in a dirty and dark room
coughing, feeble, foul-smelling. His sister had given him this room and
taken care of him as best she could.

When he got his pension she told me that all the brothers and sisters
began to be interested and came to see him. She said that all the pay the
half brother would give her for taking care of him was a dollar and a half
per week, that he had paid her 25 dollars in all, and that he kept his
money under his head in the bed so no one could get it. Poor fellow. He
probably never had so much money in his life before and the joy of having seventy five dollars of his own, where he could put his hand onto it,
probably will make him die happy.

JAN. 20—This morning, at 20 minutes after one, my doorbell rang. A
man had come for me to go out onto the Miller Road, a distance of nearly
3½ miles. He harnessed my horse for me while I was dressing. At 20
minutes to two, just 20 minutes from the time the doorbell rang, I was at
his house.

JAN. 23—Last evening was the fifth meeting of the Plattsburgh Institute.
Lieut. Schoefelt read an interesting paper on "The Nicaragua Canal and
Its Commercial and Marine Aspects."[3]

1894 FEB. 1—We had two chapters of accidents today. Bess and David were walking downstreet and she slipped and struck her head just at the left of her eye on the stone sidewalk. It cut her face and the whole place swelled up purple, as large as a hen's egg. A Normal School girl helped her back to the house. Tonight it is swelled and discolored all around the eye, and she does not see so well as with the other eye. She says it blurs.

This afternoon I was driving out on the Moffitt Road where the wind had blown the road tracks quite bare. So a track had been broken out in the ditch. While driving along, the cutter shoe struck a stone and broke, also the runner, and two or three knees were broken out. This pitched the side of the cutter down and me out. The horse started; I clung to the lines with my right hand. I suppose I did not pull evenly for he turned around, dragging me on my back on the buffalo robe. I held on to him and stopped him. I was not hurt at all but my right arm is lame from holding onto him. The cutter was pretty well smashed.

FEB. 18—Last evening George W. Cable read, or rather recited, in Academy Hall from one of his stories, *Dr. Sevier*.[4] To say that he was delightful and pleasing but faintly expresses the reality. He gave a Creole song which was wonderful. His description of a street in New Orleans was charming. Mary's getting through the rebel lines was thrilling.

This afternoon I was on the sidewalk in front of the house when Mr. Cable and Mr. James G. Riggs came along. Mr. Riggs introduced me. I asked them to come in but as they were walking "to stretch their legs" they thought they would better not. I asked Mr. Cable if he had any hobbies like mine such as Indian relics, old blue dishes. When I mentioned the latter he said, "Let's go in."

We spent nearly an hour looking at the dishes and I think he had a genuine admiration for them. I asked him if the Taxidermist was not a real character. He said no, it was from his own brain. He had been congratulated on that and ever so many people had told him who the Taxidermist was or asked him who he was. He said he was glad I liked the Taxidermist because he had made it in his elder age. Mr. Cable is short, small, full-bearded and mustached and has a pleasant face.

FEB. 20—Last evening was the seventh meeting of the Plattsburgh Institute. The papers were by Mr. Frank N. Hagar, Mr. Stair and Mr. William R. Eastman, "Inspector, Public Libraries Department, Albany." It looks as if we should yet have a good public library here.[5]

FEB. 28—The dog called Jove was found dead in the barn this morning. I borrowed a pick-axe and after school the boys dug a hole in the garden about 4 feet deep. They put him onto the wheelbarrow, and so he rode to

120

his grave. They had straps around him with which they lowered him into
the ground. Nelson felt he ought to use the Episcopalian burial service,
but instead he sprinkled in a lot of rose leaves from a jar. David was
around in glee. Elspeth stood behind me on the back piazza, peeking out
to see the ceremony, while Mrs. Kellogg stood in the north dining room
window.

Poor old dog. He has chased his last cat, he has fought his last battle,
he has barked his last bark. Meanwhile the marks of his teeth remain on
the doors at the office and in various places about the barn. Next summer
a fine hill of squashes will be grown on his grave.

MAR. 2—Went to Peru today on the cars to see a patient with Dr.
Kinsley. It was a young girl 13 years of age, ill with meningitis. It was hard
to tell the father and mother how poor the outlook was for their daughter.

MAR. 6—Was telephoned a little before 6 this morning to go about 2
miles beyond West Plattsburgh. I made a couple of calls and got started
about 7. It was fairly good wagoning, but the horse and wagon would
sink through to the ground in places where the snow was 2 or 3 feet deep
and hard. Once I had to take the horse off and lift the wagon out.

MAR. 7—Today no sleighs are on the street. We have had continuous
and mostly good sleighing from December 3, 1893 to March 6, 1894,
including both days. This is 94 days so far. We probably shall have some
more.

MAR. 20—Last evening was the ninth meeting of the Plattsburgh Institute. Mr. John Martin reported that a man from Chicago had asked the
Commissioner of Navigation for permission to remove the *Royal Savage*.[6]
He was a professional diver and evidently wanted to get the hull for relics.
It was unanimously voted that the president write to the Commissioner,
asking him not to grant the request. This the president has done this
morning.

MAR. 23—This morning I received from "Back Number Budd" of New
York 35 numbers of *The Nation*. I needed something over a hundred to
complete my set and wrote him some weeks ago, giving him my lists of
wants and also of duplicates. He wrote what he would furnish my wants
for and what he would give me for my duplicates. I sent him checks and
my duplicates and so paid him his price. Still I did not get *The Nation*.
I wrote him and he would make some reply.

Finally, the fore part of this week I wrote him that unless I received
The Nation this week, I should put the matter into the hands of the Post
Office Department. He wrote back at once that he would send me what

he had on hand and would get the balance from Long Island in a few days and would send them on.

MAR. 27—Have finished *Dr. Sevier*. Had I not heard Mr. Cable read I should not have enjoyed the book nearly so much. He taught *how* to read it understandably, and I have wonderfully enjoyed every word of it. It is the product of a master.

APR. 17—Last evening was the eleventh meeting of the Plattsburgh Institute. I brought up the matter of marking historic places, recommending that a hundred-dollar granite monument be placed at Culver Hill to commemorate the battle there. This was received with some enthusiasm and considerable opposition, so it is not really settled yet. Nearly 40 dollars were pledged toward it.

MAY 7—Last Friday afternoon, with Mr. Riggs of the High School and Mr. Botsford, I went to Mooers. We three were judges in a prize rhetorical contest. There were 8 contestants, 6 girls and 2 boys. There were three prizes for each sex; as there were only two boys, the male sex received only two prizes. Had the sex question been left out no boy would have received anything, for each girl did better than either of the two boys.

I happened to be where I could see five of the girls when the successful ones were announced. They did not cry—I wish they had—but they looked heartbroken. It hardly seemed fitting that such a contest should cause such misery.

MAY 22—Yesterday Bess and I drove to Wilmington and back, starting about 5.20 in the morning and getting home a little after 7 in the evening. The whole distance for the round trip is about 70 miles. We expected a man to come up on the train to Ausable Forks to take the horses back. We were at the station when the train got in at 4 but the man did not come, so we had to drive all the way back.

MAY 25—Yesterday I had to go to Dannemora to examine a pensioner. Bess went with me. We had a good dinner at Cadyville. Reached Dannemora at 2.10 and left at 2.40. We thought we would come via Saranac Hollow.

Through Mrs. Wm. Starr Dana's *How to Know the Wild Flowers*, which we took with us, we learned the name of the bunchberry, which now was in full white blossom. We came down into Schuyler Falls, passing on our way the "Celebrated Indian Mound" that about 15 years ago we foolishly attempted to excavate, and then to Plattsburgh at 7.20, a distance of between 40 and 45 miles for the round trip.

MAY 29—Last evening was the fourteenth regular meeting of the Plattsburgh Institute. Mr. James G. Riggs read his paper on Tennyson's poetry
and a visit to Tennyson's home. This was followed by a paper, read by
Capt. George E. Pond, giving an account of the capture of Plymouth,
N.C., in the War of the Rebellion, and the prison life and escape from
the Columbia prison of Captain Morris C. Foote of the Infantry, now
stationed at Plattsburgh Barracks. General Stephen Moffitt, General Alden
of Troy, Dr. F. Madden (lieutenant, retired) and Capt. George E. Pond
sat on the stage. Gen. Moffitt was next to me and every little while he put
his hand up to his face and wiped off the tears. Dr. Madden could not
control himself at all, and there were many faces in the audience that were
not dry.

JUNE 14—B. Turner brought into my office some human bones in a pail,
found near Fredenburgh Falls. I shall investigate tomorrow.[7]

JUNE 18—Mr. Henry W. Nichols of the Institute of Technology,
Boston, visited me today. He had my article in *Science* of July 1893,
typewritten, and was using it for information in this locality. This article
of mine brought him to see me.[8]

JULY 21—On Thursday of this week there was an excursion to St.
Johns on the steamer *Reindeer*. Helen, Nelson, Miss Hawes and I went.
We reached St. Johns about 2.15. I immediately hurried out to a livery
stable and secured a carriage to take us to Chambly. The livery man said
this one horse would take us to Chambly in one hour and thirty minutes,
a distance of 12 miles. I hardly thought it possible, but it was.
Our time was greatly limited and we had to hurry away. We came back
to St. Johns through Iberville on the east side. Our good horse did his
duty in spite of the heat and we reached the railroad station at 7 o'clock.
Our train reached Plattsburgh half an hour sooner than the *Reindeer*.

JULY 28—Today Col. Richard Malcolm Johnston left for his home in
Baltimore. He had delivered a series of five lectures at the Catholic
Summer School, one on Dante, one each on Spencer, Milton, Scott and
Byron. Each lecture in itself was a poem in addition to the delightful
quotations he freely made.
We had him at the house to tea on Thursday evening, and when he
came to us at 6 he was very tired. He asked if we had some whiskey.
Fortunately, Helen had brought home a bottle of good whiskey from
Kentucky. He poured out from this a large goblet nearly half full, poured
in a little water and drank it with a relish. He ate a good supper at which
he was highly entertaining.

He talked for more than an hour, chiefly of his early life in Georgia. He said that the state of Georgia was indebted to Middlebury College for its higher education. In the fore part of this century quite a large number of learned men came from Middlebury and taught there and raised the standard of education. Among these was my great-uncle, Adiel Sherwood, who was a professor in Crawfordsville College where Col. Johnston attended when a young man. He was very fond of Uncle Adiel.

He also knew and greatly admired Aunt Harriet Florence. He said that Aunt Harriet was stately and fine-looking and he, R. M. J., as a boy fell in love with her! He was perhaps 9 or 10 years of age. Some portions of one of his stories, "The Early Majority of Tom Watts," was founded on his love for Aunt Harriet. He was quite sure that Alexander H. Stevens never wanted to marry Aunt Harriet, as we had often been told.[9]

On leaving he wanted to smoke but we had no cigars, though I wanted to get him some. He would not let me. If I did not smoke nor drink nor *cuss*, he wanted to know what vices I did have, for he was suspicious of a man who had no vices. I had to tell him that I *cussed*.

AUG. 1—Yesterday was an excursion on the steamer *Maquam* for the Plattsburgh Library. The party was to take dinner at Rouses Point and sail thence down the Richelieu. Just after leaving Isla La Motte, some portion of the steamer gave out so that the motive power was gone. By good luck we turned around and got back to the dock at Isle La Motte. About 3 o'clock Mr. Rutherford went past on his yacht. He came over to the *Maquam* and towed her back to Plattsburgh, reaching the dock at 8, a journey of 4½ hours. The passengers gave him a vote of thanks and three cheers.

AUG. 4—Helen has become engaged to Henry Russell Platt, formerly of this town. He was graduated from the Plattsburgh High School in 1883, I think, and from Williams College in 1887. He is now a lawyer in Chicago and is a very nice fellow.

AUG. 17—Yesterday I went to a farmers' picnic in Peru. I judge there were as many as 2,000 people there, a nice-looking audience. The only speaker I heard, a Mr. Kenner, I believe, was a natural orator, holding his audience from beginning to end. His English was not the best but he had force, ready use of language, and wit, so his audience was intensely pleased.

AUG. 27—Last Saturday was an excursion. I took advantage of the cheaper rate and went up to Chateaugay Lake. Mr. Shutts was fishing in a boat but came ashore soon. We started in a rowboat and went to a long arm of sand that is about 3 miles down the lake. On this arm was an

Indian Point on Upper Chateaugay Lake, where Dr. Kellogg discovered an important Indian site in 1894.

1894 Indian encampment at a period when stone implements were in use. We took off our shoes and stockings and waded along the sandy shore. I found 5 Indian axes, one of them a fine granite one, also a good drill and some points. We got 20 in all, and one piece of pottery.

SEPT. 2—A dense smoke filled the air so that at 11 a.m. the sun, even without the clouds, looked round and red, not hurting the eyes at all to look at. After noon the wind blew from the north and the smoke was driven away, leaving clouds.[10]

SEPT. 6—This day, at 20 minutes to 12 in the forenoon, a son was born to Dr. and Mrs. D. S. Kellogg. He weighs nearly 10 pounds. He came by a long route in time, but not unusually difficult. We intend naming him Francis Fellows, the family names of the two grandmothers.

SEPT. 10—This morning Nelson came up to the house from school radiant. There has been an effort to prevent pupils from skipping the eighth grade, and he was not allowed to take the Regent's examination last spring. This fall when school opened he was in the eighth grade and had no Latin, as was expected. I asked the Board of Education to come together and as a result Nelson took an examination in arithmetic last Saturday, and this morning enters the High School.

SEPT. 22—This morning from 10 to 11 o'clock at Culver Hill, Beekmantown, were the exercises in connection with placing the monument there by the Plattsburgh Institute. At least 500 people were present and things passed off delightfully.[11]

OCT. 9—Yesterday at 8.15 a.m. I started for Ticonderoga and returned at 6.30 p.m. I went down to the ferry and signaled for the boat to come over. While it was coming I looked around on the shore and picked up a large number of Indian relics, mostly knives, cores and flakes. When we got to Larrabee's I went to the hotel and got dinner, after which I walked out to the railroad trestle. I found some fine flint knives along the shore.

OCT. 15—The other day Nello said he was glad the new baby was not a girl. One girl was enough. He knew Bessie was pretty and all that, but then she acted so!

Today I looked over the relics I got from Ticonderoga and find there are 106 in all. They are mostly knives and cores. One marking stone is very fine.

OCT. 26—I went to Ticonderoga this morning and returned at 6.20 this evening. The result of my trip was 575 stone weapons and implements picked up by me and Myron Bennett during the 4 hours I was there. This is the largest one-day find I ever had.

126

OCT. 30—I spoke to the pupils of the Normal School for 35 minutes this afternoon on "Early Plattsburgh." Among other things I told them how the bridge on Bridge Street was fought over after the planks were taken up. I suggested that at an expense of 25 cents each they could place a suitable tablet of bronze commemorating the event. Mr. Jones put the motion and it was vigorously voted in the affirmative. He then asked for a rising vote and it seemed as if every pupil rose. I have written to H. H. Upham and Co., New York, who have previously given me terms. It looks now as though a second place were to be marked this year.

NOV. 24—I have just read Hall Caine's *Scapegoat*. This is a return to the old *New York Ledger* stories of 1859 and 60, which we children were taught were infamous. This is the "dime novel" enlarged up to 50 cents in paper and a dollar in cloth. The veriest trash imaginable, and inconceivable.

NOV. 27—Last evening was the first meeting of the second season of the Plattsburgh Institute. I made a report of the work done during the summer and Mr. Walworth read the report of the expense of the Culver Hill monument. I also reported that the Normal School students had voted to put up a tablet on the bridge and that the Sons of the Revolution might put up a monument on Valcour Island.

NOV. 29—I got last night Emily Dickinson's letters, two volumes edited by Mabel Loomis Todd. I am having a delightful revel in them.

DEC. 10—George F. Tuttle, David S. Kellogg and Francis K. Kyle have formed a partnership under the name of Tuttle, Kellogg and Kyle to do business at Saranac Lake. The business is printing, job printing, and printing and editing the *Adirondack Pioneer*. Francis K. Kyle is editor and manager. I have put in 250 dollars, Francis has put in 250 dollars, and George F. Tuttle puts in whatever balance is necessary up to 1,500 dollars, whole amount. The *Pioneer* company has sold to us their entire property for 350 dollars and the new *Pioneer* is to be issued December 21, 1894.

DEC. 15—I have some patients with scarlet fever. In one house, consisting of two rooms below and a woodshed, and one room upstairs, are 3 children ill with it. One child, the oldest, a girl of ten, is the sickest one I have seen this year with scarlet fever. She had not eaten much of anything and I told her mother to let her have milk and eggs. This morning the mother told me the child had taken about two quarts of milk since yesterday morning and that she had got down her almost *seven* eggs!! The child was really better today.

DEC. 28—In the night about 12 the night before last I was telephoned to go to West Plattsburgh and about 1½ miles north. The wheeling was magnificent, although it was a little icy for the last mile or so. I got home at 1.30 yesterday afternoon, attending to examination of pensioners, and went to Valcour at 3.30 p.m.

DEC. 29—Thursday evening about 10 I went to Treadwell's Mills. The wind was blowing cold from the north and the mercury was far below 0. The house where I went was very cold, so much so that when the new baby came it steamed like a hot pudding.

DEC. 31—This is the last time that I write 1894. In many respects it has been the pleasantest year of my life.

Notes on 1894

1. On September 3, 1814, as the British approached Plattsburgh, 15 boys, ages 14 to 16, assembled and chose Martin I. Aiken as their captain. Aiken's Company helped in the defense of the town. Years later Congress gave each member a rifle.

2. Austin Dobsen, *Four French Women*. New York, 1890.

3. A Nicaragua canal received considerable impetus this year. A Panama canal was not seriously considered, partly because a French company, although it had gone bankrupt, held building rights until 1904.

4. George W. Cable (1844–1925) achieved considerable prominence with his novels of the South. His dialect portrayals of Creole and Negro life are effective, and he was one of the first regional writers.

5. Eastman's talk stimulated a group of citizens to apply for a state charter under the act of 1892, which carried with it $200 of state funds to match a similar local amount. Plattsburgh's first free public library opened in September with about 600 books.

6. See entry for October 7, 1886 for an earlier attempt on the *Royal Savage*.

7. Local historians remembered Charles de Fredenburgh's mysterious disappearance. As Plattsburgh's first settler, he had a mill at the Falls. All his property was destroyed in the Revolution and he disappeared suddenly after the war. Murder was suspected, and the discovery of the skeleton led many to assume that it was de Fredenburgh's.

8. The article appeared in *Science* on June 17, *1892* and was entitled "Glacial Phenomena in North-Eastern New York."

9. Harriet Fellows was a sister of Dr. Kellogg's mother. Alexander H. Stephens became vice president of the Confederate States but never married.

10. The smoke was caused by forest fires, accompanied by great loss of life, in parts of Minnesota and Michigan.

11. Dr. Kellogg planned most of the financing and placing of the monument, which still stands on route 22. Four survivors of the battle of Plattsburgh, ages between 87 and 92, were recognized and cheered at the dedication. The monument commemorated a sharp skirmish with the British which resulted in the death of the nephew of the Duke of Wellington.

1895

Doctor Kellogg lectures in Montreal on American folklore, including some tall claims he has recently collected from an old resident of Plattsburgh who professes to be a "mineral witch." The venerable Gazette *gives the Doctor's talk an impressive notice. Another intellectual pleasure of the year is Southern author George W. Cable's return to town with more readings from his books. The Kelloggs enjoy having dinner with him and listening to additional entertaining stories.*

The Doctor estimates that he has now brought one thousand babies into the world. He is obviously far better at that than at riding a bicycle, which he learns to do this year but with humiliating early results. He successfully guides the Plattsburgh Institute through another year of stimulating meetings, and finds time to steal off to revisit a fishing hole of his boyhood. He delights in meeting a daughter of General Alexander Macomb, who led the American land forces at the Battle of Plattsburgh, and she enjoys looking at the Doctor's many relics of that war.

The year goes out with a hurricane's roar.

JAN. 4—Last evening I was at a house where I wanted a consultant and sent the husband for another doctor. He was gone a long time, much longer than necessary, and his wife, the patient, got somewhat uneasy. She said, "Henry would be a good one to send after death."

JAN. 8—Last evening was the third meeting of the second year of the Plattsburgh Institute. The matter of ascertaining the number of dead on Crab Island was brought up, as Capt. George E. Pond wanted to learn for the proposed monument to be erected there by the U.S. Government.[1]

JAN. 18—I have been invited by the Montreal branch of the American Folklore Association to read a paper before their society in Montreal on March 11. I have consented to do so and am now trying to find out what material I have.

1895   I have had several talks with Callanan, an old man of this town who says he is a "mineral witch." He defines this to be one who locates minerals in the earth by means of minerals. His processes are his own. He claims to have certain instruments of his own manufacture by the use of which he locates minerals or metals. He says there is a British battery sealed and buried in Bernard Young's meadow. He located a gold watch once, lost in the lake the other side of Grand Isle. There are 475 dollars in silver in 75 feet of water in a trunk off Port Kent. There is also a lead mine on Isle la Motte, which he located.

He finds what he does find by means of affinity between minerals. In the hands of the right person the minerals have affinities for those of their own kind. He thinks this is by means of animal magnetism. If he should sell his instruments he would get very rich, but not every person can use them. He himself is not superstitious, but has been at this business for over 25 years.

Another kind of person is a "water witch," who hunts for water with a witch-hazel or apple-tree stick. This stick is forked, not sharpened, and each branch of the fork is about 9 inches long. He himself can find water with muriatic acid because muriatic acid is made from muriate of sodium, which is common salt, and salt has an affinity for water. This acid must be carried in a sealed vial and when it comes over water the acid will vibrate because of the animal magnetism passing from the man through to the water.

JAN. 28—The Reverend N. Richards, pastor of the Baptist church of this place, resigned one week ago yesterday. His parishioners thought it better for him to resign because he had been dealing in stocks in New York through a local dealer here. They call it gambling.

JAN. 30—We examined for pension today John Cassavaugh of West Chazy. He was 84 years old. He lost his right index finger in the war. At Drury's Bluff he had three sons killed in the morning of May 16, 1864 and two others wounded in the same battle. The other son, the sixth, was not wounded at all.

FEB. 11—In the Normal Hall were the exercises in connection with the placing of the bronze tablet on the bridge over the Saranac on Bridge Street. The tablet was on an easel and veiled with the American flag. The tablet is 20 x 24 inches, is of antique bronze, and cost 45 dollars. A committee of Normal School students went down and placed it.

FEB. 22—Francis K. Kyle has sold out *The Pioneer* so that the firm Tuttle, Kellogg and Kyle does not really exist now. It was with the full consent

130

of the firm and he had a chance to make about 300 dollars by the trans-
action.

FEB. 23—The people of the village are agog over the Revolutionary Societies. A chapter of the Daughters of the American Revolution has been formed here, of which Theo Kyle is one of the charter members. John Henry Myers had joined the Sons of the Revolution, of which I have the honor to be the first member among the residents of Plattsburgh.

FEB. 28—Last evening George W. Cable read at Academy Hall to a large audience. He sang a few Creole songs. Then he recited "Passon Jone," which was capital. He stayed at John H. Myers'. Bess, Theo and I dined there with him. He was very entertaining and told some fine stories.

In speaking of Mrs. Riley in *Dr. Sevier*, he said she was a real character in a New York boarding house. He had come up from New Orleans and wanted a place to stay and be quiet so he could write. In some way he came across a boardinghouse whose landlady was new to the business and wanted to get boarders. As he liked the place he said if she were satisfied to take him without references, he would her. Before he had been there long he found she was a veritable character and must go into a book, and before she knew it he had her in a book and he did not know that she was ever aware of the fact. He could not even remember her name now. He said that the chapter in *Dr. Sevier* about the departure of the troops from New Orleans was all true and that he himself was one of them.

MAR. 12—Bessie and I went to Montreal yesterday morning at 5.15 and got home at 11.35 this morning. We went to the Windsor where we stayed at 4 dollars per day. I read a paper before the Montreal branch of the American Folklore Society to an audience of about 35 gentlemen and ladies.

A funny thing happened. I had taken a clean shirt to put on in the evening. When I got it out, lo and behold it was Robert's. I could get into it but my arms and hands stuck through very lengthily and I could not make the collar go around my neck. Luckily John Bailey came in just then (7.20) and he hustled out to a store and bought me a new one.

MAR. 20—*The Gazette*, newspaper of Montreal of last Friday, gave my paper a notice of nearly one column. As this paper means what it says, the notice was very complimentary.

On Monday, about 6 a.m., I was telephoned to go out on the Turnpike, a distance of eight miles. I hurried, made a couple of calls, and got started before seven and reached the place before eight. There was no haste and I had business to attend to in town, so I came back and returned again at 2 in the afternoon. Such a terrific wind I hardly ever knew. It blew my wagon around in one place. It blew the horse blanket out part way and my obstetric forceps were missing and I have not seen them since. When I was coming home at midnight I had such a terrible headache I could hardly sit up in the wagon part of the way.

MAR. 30—I received a telegram the other day from a man in California asking me to prescribe for him by telegraph, which I did. This was the *longest* prescription I have ever made. The man had recently left Plattsburgh and had been a patient of mine.

MAY 15—Last evening was the twelfth meeting of the second year of the Plattsburgh Institute. The lecture was by Benjamin Norton, formerly of Plattsburgh but now president of the Atlantic Avenue Railway Company of Brooklyn. Subject was "Electrical Railroads." About 130 people were present and the interest was great. Many questions were asked and answered. This may lead to an electric railway in Plattsburgh.

JUNE 11—It is now 20 minutes to four in the morning. I am sitting on the east piazza and can easily see to write. I have just been out on a sick call.

JUNE 12—Yesterday I had the honor of assisting into this world my one thousandth infant. He was a fourth son, named Owen Conley Fagan. No daughters. Today I had a fourth son, no daughters, in another place.

JUNE 13—We expect Rebe and Bessie Gallaher on every train from Montreal. She was to start from Sloan on Monday last.

JUNE 15—Went on the High School Cadets' excursion on steamer *Reindeer* to Vergennes today. It seemed strange to go through meadows and pastures on a large steamboat.[2] Robert, Nelson, Elspeth and Bessie Gallaher went too. After dinner at the Stevens House I got a horse and buggy. We went out to Panton, where I taught school three of my four college winters. I looked into the window of the schoolhouse and saw the new seats which had taken the place of the old ones. But the local changes could not alter the views of such marvellous beauty as the Adirondacks in the west preserved, and the Green Mountains in the east.

JUNE 17—The other day I got some eyeglasses to find out whether I could read any more easily. Elspeth was constantly putting them on as she walked downstreet with me, and was peering at the girls and boys whom she passed. Little Charlie Barber came along on his bicycle and called out "Hello, Grandmother," which made her hand the glasses back to me.

In the heart of Dr. Kellogg's beloved Adirondacks—Upper Au Sable Lake as photographed by S.R. Stoddard in 1887.

1895   JUNE 25—Yesterday Robert had his first shave. He has been quite hirsute for some months. His appearance is greatly improved.

JUNE 26—I went over to Burlington yesterday afternoon to attend the fiftieth anniversary of the Sigma Phi's existence at the University of Vermont. We had a delightful reunion, there being about 70 present.

JULY 24—Today the Saranac Chapter of the Daughters of the American Revolution placed a tablet on the house in which lived Maj. Gen. Benjamin Mooers.[3]

AUG. 3—This week, have attended Fr. Zahm's lectures on "Evolution" at the Catholic Summer School, also Col. Richard Malcolm Johnston's on the "Evolution of the Novel." Both were wonderfully fine. We had Col. Johnston to tea last night. He was just as delightful as ever.

AUG. 21—This morning at 8 o'clock went to St. John's church to attend the funeral of Thomas Hafford. He has been sick with consumption for nearly a year, and his wife died of the same disease less than two years ago. It was a sad sight, the four little orphan children huddling close to their father's coffin. I do not think the oldest is over 10 and the youngest is perhaps 4 to 5 years. While the Mass was being said, the sun came out clear and the light came in through the windows cheerfully, a good omen, perhaps. Poor Tom. Poor Tom.

AUG. 22—I am learning to ride a bicycle. I have so far succeeded that I can get on sometimes and go quite a good many rods. But our wheel has some peculiar perversities. When there is a good ditch by the side of the road it will make for it. If there is a stone to avoid, or a team to get out of the way of, just at the last instant, when it should be entirely distant from the obstacle, it turns right up to it. For some time I could not turn and pass. It took some time to get it to go by C. W. Bromley's back door. It would turn up there in spite of all I could do. One of our neighbors hinted it was a second-hand machine and that its former rider had always stopped there. Certainly if in ancient times there was a "Deus ex machina," there is now a "Devil ex machina," so far as this wheel is concerned.

Later. I was riding up the street going past George H. Beckwith's house. He was on the piazza and said, "Wonders never cease." This one did cease soon. After a very few rods more I was in the ditch.[4]

AUG. 28—Yesterday evening at 7.30 Helen Sherwood Kyle was married to Henry Russell Platt. The ceremony was performed by Rev. Dr. W. T. Poynter of Shelbyville, Kentucky. He was head of the school where Helen has taught Latin for the last 5 years.

All during the day the various members of the family had been getting the house in order. Chairs and sofas were taken out. The pictures on the walls, the radiators, every place possible had flowers and vines. There were roses, sweet peas, goldenrod, asters and many other flowers. Everything was just as pretty and pleasant as could be.

About 8.30 Helen had put on her travelling suit and the family were upstairs bidding her and Russell good-by. The crowd below filled the hall waiting for them to come down. Francis Kyle and Dr. Platt took their trunk out to the carriage. Suddenly there was a shout. The bride and groom had hustled down the backstairs and were in the carriage before those waiting knew it. Some rice was thrown, but not disagreeably. I saw on the top of the carriage two old slippers which I recognized as mine and which I think Nelson placed there.

SEPT. 2—Last Friday, yesterday and until this morning Mrs. Gen. S. Miller (born Jane Octavia Macomb) was at the Fouquet House. Mrs. Miller is a daughter of Gen. Alex. Macomb, who commanded the land forces at Plattsburgh in September 1814. Mrs. Miller was born in Washington, D.C. and lives there now. She was the youngest, and the only now living, of Gen. Macomb's 12 children. One of her brothers who was born after the battle was named Alexander *Saranac* Macomb.

Yesterday Mrs. Miller rode up to the house with me to look at my war relics, in which she was greatly interested. On the way down we stopped at H. K. Averill's and he showed her his father's flintlock breech-loading gun, presented to him by Act of Congress in 1826. He also gave her many photographs of local interest, including one of her father's house here. She was greatly interested in Plattsburgh. She had great admiration for her father. She said he was so modest he would never talk about his war experiences. She was quite exercised over the misspelling of her father's name on the street in Plattsburgh, called after him. It is MACOMB. The o has the sound of oo in booth. The last syllable rhymes with *tomb*.

SEPT. 11—We got the Halsey's Corners monument in place and were just ready to do the ceremonies when a terrific shower broke in upon us and we all retreated. The soldiers got very wet as they marched in the tremendous rain.[5]

SEPT. 13—Today for the first time I came downtown on a bicycle. I cannot yet touch my hat to a lady while riding, and if a hair gets onto my nose I have to suffer in silence, for I cannot let go my hand to get it off.

It was the Doctor's frequent custom to write reminiscences of his boyhood days for the entertainment and edification of his children. The following nostalgic account of Colchester Pond, Vermont, is one of the most charm-

ing of these accounts. It is inserted here in the body of Doctor Kellogg's Journal because it provides a perfect introduction to his Journal entry for October 3rd, describing a sentimental return to this beloved fishing hole of his youth.

Around over the hills, about three miles from our home, was a body of water named from the town in which it was, Colchester Pond. It was perhaps a mile long and half a mile wide and, as usual with such ponds, was said to have no bottom. I suppose in reality it was a hundred feet deep in some places.

One day I saw Philo Pierson scaling some fish at his house. He said he got them at Colchester Pond. He told us it would not do for us to go there alone for the "water was as deep as from here to that bench, or deeper," pointing to a bench perhaps 30 feet away. From that time on, one of our greatest desires was to go to this pond. How soon after this we went, I cannot tell. We may even have been there before. We certainly had heard of it, but these fish impressed us greatly.

The whole eastern side of the pond was close against a high, steep, rocky hill, but there was a path near the water all the way. In some places there were ledges nearly perpendicular, but these projected enough to form the path close to the water's edge. I believe in high water this was sometimes covered. Yet here was the best fishing place. And what do you suppose we caught? Chiefly small pumpkinseeds and perch. Occasionally a bass would be hooked up, or a bullpout, but not often. I should like to know how many hours I have stood or sat here fishing.

One time Osman Seaver came up from Burlington and we all went over to the pond for the day and took our lunch with us. He had a bunch of firecrackers which he gleefully shook in my face. But they made no impression on me, for I had never seen any before. We had our lunch near this ledge, after building a fire and roasting our fish. These fish were good, too, even if we had no salt.

The land at the north of the pond was a sloping pasture through which, after a heavy rain, two brooks ran to the pond. Wonderful as it seems to me now, for a short time in the spring of the year these little streams at night would have large numbers of suckers. I believe they used to go back into the pond in the daytime. I remember one night when these brooks were high some men waited until near midnight, when they found the suckers had gone up one of the streams. They made a stick dam across this brook near the pond, through which the water but not the fish could go. Then by the light of a lantern they reached into the water and threw out the fish with their hands. This night they must have taken at least two bushels. They were very large, perhaps a foot and a half long. We supposed that the pickerel, which had been put into the pond only a few years before, had eaten out the small ones. The light of the lantern either blinded them or they were not afraid of it. The water was so shallow that their backs would almost, or quite, stick out. I recall that on one small ripple these large, dark-backed suckers, with heads upstream together, allowed themselves to be picked out one by one, almost without attempting to get away.

The land at the south was meadow and pasture, with some alders and willows scattered here and there. Quite a large inlet entered near the southeast corner, while the one outlet was from the southwestern part. This inlet was so long the suckers did not return as they did in the north ones, the same night. They hid themselves under projecting sods and banks and stones. There we used to find them and catch them with our hands or with spears. Ever so many times, by putting our hand or spear or a stick into the water under a stone or bank, a sucker would be frightened out and dart up or down stream, wherever he could go the most quickly, and then a chase would follow. Ofter he would get into deeper water and hide again. Often the cruel iron pierced his back and he was thrown quivering onto the land. We always took them home and ate them. Sometimes as the water in the brook grew less, a large fish would get into just water enough to keep him alive, but after a time he would have to drown in the open air.

It seems the owner of the land south, being so much annoyed and injured by the men at night burning up his fences, determined to stop the fishing by not letting the fish come up. So he dug a long ditch from the inlet to the outlet, half a mile or so from the pond, and turned the water out of its usual course so it did not run into the pond at all. Where this ditch started from the inlet, he built a strong stone and earth dam. But every spring someone would make a large opening in this dam and let the water run as usual. Often this opening would let the water down but *not* the fish up. I came one day to the pool just below this dam, and such a floundering and flapping and splashing I never heard before. This whole place, which was perhaps 20 feet square, was full of monstrous suckers. A man coming along then told me he got a whole barrelful there the week before and salted them down.

The pond itself was of great beauty. The water was clear, but the bottom of the south end was muddy and the surface here covered with large lily leaves. We used to go in boats to the edge of these leaves, anchor, and catch larger fish than we could at the rocks. The boats used were leaky and unsafe. A boy named Johnny Carty, who used to work for us, was drowned here. His boat filled with water and he could not swim. When the city of Burlington began to talk about supplying itself with water, there were many who thought the water of Colchester Pond would be better than that of the Winooski or of Lake Champlain.

One night we went over to "spear" on the pond. Our boat was loaded too full. We had a highjack filled with burning pine roots for a light. We could see the bottom distinctly. After rowing a good many hours and getting thoroughly chilled through, about daylight we started for home without a fish. I shut my eyes while going through the pasture about sunrise, and found myself walking out of the path, asleep. I went to bed after getting home and had a good sleep. My brother Abiel would not go to sleep, but went to work instead and was made sick in consequence.

One day in the spring, after a rain, Horace Kelly came along after dinner and wanted us to go over to the pond with him. Father, after much teasing, told us we might go, but we must be home at milking time, *without fail.* As that was nearly five hours later, it seemed absurd that anyone should even *think* there was a possibility of our being gone so long as that. We went and played around, but had no luck catching fish.

After a time an old fisherman, smoking a stub of a clay pipe, told us the fish wouldn't bite well until about sunset. Before we knew it sunset was on us. Then we learned that the bullpout would bite after dark when we had a fire. The dark came and the fire, but not the bullpout. By this time it must have been 9 o'clock and we wanted to go home. But the men told us we had better wait until after the moon rose, about 11. After the moon came up we three started, in much fear. When we got to Horace's house Harrington, his brother, said, "Are the Kellogg boys there?"

Horace said, "Yes."

"Their father has been here after them."

That made us the more afraid, so we took hold of hands and ran nearly the rest of the way home. One of us said, "I'll bet he'll lick us." That was the extent of our conversation, and our expected fate. However, when we got home Mother told us they thought we were in the bottom of the pond. In the morning Father said, "Boys, don't let this happen again," and that was all. We always thought the only thing that saved us from a "licking" was that they were so glad we were not drowned.

I can shut my eyes now and see this beautiful sheet of water. I can smell the fish we caught and feel them biting our hooks. I can put my hand under the bank and start out a sucker and jump after him and murder him with a jagged spear. I can feel the chilliness of the night when we rowed around the pond without catching a fish. I can see the moon coming up through the trees on the hill the night we didn't get home at milking time, and I am glad even now that we didn't get our expected and much-deserved "licking."

OCT. 3—Went over to Colchester Pond today. It is over 22 years since I have seen this pond. It has not changed much. The same path along the rocky east shore, the same fishing places, apparently the same abandoned

The Doctor's wife, Bessie, pictured in her home about 1895.

fish poles on the shore were to be seen. I took up one and held it out as if fishing. I do not doubt, if I had a hook and line, the same old pleasure in fishing would have returned.

OCT. 8—Went to Malone to the Northern New York Medical Association meeting. Twenty five physicians were present.

OCT. 10—Although Francis F. took his first step alone on Saturday, he did not realize that he could really walk alone until last evening. He then walked several steps alone and received much applause for it. This encouraged him to try again and again, with greater success and greater applause. He could sit on the lower stair, get up alone, and walk into and nearly across the front sitting room alone. He is a remarkably fine young fellow.

NOV. 9—Yesterday I went to Ticonderoga to look for relics. I went at 8.15 a.m. and got home at 6.15 p.m. James A. Stratton went with me. We looked on Willow Point and on Wright's Point. We found and brought home over 300.

NOV. 22—We found this morning it was cold. The door to the bathroom upstairs was shut all night and the window open. The water would not run because it was frozen in the pipes. A joint of pipe that runs to the overflow reservoir of the heating apparatus burst and we had quite a little deluge. So much for winter coming unannounced.

NOV. 28—Thanksgiving Day. To our delight Francis Kyle came down rom Saranac Lake and took dinner with us. He has been working on the Adirondack Survey in one of Colvin's parties under Prof. Parks.

DEC. 18—Last night I started about one o'clock and went out on to the State Road 6¼ miles to John Conroy's, at the old Farnsworth place. The house, made of stone, stands on a surface ledge. Its walls are 3 feet thick. In the "attick" are the remains of an old district school library.[6] I found 8 volumes of Jared Sparks' *Lives* and some other things.

DEC. 23—David wrote a letter to Santa Claus. He took a sheet of my paper with my name on it and scratched out the M.D. and put Jr. after it.

DEC. 27—The wind blew so hard about 4 this morning that the heavy iron girders they were putting up for the roof of the Normal School blew down, doing considerable injury.[7]

DEC. 31—It seems as if the year is to be blown out. Towards morning the wind changed and there has been almost a hurricane today. On the lake the waves are tremendous. The wind would take up the water and drive it along like mist so the surface of the lake looked foggy. Down by the Creek the heavy roaring of the invisible winds in the trees, over the ground and on the lake was as if the air were full of rumbling trains of unseen cars. No wonder people have thought the air was filled with conscious beings who were terrible or otherwise according to the violence or quietness of the atmosphere.

Notes for 1895

1. Crab Island, or Isle St. Michel, served as an American military hospital during the British occupation of 1814. Armed with a cannon, the invalids on the day of the battle on the lake received the surrender of a British warship that drifted out of control. The Island was the burial place of the 300 battle dead of both sides.

2. The steamer sailed up Otter Creek as far as the falls at Vergennes.

3. The house stands at the corner of Peru and Bridge Streets. Mooers (1758–1838) was an officer in the Revolution, an early settler of Northern New York and commander of its militia in the War of 1812.

4. Dr. Kellogg was one of many to succumb to the bicycle craze. In 1895 about 400,000 of them were produced in the nation. In Plattsburgh its hazard to traffic gave rise to demands for regulating speeds in town.

5. Halsey's Corners was the site of one of the brief stands made against the British army as it approached Plattsburgh in 1814.

6. The Conroy-Farnsworth house, now an inn, was standing in 1814. According to tradition the British mistook it for a fort and fired on it. The third floor once served as a school.

7. A large south wing was being added to the original Normal School building.

1896

The Doctor mourns the deaths of two young Plattsburgh boys, one of whom drowned in an icy pond, while the other froze while lost in a blinding snow-storm on the lake.

His reputation as an authority on the archaeology of the Champlain Valley is enhanced by two important lectures. In Albany for a medical con-sultation, he finds time to hunt up ancestors at the State Library and is pleased to discover that one of them came over on the Mayflower.

After bicycling home from a call at three-thirty on an April morning, he puts off sleep a few minutes longer in order to wait on his porch to hear the first birds sing. In June his oldest child, Robert, graduates with honors from high school, and in September enters the University of Vermont, "the beginning of his always being away from home."

The Doctor wearily notes, but hardly celebrates, his forty-ninth birthday. He hails the coming of the trolley to Plattsburgh, but the year's greatest gratification to him is McKinley's victory over Bryan in the fall election. In this the Doctor sees clear indication that God has not forgotten the Ameri-can people.

JAN. 6—It is 11° *below* on our east piazza. The ink froze in the office, though I had a fire yesterday and I had wrapped the bottle in paper.

JAN. 7—Last evening was the third meeting of the third year of the Plattsburgh Institute. The Institute passed a resolution requesting Congress-man Wallace T. Foote to do all in his power to further the appropriation of 15,000 dollars by Congress for a monument on Isle St. Michel. A resolution was also passed against any raising of the *Royal Savage* for purposes of relics, or anything else.

JAN. 18—Yesterday afternoon Edward Hudson, a little son of Charles F. Hudson, aged 6½ years, was drowned in the Normal School pond. There was an open place near the center, where he got in. A little boy ran and told his mother, who ran to the place. The ice broke through with her. A man took her out. When I got to the Normal School building, some men had carried him in and his uncle, Mr. George H. Hudson, and John Blanchard were working over him, but all to no purpose. The life had gone out of him.

Only that day noon he had come home from school shouting that he had stood 99 in his arithmetic. He told his mother to look at the two nines. He said that next he would stand a hundred. His twin sister had always admired him. Only the day before in school this sister tried to comfort him. For some little thing he had had to stand on the floor for a time. The sister asked if she might leave her seat. She went to him, put her arm around him, and told him not to mind it. When they got home their mother would give them something good and he would forget all about it.

JAN. 22—I went to Albany yesterday and read a paper before the Albany Institute entitled "Notes on the Archaeology of the Valley of Lake Champlain." I took a heavy load of relics with me. The audience seemed very appreciative.

JAN. 29—The other evening I was talking with Congressman Foote about a monument on Crab Island and on the Reservation. David was with me and we talked until a little after 6, which is our supper time. David was quite restless but did not say anything. After we got onto the street he wanted to know why I stayed talking so long when it was past our supper time. I told him, but with all the dignity he could muster he said, "Well, I should think it of a good deal more consequence to be talking about getting something to eat than to be *talking about putting up monuments.*"

I am struggling with my second attack of grip for this season. In my case I might call it *back* instead of *grip* if the pain and size of the pain are any index.

FEB. 10—Yesterday was a heavy fall of snow, perhaps more than a foot. In the storm two little boys, aged about 14, went on the lake skating. They went to the Head and only one of them got home. A large party, including many soldiers, searched for him in the night but did not find him.[1]

FEB. 22—Fred H. Chase, Theo's young man, came yesterday. We expect Francis Kyle in the morning.

FEB. 29—I spent the time from about 3 this morning until near six this evening in a house at Culver Hill, where a new boy was born. Poor fellow. He will not have a birthday until 1904. His brothers and sisters which probably will follow will have their birthdays many times before he does. How they will lord it over their *baby* brother.

MAR. 3—Last evening was the seventh meeting of the third year of the Plattsburgh Institute. Mr. H. Walworth read an account of "Don" Caleb Nichols, a former resident of Plattsburgh.[2] The paper of the evening was by Lieut. Charles H. Bonesteel, Co. G, 21st U.S. Infantry, on "A Winter Camp at the Rosebud Agency."[3] About 175 persons were present, ladies and gentlemen.

MAR. 10—I went to Albany yesterday, leaving Plattsburg at quarter to twelve and reaching Plattsburg on my return at 5 this morning. I took a little patient, Katherine Buckley, to see Dr. VanderVeer. I spent about an hour and a half in the State Library looking up my ancestors.

MAR. 12—The other day I told the children not to take too much butter onto their plates and then eat only a little and let the rest be wasted. David said, "Papa, that isn't wasted. Lizzie puts it onto the toast in the morning. I have seen her do it."

MAR. 28—I wrote to Mary two weeks ago about father's singing the old tunes and also about Uncle George Whitney's singing at Aunt Eliza's funeral, to the tune of "Robin Adair," the following:

> When shall I see the day
> Dear Jesus, when?
> When all the heavenly host—

This is all I can remember. I asked Mary if she remembered and she wrote as follows:

Dear Friends,

Your March 16 is at hand. When Nettie was here we used to sing so many of those *old* hymns. She remembered so many of the words. "When marshalled on the nightly plain" Miss Cubley used to sing the most. From her I learned to sing the alto, though I have heard Aunt Tabitha sing it but not so much as

> True Retreat
> From every stormy wind that blows,
> From every swelling tide of woes
> There is a calm, a sure retreat,
> 'Tis found beneath the mercy seat.

I think I have heard of Uncle David playing the bass viol in church. I think you are mistaken in the hymn Uncle G. Whitney sang at Aunt Eliza's funeral, for Nettie and I found it. It is in an old hymnbook of Henry's, tune "Sonnet."

He may have sung the one you spoke of. I know it, for it is very familiar. Father used to sing so much while milking. "China" is the tune I remember mostly, also the one you spoke of, "How long, dear Savior," etc. I think them over and over again and never sing them, but it brings to mind the pleasant past.

APR. 12—I have just come down to the office, a thing I do not often do on Sunday evenings. I had some new sugar on snow with the family, which tasted good. The robins are singing, the young people are riding on their bicycles and spring has come. I hope the adders'-tongues and liverworts will be out soon. Just now the church bells are ringing—tolling, rather. The

The Plattsburgh trolley line, which began operations in 1896.

APR. 20—I found yesterday that John Howland, one of the Pilgrims who were on the *Mayflower*, was an ancestor of mine. His daughter in 1643, *Desire Howland*, married John Gorham. *Their* daughter, Linda Gorham, married Col. John Thacher and was his second wife. *Their* daughter, *Hannah* Thacher, married Nathaniel Otis and *their* daughter Lydia married Abner Kellogg. I feel prouder of this Mayflower ancestry than of any other I have yet come across.

APR. 25—This morning I was called out about 3. I took the wheel and went down onto Oak Street. I reached home again about 3.30. It then was so light from the morning that one hardly needed a lantern. I waited on the steps to hear the robins begin to sing. At 20 minutes to four there was heard the voice of a single robin for an instant. At ten minutes to four there was the same sound again, followed by quiet. In just five minutes there came a different call from a robin in another direction and during the next three minutes the whole robin chorus was in full swing.

MAY 14—Mr. Edward Barber told me yesterday that a few years ago at one election a member of a family voted early in the morning and got only two dollars for his vote. In the afternoon the other voters got 5 or 6 dollars apiece. The mother expressed her regrets as follows: "Too bad to take the provision right off a poor man's back in that way."

MAY 16—Went to Saranac Lake yesterday afternoon to examine two pensioners. I stayed at the Berkeley Hotel. The cars left to return at 7.30 this morning. The ride was very beautiful. The clear sky, the cool north wind, the new life which the ground and trees were putting on, made one appreciate the luxury there is in mere existence.

MAY 19—The other day a man wanted to know how to make the tincture of iodine. He used to be a prosperous farmer, or at any rate one who got a good living. A few years ago he became blind in one eye and nearly so in the other. He had to consult Dr. Bullen in Montreal and as a result the sight of one eye is partly saved. Now he can see to drive in the road in the day-time, and can walk around if it is very light.

He lives on the State Road in a little house for which he pays one dollar and a half per month. He keeps a cow and horse. His wife and her mother live with him. In his nearly total blindness there is but little he can do. So he has taken to selling tinctures and essences, driving through the country as best he may. He generally sells his articles by the ounce. He said the other day he made 57 cents, and another, 35 cents. He seemed to think he was getting a good living and was cheerful and contented.

JUNE 20—Theo left last night for New York on the sleeper. She expects to sail for Hamburg today on the steamer *Polatia*. She was very happy. A

1896 small bundle of letters was handed to her just before starting.

JUNE 25—Today Robert was graduated from the Plattsburgh High School. There was a class of 17 and he stood second, thus having the honorable position of salutatory. His subject was "Pasteur." No one of his class did any better than he.

JUNE 30—Today Robert and Fred Mason went over to Burlington and picked out their room in the new Converse dormitory. They both have really become members of the freshman class, U.V.M., on certificates from the Plattsburgh High School.

Last Saturday night the first trolley car ran in Plattsburgh.[4]

JULY 3—Today I received a notice signed Philip Livingston, Secretary, to the effect that I was admitted to membership in the Society of Colonial Wars.

JULY 10—Today the whole family, myself alone excepted, and the horse No. 2 has gone to a cottage for a few weeks. They are to stay there so long as they can under the aspect and name of comfort—make themselves miserable.

AUG. 8—I delivered at the Summer School last night my lecture entitled "Notes on the Archaeology of the Champlain Valley."[5]

SEPT. 5—This afternoon a French fellow tried to play a shrewd game on me. He came in haste to have me go up to his house. He had not the money now, but would have it at such a time next week. He had done the same thing to me before, but still he had paid me something. After some little talking, although he thought the case was urgent, I told him if he would get me an order from Mr. Rising, the man he worked for at the pulp mill, I would go. He put his hand into his pocket and took out an order from Mr. Rising that he had ready to give me, unless he could get me to go without.

SEPT. 17—A telegram came from Russell Platt today saying that Helen had a daughter weighing 7¾ pounds and that both were doing well.

SEPT. 28—Rob, having entered the freshman class at Burlington, leaves tomorrow. It seems as if this were the beginning of his always being away from home. Fred C. Mason of this place is to be his roommate. Robert takes the classical course.

OCT. 3—Francis Kyle came up from Troy this evening. He seems to be doing very well in his new position on the *Troy Times*.

OCT. 4—A couple of weeks ago a poor man came for me to go to his house to help a new baby into the world. It was raining hard. He had an open buggy and no overcoat. I rode down to his house with him and was

146

The Catholic Summer School at Cliff Haven, near Plattsburgh. This site was first used in 1896, after several seasons in temporary quarters.

ready to come back in about an hour. He took out five one-dollar bills and said that was all he had been able to save during the summer, above what he had to pay for food for his family to eat.

OCT. 5—A letter came from Rob today saying he was pledged to the Sigs last Wednesday evening. That was quick and good work. I soon "shall have a son in the Sigma Phi."

OCT. 17—I went over to Burlington last evening and was present at the initiation into the Society of the Sigma Phi. Robert enjoyed the initiation services and is enjoying his studies in college. His room has a beautiful outlook east onto Mansfield and Camel's Hump and the valley of the Winooski.

OCT. 21—I can say seven times seven today. I used to think that a man between 40 and 50 years of age was old enough to die. I have changed my mind on that point.

OCT. 23—Yesterday afternoon I took the train with Dr. Holcomb to go to Isle La Motte to see Mr. Hill. We left the cars at Chazy and drove to Saxe's Landing. There we took a scow ferry and went to Isle La Motte. I remained there about an hour. Returning, the Doctor's team was coming to Plattsburgh. I rode in this, leaving Saxe's at 6 and reaching home at ten minutes to nine. Then I had to go out onto the West Beekmantown Road, about 3½ miles. I got home and to bed and to sleep. A little before 12 a gentle rap was heard at the door. I got up and had to go to a confinement case. Luckily I was not long detained, but today I feel more than 49 years old.

OCT. 27—I went again last night to Isle La Motte to see Mr. Hill. He is very sick indeed. I went on the 6.15 evening train to Chazy to see a patient with Dr. Fairbank. This patient died just before I got to the house. Dr. F. then took me down to Saxe's and the ferryman took me over to Isle La Motte in a sailboat by moonlight. I got to Mr. Hill's about 9, remained there overnight and came back on "the scow" to Saxe's, thence to Chazy and on the train reached Plattsburgh at 8.10 a.m.

A boy nicknamed "Peekie" took me in a hay wagon from Mr. Hill's to Chazy. Peekie seemed to be quite a character. The advice given him, had he taken it all, would have been sufficient to sink the scow. He got up about 4, milked 10 cows, had his breakfast and was ready with the horses at 6.05 in the morning. It was "Peekie, hurry up, you'll be late." "Peekie, make that team go right along." The ferryman, whose son was with him, encouraged him by reiterating "Peekie, you're late." As soon as we were landed, Peekie jumped up and handed the barrels out to the ferryman's son without a word. I concluded that though it was "Peekie do this, Peekie do that," when it came to business Peekie had a way and mind of his own.

NOV. 2—The night before election. There is much deep feeling, not much outward expression. David Dobie said he felt like the old Universalist who all his life had claimed that everybody would be saved and go to Heaven, but when he was in his final sickness said he *would give his best cow to know positively.*

NOV. 5—Well! Election day has come and gone and Major McKinley has been elected beyond a peradventure. I said to a man it showed "God had not forgotten the people of the United States." He said, "It shows that the people of the United States have not forgotten God."

NOV. 14—I went to Fort Ticonderoga yesterday to look for relics. James A. Stratton went too. We looked exclusively on the Orwell shore. The water was much higher than last year, but we made good finds. I have not counted them yet.

DEC. 15—Elspeth has an invitation from Dan Cornman, Capt. Cornman's little son, to go up to the Administration Building to a dance tonight. It is for the children. Like a true daughter of Mother Eve, when I told her about the invitation she said, "Well! I can't go. *I haven't anything to wear.*"

DEC. 29—There has been little or no snow but the ground is so hard the sharpenings of the horses' shoes wear off quickly. I had my horse sharpened twice but in two days with little driving he became very slippery.

DEC. 31—The year goes out tonight. 1896 has been a good and moderate year. I am watching to see if there is any noise or other indication of the annual change.

Notes for 1896

1. He was found dead next day two miles out on the lake.
2. Caleb Nichols was a lawyer in early Plattsburgh. He owned Crab Island and after the battle of Plattsburgh he billed the government for $615 in damages. Unknown to his neighbors, he made wartime intelligence reports direct to Washington. His nickname originated when someone ridiculed a grandiloquent poem of his by adding two lines:

> And the frightful fish, hearing the clatter
> Cried out, Don Caleb! what in h—l's the matter?

3. Bonesteel talked about the winter of 1890–91 at the Rosebud Indian Agency in South Dakota.
4. When completed, the trolley line connected Bluff Point, the steamship dock, the fairgrounds and the Normal School. The first run took place on June 27. On the 28th hoodlums piled stones on the track and derailed the car. The passengers were shaken up but no one was hurt.
5. The Summer School consisted of 75 lectures between July 12 and August 16. For the first time it was held at the permanent site at Cliff Haven.

1897

On a not untypical night of winter, Doctor Kellogg is called out at dinner time and doesn't get back home until time for breakfast. Meanwhile, he manages to catch two hours' sleep on a bench in a small railroad station, in front of the stove. On a February day, he covers ninety miles in his cutter while visiting patients between 4 A.M. and evening. Some of them are abjectly poor, but his sympathies and energies never flag as he dashes around to deliver their babies. In the course of two months, he is summoned to patients' sides on eighteen nights.

The Doctor writes delightfully and often of various birds he has watched and listened to on his rounds. He reports also on two most uncommon natural phenomena for Plattsburgh—a couple of earthquakes, one of which seemed to be heralded by the neighborhood cats.

Less turbulently, Plattsburgh is visited by the President, Vice-President, and Secretary of War with their families, vacationing en masse. Nelson Kellogg manages to meet President and Mrs. McKinley.

Faithful old Fly is put out to pasture for the last time, and Belmont, "a good walker but not yet well broken," takes his place. The Doctor feels he has betrayed Fly but consoles himself with the thought that it's really a kindness.

In far-off California, Doctor Kellogg's mother dies, in her ninetieth year.

JAN. 1—I have been out for consultation with Dr. Jabe Bidwell. This Dr. Bidwell has been practicing medicine in West Plattsburgh for many years. He has paralysis agitans terribly. He cannot really get into or out of a wagon alone. His hands tremble terribly. He only speaks in a whisper and people have to put their ear close to his lips to hear him. He can't put up his own medicines into powders or liquids, and yet he has a large practice. It seems strange that a doctor can hold his practice when in such a wretched physical condition. I hope when I get so debilitated my clients will stick by me.

JAN. 20—I went to the Creek this afternoon and got much Indian pottery. The children had saved several boxes and I found a number of good pieces myself. What fun it is to search, and find.

JAN. 21—I drove up onto Lyon Street this afternoon. While returning, a long swarm of crows began to pass overhead, making for the pine woods just south of the old Barracks. They were flying rapidly, flapping their wings until they were 30 or 40 rods from the woods, then they held still like hawks and sailed majestically onto the pine branches. We watched these for a time and there seemed to be no end of them. I do not think I exaggerate when I say there were tens of thousands of them. Stanton Day, whom we met, said that crows had wintered in this grove for 5 or 6 winters, but never so numerous as this winter.

JAN. 25—Yesterday was Mother's birthday. She was 89 years old.

FEB. 2—I have been quite busy for the last few days. Friday night I started at 11 o'clock to go to Cadyville. I rode with Albert S. Martin. Above West Plattsburgh we had to get out and walk and lift the cutter to get through the drifts. However, it took only 1½ hours to complete the journey. Bert's new baby came about half past nine in the forenoon and I reached home at 12. About 6 p.m. I received a telegram to go to Willsboro on the sleeper, which I did. I got back to the station at Willsboro about 2 a.m. I drew up a settee to the fire, got a small box for my pillow, and slept nearly two hours. I reached home a little before 6 in the morning and had a little sleep. In the forenoon I went to Cadyville again and in afternoon I went up onto Lyon Street, 6 miles.

Monday I was called out at ten minutes to four but got home i time. I had some work to do with the microscope which mu After finishing that I slept a little. Then in the forenoon Cadyville and Hardscrabble. 'Twas a hard ride but I g before six. These cutter rides alone were about 90 mi include what I rode around town.

Today has been Charter (village) election. It money was used. I stayed in my office as muc 14 dollars by three different men. Some of this, a these men had received for their votes. Who says u a good thing!

FEB. 6—The rush of business has continued. Wednesd Eleazur L. Chauvin's on the Turnpike, 8 miles out. I got home a 3 Thursday morning. Then I had to go to Cadyville. Yesterday I st 7 a.m. for Chauvin's, went thence via West Plattsburgh and Cadyv thence to Saranac to examine an insane woman, thence to Dannemora with

Dr. Madden to examine four insane convicts, thence back to Cadyville and home, a distance of about 54 miles. If my day's work pays me 55 dollars, as I expect it will, it will not be a day misspent.

MAR. 1—I was at a house last Friday where a new baby came. There was only one room downstairs and this was heated with a wood stove. The mother told me she let the fire go out at night, that a few nights before she had a cup of water standing near her bed to drink from in the night, and in the morning the water was frozen solid. At the time the baby came she congratulated herself because she had some *hard* wood to burn. They generally used the wood from the pulp mill. After the baby came the twins, 2½ years, and the older children were brought back to the house and there was no rest for the mother then. Still she was happy. The house was hers and her husband's and they were not among the very poorest.

MAR. 24—Last evening while sitting at the supper table, we heard and felt a distinct shock of an earthquake. At first I thought it was a heavy wagon passing, but the radiator in the northeast corner of the dining room rattled so hard it was immediately apparent it was an earthquake. The whole thing subsided in less than a minute. The newspapers report it all around us and also in Montreal very hard.[1]

APR. 3—Last Sunday afternoon I was driving in on the Miller Road above Mr. Weir's. I saw a large hawk sail in from the southwest and circle around Mr. Weir's barns. In about 3 minutes after I had passed the house, I heard some crows overhead making a great fuss. Mr. Hawk had a dove which he had brought out from Mr. W's barn and which had gotten away from him. The dove was darting around, the hawk following as best he could, the broadness of his wings towards me and then the edges. Haste was necessary, for the three black enemies with louder noise were bearing hard upon him. Feathers flew from the dove, though Mr. Hawk could not get him again. Then he had to leave his prey and take care of himself. At this instant the dove took a beeline for the barns, and no runner could better manifest determination to win than this dove to reach the protection of his home. With head down and rapid wings he reached his refuge. Meantime the hawk flew near the ground but was not permitted to light. The black demons followed him clear across the meadow to the grove north, where his pursuers allowed him to stop on a limb of a tree. Then they turned around and resumed their journey southeasterly, talking to one another exultantly, their hated enemy having been driven from his prey and deprived of his supper.

APR. 26—Yesterday Elspeth must go to church because she had a new dress. The day before she had come to me in the office and must have a dollar to get some ribbon with, because she wanted her dress to be finished. She did not get the dollar but went to Lizzie and borrowed 75 cents, and this amount proved to be amply sufficient. She has many and increasing characteristics of a true daughter of Eve.

MAY 3—Yesterday was the funeral of Col. Horace Jewett, late commanding officer of the 21st U.S. Infantry stationed at the Barracks here. Col. Jewett was sick only about one week. He was cousin to Sarah Orne Jewett, my favorite New England story writer, and a fine man. The funeral was of course military. I understand there was a great crowd of people, several thousands, from town.

The sadness of the affair impressed me so I did not want to go. Mrs. Jewett, only the three days before, was the first lady of the Post. Now she was no more than a stranger and outsider. She will have to leave her house at once, to make way for the successor of her late husband. All of the infantry officers are advanced one step by this death, so this could not bring them unalloyed grief. And then this great crowd of unsympathizing sightseers!

MAY 8—I was called out at 2.30 this morning and reached home at 4.10. When I got 'most home I heard the first crows. I stood and watched the one nearest me for some time. His wings and feathers and tail did not seem to fit, for he kept shaking and moving them in a very nervous manner. Perhaps he was only trying them to see if their machinery was in good order for use during the day. But he sang while there most of the time, using two different notes or tunes. The first note was *cawuh, cawuh, cawuh,* repeated over and over again, being the same thing, tune or note. Then he changed and gave *ahuh, ahuh, ahuh,* in entirely different and higher key. And this was repeated many, many times. When he sounded his *cawuh* he would contract himself, head down, and as the note was coming out, extend himself and raise his head as a man does when he emits a long, protracted and loud cheer. When he said *ahuh* the effort was more with the head, neck and chest. His mate did much the same things, but soon flew off to another tree at a distance. But my crow remained and continued his lecture to me as long as I stood to hear it.

MAY 11—Last evening was the tenth and closing meeting of the fourth year of the Plattsburgh Institute. A paper was read by Prof. George H. Perkins of the University of Vermont on "The Position of Evolution in Modern Thought."[2]

MAY 12—Today Bessie received a *Hartford Courant* of yesterday announcing the death of her Uncle Roland Mather, who married her mother's half-sister. Mr. Mather was born in 1809 and was a descendant of Richard Mather.[3]

1897   MAY 25—Saturday I went up to Ausable Forks in consultation with Dr. E. S. Howe. We had to drive a few miles over into Jay. When I got home at night I found a telegram awaiting me, asking if some of the Plattsburgh people would accompany the Montreal Numismatic and Antiquarian Society on an excursion to Fort Ticonderoga on Monday.

So on Monday morning at 10.30 on a special, we started for Fort Ticonderoga. Nearly 150 Montreal people were aboard, intelligent, well dressed, refined—in short, ladies and gentlemen. Judge Baby gave an address near the Fort on the battle between Montcalm and Abercrombie. I followed with a short speech. We got to Plattsburgh at 7.30 in the evening. I was tired and went to bed at 9. I dozed a little until ten when the telephone bell whanged me out, and I went into the country and did not get home until 2.45 a.m.

MAY 28—Last night at 10.20 there was a heavy shock of earthquake. It was perhaps the heaviest one I have ever heard. The radiators shook and I thought the water pipes had burst. It lasted about a minute. In about half an hour, just a little before eleven, there was another mild one.

During the first shock and for *some time before*, the cats were making a tremendous yowling, and the noise of the shock itself and my efforts to quiet them after it was over did not stop them for some time. They yowled and yowled and yowled. They evidently thought it was a *cata*strophe.

JUNE 15—Last Sunday about 6 p.m. a man came for me to go to his house, as the seventh addition to his family was expected. He remarked that his wife's mother lived in the same house but that she had a mean, ugly disposition and had got mad at his wife and would not speak to her. His wife was of that disposition that she would not speak to her mother unless the mother spoke first, so they had not spoken for some time.

After reaching the house I found a neighbor's wife but not the mother assisting. In a few hours matters began to look serious with the sick woman, and occasionally the mother's voice was heard at the outside door asking for someone to come out. These calls became rather more frequent, until at last the mother came in and stood by the foot of the bed and said, "Don't you want me to make you some warm tea, Mary?" This complete surrender on the mother's part doubtless helped matters on to a speedy and favorable termination.

JULY 2—Francis Fellows wants to go with me when I go anywhere. Today I was going up near the Normal School. He wanted to go with me and thought he would stay outside while I was in the house. He was bareheaded. When he got 'most to the house his courage failed him to stay outside. He said, "I must go home to get my hat." I got him off that notion

154

President and Mrs. McKinley being entertained by the staff of the Plattsburgh Barracks in August 1897.

and in a minute he concluded he must go home to get his face washed. However, when I came out he was sitting quietly on the stepping block.

JULY 28—President McKinley, Vice-President Hobart, Secretary of War Alger and their families come to Bluff Point Hotel tomorrow morning to stay nearly a month. So the executive part of the United States government will be in Plattsburgh now.

A letter from Mary last week said that mother had fallen and hurt herself. A later letter seemed to think her better but that it was probable she would not last long.

JULY 31—I have purchased one mare five years old for seventy-five dollars. She is a Belmont and a good walker but not yet well broken. Poor Fly. He has gone out to pasture and probably he will come in contact with chloroform before too long. It is treachery on my part to a faithful horse who has served me faithfully for 21 years and is now 27 years old. But it is a kindness to him, too.

AUG. 7—Today on the *Chateaugay* Robert, Nelson, David and the new horse Belmont went to the Island to occupy the same cottage where they were last year. Some more of the family are to go next week.

AUG. 19—Last evening Nelson went up to Hotel Champlain to a ball or reception. He walked along and, as did the others, introduced himself to President McKinley. The President did not catch his name and asked him again. Then he said, "I am glad to see you, Mr. Kellogg." The President then introduced him to Mrs. McKinley, who said that she had to look up to him. Nelson replied that people often had to do that. She introduced him to Mrs. Alger, wife of the Secretary of War.

AUG. 30—This beautiful autumn morning I received the following telegram:

From Whittier Calif.

Mother died at four this afternoon.

H. F. Griffin

SEPT. 2—No further word has come yet concerning Mother's death. I had been expecting to hear of this event for some time. I can see the look on Mother's face which I saw when Louisa died. She was tossing with pain and moaning and said, "Oh! I shall die, I shall die." Mother said, "I expect you will, my daughter," and this look spread over her face. Again when 'Biel died, this same look came. I seem also to hear her voice singing around the house.

I remember that she told me when she first came up to Essex to make a visit it was in the dead of winter. Then she had been living in Cohoes after her marriage in Sandy Hill. This cold winter morning after her first night in Essex she looked out the window over a desolation of snow. The thought suddenly came to her, what if she should have to come here to live. It was like a knife cutting into her heart. She put it away from her as an impossible thing. But after all it came to appear best for her to do so, and she did. And her many years in Essex, from about 1837 to 1882, had their influence on the people there. With father's help they kept out of debt, educated their children, made a journey nearly every year and were the best people in Essex. Religion, honesty, good life, good sense must always win, and they did in this case.

SEPT. 10—We examined an applicant for pension on Wednesday from Colchester, Vermont who used to know Dr. Lyon's father, who was a Methodist preacher in Vermont many years ago. He said that when a boy he heard that Mr. Lyon said, "Preaching in Colchester Borough was like shooting chipmunks on a stone wall. The ammunition was worth more than the game."

SEPT. 11—Last night at 10.30 I started for Salmon River. It was another clear night. I was sure there was occasion for haste, so I did not wait to harness a horse but rode with the man who came for me. The event justified my expectations. If I had waited to harness, Harry Tyler's first boy would have gotten there before I. His daughter was born one year ago last Monday.

SEPT. 12—Another ride last night led me by moonlight up Rugar Street about 3 miles from home. I seem bound to spend my midnights away from home.

OCT. 11—Francis Kyle came up from Troy this morning for a week's vacation. He is thin and has a cough that cuts me to the heart. I hope it is temporary, but it brings back his father's cough very vividly.

OCT. 13—On Monday evening the physicians of the village gave a farewell dinner to Dr. Philip F. Harvey, Major and Surgeon, U.S. Army, who leaves here soon for Fort Snelling. I got home about 11.30 and went to bed. About 12, before I had gone to sleep, a man came and begged me to go to Salmon River to see a sick baby. As I expected to go to Vermont at seven in the morning I did not want to go, but he urged so hard and said he would carry me both ways I finally relented and went. A more unpleasant ride I do not remember. The moon was giving enough light, but the south wind was blowing hard and the dust was terrible. It filled my eyes, ears, and nose and hair and was altogether too familiar. I got back home at 2.30 a.m. and to bed. I was too tired to sleep and at 3 a man came for me to help a new boy into the world, which was accomplished, and I got home again about 6.

The steamer Chateaugay *on Lake Champlain. It is mentioned frequently in the Journal, for all the Kelloggs used it in their lake travels.*

The wind was blowing hard but Francis K. and I started for Burlington at 7 on the *Chateaugay*. Before we had reached Valcour Island it began to rain. After reaching Burlington Francis and I went up to the college to see Robert. We took a trolley car for Essex Junction. It was still raining but we took a horse and top buggy and drove out to see Philo Pierson, who is yet living at Frank Adams', where he has been for some years. Poor man. He had become so blind he could not see us but recognized us by our voices. It was sad to see him with that uncertain expression of a blind person trying to look at us and still looking beyond or to one side of us. He seemed quite cheerful and contented and otherwise well.

At the Center we stopped a moment and Francis went into the graveyard to see the place where his mother lies buried. We took the trolley again and before three were in Rob's room. After a short stay we took the trolley again and reached the *Chateaugay*, nearly ready for her return trip to Plattsburgh. In spite of the rain and weariness we had had a very enjoyable day.

OCT. 31—The day before yesterday Bess and I went to Fort Edward and Sandy Hill and returned last evening. We had a delightful time visiting those places which Mother roamed over as a child. Many things she used to tell us we saw or heard about.

NOV. 6—Saturday evening. I am alone in my office. I hear people's voices, wagons passing, boys whistling, footsteps on the stairs and upstairs. I am so tired I feel like going to bed. Since September 1, I have been up 18 nights.

NOV. 22—Rob came home from college tonight hearty and well, weighing 161 pounds. He is bearing his sophomore year quite well. He wears his hair long because the others do, I suppose.

NOV. 30—Last evening I went to Chazy to a dinner at Dr. Brook's house. It was the day of Dr. Brook's birth, multiplied seventy eight times. I went on the 6.15 train, which was more than half an hour late, and returned on the 9.30 train. They did me the honor to wait dinner for me from 6 to 7.30 p.m. Twenty one gentlemen sat at the table. I was greatly impressed by the fine appearances of these men, the backbone of our country.

DEC. 8—Henry Fagnant has been doing a little cementing in the cellar. He is a peculiar man. He was complaining about the anxieties and cares in bringing up a family. He said he agreed with the apostle Paul who said, "To marry is well but not to marry is better, a devilish sight better." He wanted some sand for his cement as he had not saved enough in the cellar. I told him he could get some in the garden as he wanted only a couple of bushels or so. He demurred somewhat. He said, "I don't know whether I can or not. You ought to get a *laboring man* to do that."

DEC. 24—At ten minutes to two this morning the doorbell rang and a boy about 14 years old was there for me to go up on the Turnpike towards

Treadwell's Mills. His mother was sick but he did not know what was the matter with her. The wind was cold from the west, thermometer 10 above. I harnessed and drove out.

The house was heated by a defective cooking stove in the kitchen. I had hard work to keep warm, even close by the stove, much less in the room where the seventh child was approaching. The wind blew the curtains. There were no double windows and the house itself, a thin-shelled frame house, not warm enough for a barn. But all were happy inside. The man worked at the pulp mill at Treadwell's Mills and had a fine job. He works every day, Sundays and all, but once in two weeks, while shifting from the day to the night tour, he got in an extra day by working 18 hours. So one week he got $7.70 and the next week he got $8.80, all in cash, and nothing must interfere with his work so as to endanger his job.

But he had other blessings. When he worked the 18 hours his oldest boy could help him so he could rest a little. His (now) seven children had never been sick a day in their lives. Just the evening before he and his wife had ridden into the village, getting some things for the children for Christmas tomorrow which, as nearly as I could make out, was some candy. A more contented man, and family too, I do not remember to have seen.

DEC. 25—Theo gave me the four volumes of McMaster's *History of the United States*. Mrs. Kellogg gave me *Captains Courageous* and each of the children gave me something. Francis Kyle gave me a fine wrapper to wear when I get out of bed in the night.

DEC. 31—9.30 p.m. Tonight a light snow is falling with a heavy north wind. The Frenchmen are going from one saloon to another, drinking, drinking, drinking. The electric cars are bravely pushing along, the lightning flashing under the wheels like a summer thunderstorm. Good-by, 1897.

Notes for 1897

1. A series of earthquakes occurred during the spring, centering in a well-known fault line in the St. Lawrence Valley. At the time sunspots were given as one explanation.

2. Dr. Kellogg remained the chief promoter and president of the Institute this year. At a meeting in January it was decided to invite ladies to future meetings.

3. Richard Mather (1596-1669), colonial American preacher, was the first of the famous Mather line in Massachusetts, father of Increase and grandfather of Cotton Mather.

1898

A snow-burdened February rivals the wild winter of '88, though in this month the Doctor enjoys a triumphal return to Montreal with choice implements and weapons and a well-received lecture on the archaeology of the Champlain Valley.

In the spring and summer, the short war with Spain affects this military town deeply. Its citizens long ago adopted the 21st Infantry as their own, and the regiment's departure and return are occasions for great popular demonstrations. Doctor Kellogg accepts temporary medical duties at the Barracks, which, when the war ends, include sick call for as many as one hundred and fifty-five convalescents a day.

During the very busy year, the Doctor's second son graduates from high school, his second niece is married, and he delivers his thirteen-hundredth baby, though on one extraordinary day four of them arrive at various homes before he gets there.

FEB. 1—A tremendous storm, threatening to rival the blizzard of 1888. The wind blew hard all night and a heavy snow was falling all the time. The tracks filled in at once as soon as opened. The trolley cars gave up the contest at 11 a.m. The last night's sleeper from New York, due here at 4.40 a.m., reached Plattsburgh at 5 p.m. No train has come through from Montreal today, though it is expected the usual one at 9.30 this evening will get here.

FEB. 3—The heavy storm abated, leaving the snow piled up and deep all around. Last night just as I was going to bed, about 9.30, the doorbell rang. I had my coat, vest, collar and boots off and was pulling off my stockings. I had to go over to Wallace Hill, a distance of nearly four miles. The mercury was at 10 below but the moon was bright and the roads tracked out. I was dressed warmly and when I got back at 5 this morning the thermometer was still 10° below. But it was an enjoyable ride and I got ten dollars for it.

—Went to Salmon River yesterday afternoon and up on the **1898**
West Beekmantown road in the evening, each a ten-mile ride. On the upper
Beekmantown Road many of the drifts, shovelled through, were as high as,
or higher than, the horse's back.

FEB. 26—On Thursday at 6.15 I left for Montreal and reached that city
at 8.50 p.m. Mr. William D. Lighthall met me at the depot and took me to
his beautiful home. The next morning he took me to the Chateau de
Ramezay, where I was to lecture in the evening. I took in with me over a
hundred stone implements and weapons, a box heavy and full. The chateau
is a wonder. Built in 1705, it was then the fine house of Montreal. The
Society (the Montreal Numismatic and Antiquarian Society) now has
possession of this building and, in the two years since obtaining it, has
made a remarkably fine and valuable collection of paintings. There are
pictures of old Montreal and Quebec and other Canadian localities of the
olden times, also manuscripts, old books, relics of the old wars, Indian
relics, coins and many other things. Here after lunch I arranged the relics
I brought so they could be seen at the evening lecture.

I then went back to the house and had a good sleep. After supper we
went down to the Chateau, where an audience of about 140 persons listened to my lecture entitled "Notes on the Archaeology of the Champlain
Valley, Including the Richelieu." The people were generally attentive and
were especially interested in seeing the specimens after the lecture. I think
this is one of the most delightful trips I ever took.

The snow in Montreal was unusually deep. Standing on one sidewalk I
took my cane in my left hand and with this could not reach the top of the
pile between me and the road. In another place I took particular notice and
could occasionally see the top of a woman's hat, the woman walking on the
sidewalk and I sitting in the trolley car. On coming out in the steam car,
near St. Henry the snow was as high as the top of the car in which I
was sitting.[1]

MAR. 12—A clipping from the *Record* of Troy of March 9 tells how
Francis K. Kyle and another man saved two boys from drowning at the
great risk of their own lives. It was a brave act. The boys had broken
through the ice.

MAR. 17—I have a little girl very ill with meningitis. She is French,
aged about 6, and is going to die. The family is very placid about it, so
much so as to be quite noticeable. I could not account for this until today,
when I found the child's life is insured and the parents will get about one
hundred dollars after she dies.

MAR. 29—Rob and I went up into Wilmington yesterday. I had to examine an applicant for increase of pension. I did not know where the man lived but I saw two men working in front of a house. One of them had a heavy timber on his shoulder which I saw him hold for a time and then throw down.

I asked a man on the opposite side of the road where Jacob Slater lived and he said "There," pointing to the two men. The one with the timber on his shoulder was Slater himself. I drove across and the very instant he found who I was he began to groan, and he swung himself around and got hold of a crutch that was against the side of the house. This crutch's shaft stuck through the crescent so far as to make it quite impossible to use. But that the sight of me should give a man so much pain of a sudden was a new experience to me. However, the man has rheumatism badly, also heart disease, and has lost the sight of his left eye from cataract.

APR. 1—I had a peculiar experience yesterday and last night. A man came for me about 7.30 in the morning and wanted me to go to his house in a hurry. I had not finished dressing but I hurried and was there in about 25 minutes, but a boy was born before I got there.

About half past ten p.m. another man came and wanted me to go to his house in a hurry. I dressed quickly and was at his house in about 20 minutes, but a boy was born before I got there.

About 1 this a.m. a man came to the house and thought he might want me to go to his house soon. I advised him to go back and if he needed me I would go quickly. He returned soon and I was at his house before two o'clock. But before I reached his house *two* boys were born.

APR. 16—The regiment, 21st U.S. Infantry, stationed at the Barracks, has received orders this afternoon to start for Tampa, Florida next Tuesday for the Cuban War, which we all hope may yet be averted.

Soldiers of the Spanish-American War at the Plattsburgh Barracks. These were the men whom Dr. Kellogg treated after their return from Cuba.

APR. 19—Well, the regiment went away today. There were great crowds present, but I could not bring myself to go. Two little children sat on their father's knapsack crying, and when he tried to go they hung on to his legs and begged him not to go. Leighton and Dan Cornman followed their father closely around, and their poor mother, who recently has had a severe surgical operation, had her bed placed near the window to see her husband as long as she could.[2]

APR. 30—For some months some men living in and around Morrisonville have been possessed with the idea that petroleum could be found around Cadyville by boring deep enough. As nearly as I can learn their chief evidence is from the *use of the wand,* a green stick that bends when it comes over the petroleum. Mr. Weaver has been to Pennsylvania and has proved the correctness of this experiment. They have already erected a derrick and will soon have an engine ready to bore deep enough and then they will find the oil. And this in Anno Domini 1898, when the people are supposed to have emerged from the dark ages.

MAY 16—Dr. C. B. Byrne returned to the Barracks today from Concord, New Hampshire, where he has been to examine recruits. He examined 1,121 recruits. During these days I have been acting assistant surgeon, U.S. Army, according to contract made between me and Col. C. B. Byrne, asst. surgeon, U.S. Army. My compensation has been at the rate of $125 per month.

MAY 25—In response to a requisition made the other day to the Paymaster General, U.S. Army, I received duplicate blanks on which I had to make affidavit. A portion of the blanks was "And made oath on the Holy Evangelists of Almighty God that the annexed account is accurate and just."

JUNE 23—Today Nelson was graduated from the Plattsburgh High School. The pupils all did well, and Nelson did as well as the best of them.

Today I again begin attending at the Barracks. Under my new contract I am now contract surgeon, i.e. act. asst. surgeon, U.S. Army, at the rate of one hundred dollars per month. As Narcisse in *Dr. Sevier* said, "So long my salwy continue I don care if dis war las ten yea."

JULY 1—Robert and Nelson came home from Burlington yesterday. Robert has finished his sophomore year and Nelson is, I suppose, a full-fledged freshman.

A battle is taking place near Santiago de Cuba and all here are anxious. The wives and families of the officers at the Barracks are in great anxiety.

JULY 2—The *Montreal Gazette* of this morning says that the 21st had four men killed and 15 wounded yesterday. I presume from this have come the wild reports that Capt. Bonesteel and Capt. Ebstein are wounded. Up to this time no names of the injured have come over the wires. The bulletins in front of the Postal Union Telegraph Company's office have crowds before them. It is an anxious time.

JULY 4—Great rejoicing over Sampson's victory over and destruction of Cervera's (Spanish) fleet. Also great rejoicing over the news that the 21st is not badly cut up.[3]

JULY 19—Yesterday I helped introduce into this world Baby No. 1300. The mother came near death by hemorrhage, but not quite. She is all right today.

AUG. 18—Last evening were married at 7 p.m. in the Peristrome Presbyterian Church Theodora Kyle and Frederic Hathaway Chase. The church was beautifully trimmed with flowers, plants and vines. The Rev. William A. Batt of Concord Junction, Massachusetts performed the ceremony, assisted by the Rev. F. B. Hall of Plattsburgh. After the wedding an informal reception was held at the house until 9 o'clock, then Theo and Fred left for the 9.30 train. At the church little Theodora Platt ran around and talked and shouted all through the ceremony. Her father tossed her flowers and tried to keep her quiet in many ways, and partly succeeded. Theo was the only bride I ever saw who really looked pretty. She seems to be a general favorite, as she has always been.

AUG. 20—Today Helen, Russell and the two children left for Shoreham, and will start for Chicago next Tuesday. The little Theodora is a reproduction of her mother at her age. She is the same little flyaway that Dot was in Vergennes in 1867. The boy Henry Russell Jr. is a very nice child, too. Theo is now at the Greylock, Williamstown, Massachusetts.

SEPT. 11—The streets are dotted with bluecoats, most of them convalescent from Montauk Point.[4] They have been coming for three weeks. Among them is a large contingent of Negroes from one of the colored regiments of United States Infantry who fought so well at Santiago. The 21st is expected back this week.

SEPT. 13—This evening between six and seven hundred members of the 21st came up from Lithia Springs, Georgia. These were the recruits to the twenty first.

SEPT. 14—The town is dotted thickly with soldiers. The real 21st is expected tomorrow from Montauk Point. I understand they are to come via New London and Burlington.

Robert Kellogg, 19, was a Junior and Nelson, 17, was a Freshman, when they left for the University of Vermont on September 26.

Under April 30 of this year I wrote about some men boring for petroleum at Morrisonville. They did not use the actual green stick for the wand, but an "instrument" designed for that purpose. They stopped boring about a month ago after getting down 500 feet in fruitless endeavor to strike oil. They claimed their money gave out.[5]

SEPT. 15—The 21st came home from Cuba today via Montauk Point. Two sections of the train were used. The first one had the invalids and the second the well ones. I doubt if Plattsburgh ever had a greater celebration. Thousands and thousands of men, women and children were out, and hearty greetings met their sadly decimated ranks.

SEPT. 26—Robert and Nelson started for college this morning together on the steamer *Vermont*. They seemed to feel happy.

At sick call at the Barracks 121 men presented themselves. Many of these were in the Cuban War and have had yellow, typhoid or malarial fever. Poor fellows. They are brown, yellow and white combined.

SEPT. 27—One hundred and forty eight men on sick call this morning. I prescribed for them in 160 minutes.

I received from Mrs. Mabel Loomis Todd this morning a manuscript poem of Emily Dickinson. It was written with a lead pencil. Not a single letter was joined to another. I prize this very highly.

The Hotel Champlain, started near Plattsburgh in 1888 and burned in 1910. It served as the summer White House during the vacations of President McKinley in 1897 and 1899.

OCT. 12—There were 155 men on sick report at the Barracks this morning, for whom I prescribed in 105 minutes.

OCT. 24—A portion of the 21st, about 350 in all, left today for Philadelphia to attend a peace celebration. It was the intention to take 350 of those who had been to Cuba. It was found last Thursday that only 189 were able to go. However, the men wanted to go, and Saturday from my sick report I returned to duty 32, and yesterday I returned 31 more, making 63 in two days. So the Elixir Philadelphiae is very powerful as a restorative.

NOV. 11—I finished at the Barracks today, my contract having been annulled to take effect yesterday. The men are getting better but there are yet as many as 130 on sick call, besides about 80 in the hospital. I have been acting assistant surgeon, United States Army since June 23, 1898, but was off duty from August 15 until September 25. The work has been very pleasant indeed.

NOV. 21—I have been having the stable made warmer and the yard raked. Old Myette's son has been doing the raking. I said to him today, "How much did you make election day?" He replied, "Well, doctor, I

166

didn't make as much as I expected to, but I thank the Lord for what I did get. I made about nine dollars." This was the actual amount he received, for Dr. LaRocque had told me that he paid old Myette and his son nine dollars, the highest price.

NOV. 26—I went to Dannemora on the train, returning at 6. I made thirty dollars, having examined three insane convicts.

DEC. 6—Last evening was the first meeting of the sixth season of the Plattsburgh Institute. Capt. F. H. Ebstein of the 21st U.S. Infantry gave the address, and a fine one it was. Many stood up and I learn that many came who could not get in and had to go away. His subject was "The Campaign in Cuba."

DEC. 17—Went to Mooers last night and read my lecture on "Local Archaeology." They have formed an organization there similar to our Plattsburgh Institute. I had the honor of giving the opening lecture.

DEC. 25—Christmas. Robert, Nelson, Elspeth, Francis F. and David all home. A beautiful Christmas tree was set up in the back sitting room and at 6 a.m. the children got up and soon came downstairs, nearly dressed.

Tonight after Francis F. had gone to bed, his mother had him say his prayers as usual. He insisted on her lining it off for him and he repeated after her. After he had finished all of the "Now I lay me" and had gone through with "God bless Papa and Mamma and Robert and Nelson," he took it under his own control and continued with increasing earnestness and loudness, "Bless Bessie and David and make Francis a good boy for Christ's sake, Amen, rubberneck."

DEC. 31—The year goes out tonight, an exceptionally good year for me.

Notes for 1898

1. Up until February 23 Montreal had had 12 feet 8 inches of snow and the snow season was far from ended.

2. The 21st departed gaily to the tune of "The Girl I Left Behind Me." On April 25th war was declared to have existed since April 21.

3. When Cervera brought his fleet out of Santiago harbor it was completely destroyed by the blockading American squadron. In the land campaign against Santiago the 21st lost seven enlisted men killed and one officer and 32 enlisted men injured. Total casualties of the war included 329 killed in battle, 125 dead of wounds, and 5,277 from disease.

4. Troops who served in Cuba were put into quarantine at Montauk Point, Long Island, to prevent the spread of contagious diseases.

5. This was a temporary halt for the replacement of broken parts. Drilling continued until the summer of 1899. The traces of oil found in the well were thought locally to have been put there by the drillers to encourage the owners.

1899

A widespread epidemic of grippe is followed by the departure of the popular 21st Infantry for another battlefront, this time in the Philippines. The Doctor, depressed to contemplate the probable toll that disease will take there, hasn't the heart to join the town in waving the boys goodbye.

Doctor Kellogg satisfyingly exchanges deep bows for the first time, though through a haze of dust, with President McKinley, in Plattsburgh once more for his vacation. The Doctor feels suddenly older to discover that a baby he has just delivered is the child of a mother whom he also brought into the world. A more difficult case later on keeps him away from home for twenty-three hours.

JAN. 5—Bessie went to see Theo yesterday at her new home in West Roxbury, Massachusetts.

The grip is prevailing very extensively all around. I presume there are 1,000 people ill with that disease in this village. Only a few are serious.

JAN. 7—In the *Plattsburgh Press* this morning was a notice of the death of Mrs. Colombe on Miller Street, who died with grip pneumonia. The *Press* got somewhat mixed, saying that "she was born in Chazy with the grip," etc.

JAN. 15—The grip is prevailing here nearly as hard as in January 1890. One house yesterday had each of its members flat on their backs in bed, all grown people. Still, it has not proved very fatal so far; only those are fatal which have complications.

JAN. 26—Tonight I received a letter written in good legible hand; the following is a copy:

Newman Essex Co. N.Y.
Jan. 24th 1899

Mr Dr Kellogg

Dear Sir I have been trubbled with rumatis for the last 4 weeks it has settled in the mussil of my left arm and i can hardly use

my arm if you no of something that will help me will you please
sent it to me by mail and I will call and pay you whin a go to
plattsburg in march yours truly

Thomas Barnes

my hand by times get quite cold and feels nom.

FEB. 21—One week ago last night, during a most violent blizzard, with
the thermometer just above zero, with the snow falling and blowing hard
from the north, the drygoods store of R. O. Barber and Sons took fire in
the basement. The smoke at once so filled that building it could hardly
be entered. It was a horrible event. Within an hour the things were all
removed from my office up over the Vilas Bank, mostly by the Maccabees.[1]
The family living on the third floor over the drygoods store moved their
things out early, and soon the fire and water ruined their apartments.
Twice I went up there afterwards and through their rooms and the fire was
all out. Soon it caught again up there and from my office door, the door
at the head of the stairs was one blazing, fiery furnace. That building is
nearly all destroyed except the walls. It is too horrible to write about.

MAR. 5—Dr. Barton of Willsboro telegraphed me to go to his place on
the sleeper last night. I went and returned this morning.

APR. 3—I hear that sap is running pretty well. Today while driving out
I saw 6 small boys and one small girl under a soft maple tree. They had
tapped this tree certainly 5 times, and I am not certain but six times. They
had empty tomato cans for buckets and pieces of tin bent up V-shaped and
driven in for spouts. The tree was collared with tin cans and tin spouts
and surrounded by anxious children.

APR. 10—This evening the streets are as quiet as a funeral. The Twenty
First United States Infantry left the Barracks here for Manila. They were
nearly 1,400 strong, a fine body of men, but I could not bring myself to
go out to see them start. I do not suppose they will have much fighting,
but disease will prevent a great many of them from ever returning.[2]

APR. 21—About 1.10 this morning was telephoned to go to Peru to see
a patient with Dr. Kinsley. The one who was sick was a little fellow between 4 and 5 years of age. He has been ill about one week and was dying
when I reached the house. His mind was clear and his voice strong, but he
died sometime before noon. While I was at the house a little sister was born
to him. He had one brother older and one other sister about two years of
age. The little boy that died said many times, "Papa, tum lie down by me."

MAY 2—Nelson and Howard and Louis Martin of his class came over
last Saturday night and went back this morning. Nelson is tall, Louis is a

little shorter, and Howard is of ordinary height. They go through the street by threes, with Nelson in the middle. They are called Taffy, The Laird and Little Billee.[3]

MAY 11—The new foliage, new grass and new songs of birds and frogs prevail. I think I never realized before that frogs sing. I heard them a few nights ago and discovered that what we call peeping, or croaking, is really a musical conversation in responses between them.

MAY 30—The Saranac Chapter, Daughters of the American Revolution, placed bronze markers on the graves of the 15 soldiers of the Revolution buried in Riverside Cemetery. Some of the citizens placed aluminum markers, planned and patterned by H. K. Averill Jr. and made at the foundry in Plattsburgh, on the graves of soldiers of the War of 1812. The one I contributed was placed on the grave of Sheldon Durkee.

JUNE 3—On Thursday I went to Elizabethtown to the Centennial celebration of the formation of Essex County. On Friday Bessie and Helen came, and we all returned on the 6.15 train. I was entertained at the house of Judge Richard L. Hand, and when Bessie and Helen came they were invited there to dinner. Mr. Henry Harmon Noble was a guest there, too. Our entertainment was most delightful.

The exercises, held in the Court House, were excellent. Town histories were read, speeches were made, and the whole thing was a grand success. I got several new place names with their origin.

JUNE 12—Went on an excursion to Burlington yesterday on steamer *Reindeer*, leaving here about 12 and reaching home at 11 p.m. I had telegraphed Robert or Nelson. Robert got the telegram but could not find Nelson.

We took a horse and buggy and drove out to see Philo Pierson. The cancer on his left forearm is a little larger but does not trouble him a great deal. He has had it for over 15 years, and perhaps more than 20. He got up and sat on the edge of the bed. He could not recognize my voice at first, but when he did he cried because he was so glad to see me. I do not think he can walk any to speak of. His cataracts make him wholly blind.

JUNE 13—The following is a copy of a telegram we received while at dinner today:

Girl twelve fifteen this morning everything all right.

F. H. Chase

Today while coming in from South Plattsburgh, when I was on the crest of the hill just south of the Iron Bridge, I saw a boy holding a horse by

Plattsburgh on a Fourth of July. The new courthouse is in the background. Many hundreds of gallons of Coon's Ice Cream en route—undoubtedly strawberry!

the bits. The horse was attached to a lumber wagon that had one seat and one board seat. From this wagon five women had gotten out to walk into town. They did not want to be seen riding in that conveyance.

JULY 5—Yesterday was the Fourth and the small boys had a great time. Francis Fellows and David were up early, and the voice of the firecracker was heard in the land, in our yard, soon after 6. At night I asked David how much money he had spent for firecrackers that day. He said one dollar and forty one cents, and he thought he received his money's worth.

JULY 14—The other day I saw a cluster of children, 15 by actual count, on the street below the Episcopal Church. They had a little child's express wagon in which was quite a high box filling nearly the whole of the wagon. On the top of this box sat one of the larger girls, perhaps 8 years of age. A small dog was fastened by a string from its neck chain to the tongue of this wagon. All of the children were interested in making this dog run and draw the wagon. By a grand and combined effort, they got the wagon under good headway down the street, all rushing in delightful confusion. After 10 or 15 feet of glorious success, the wagon reached a muddy place through which the dog could not pull it, and came to a sudden stop which caused the queen on the box to fall precipitously from her high position, face and arms outspread, into the very deepest part of the mud. Nothing daunted, she scrambled up again, brushed the mud off her clothes, and when I left she was trying to mount her triumphal car again, utterly oblivious to the presence of interested spectators.

AUG. 7—Yesterday I was on a trolley car, the only passenger. President William McKinley drove past in an open carriage. I took off my hat and bowed. He took off his hat and made a very low bow in return, even lower than mine. He was on the seat of the carriage and another man was with him. He wore a black silk stovepipe hat. The driver was on the seat in front, driving a span of fine grays very rapidly. It was quite dusty. This is my first interview with the President of the United States.[4]

AUG. 25—In the evening, when quite dark, I was on Lyon Street beyond Gilliland's. Belmont shied a little and a skunk waddled quite rapidly from the wagon road over into the ditch. He did not defend himself, neither did I, and both were to be congratulated.

AUG. 30—Mrs. Kellogg and Bessie Gallaher have gone to North Elba today to the reinterment of the bodies of the John Brown raiders.[5]

SEPT. 4—Drove to Peru this afternoon to see Dr. Cole's daughter, Mrs. Lapham. On my way back I stopped at the gravel pit where the Turnpike meets the road near the Little Ausable, and examined the gravel and

sand. It is more or less stratified and contains large quantities of marine
shells. It is an old sea beach.

SEPT. 21—The other day Francis Fellows told his mother if he had a
big farm he would dig nice flower beds for her. She thought that would
be nice. Then he said if she should die he would dig her a grave. She
thought it very kind in him. "Oh no," he said, "it wouldn't be much
trouble."

About 2 this morning I was called out to see a patient. When I reached
the house the woman told me when she had been asleep an hour or two
before, that she dreamed that the moon came out from behind a cloud
full and beautiful, and then suddenly it changed to a beautiful baby in a
handsome cradle. In less than three minutes after my arrival her dream
became true so far as the baby was concerned.

OCT. 11—I appeared before the Daughters of the American Revolution
and read from Pausche's, Hadden's and Digby's journals on events re-
lating to the battle of Valcour Island, which occurred 123 years ago.

NOV. 18—Today I helped into the world Wilfred Bourdon, son of William Moses Bourdon of the Maine Mill Road. The mother, Helen Picott, I
helped into the world 18 years ago this year. This is the first grandchild
that I know myself to have assisted into this mundane existence. This
girl married her sister's husband's son, and the relationships growing
therefrom are too many to enumerate.

A curious economical or political incident might be mentioned in connection with this event. The husband voted for the first time, this last
week's election. He said with the money for his first vote he was going to
pay the doctor for his first baby, and he did, as far as it went. (His state-
ment was that he was going to buy his first baby with the money he got
for his first vote.)

NOV. 21—Yesterday morning at 2.15 a.m. I was telephoned to go two
miles beyond West Plattsburgh. I dressed, harnessed and got up there at
4.15 a.m. I reached home at one this a.m., having been gone 23 hours,
nearly.

DEC. 6—At 12.15 a.m. the doorbell rang and I was called out. I got
back a little before 3, made some entries, read a little, and as the clock was
striking three I put out the lamp. Before the lamp chimney had become
cold the bell rang again and I had to go about a mile beyond Beekmantown Corners, and did not get back until ten.

This was pension day, and Dr. H. H. Reynolds of Ellenburgh Depot, the
new member of the Plattsburgh Board of Examining Surgeons for Pen-

The younger Kellogg children, pictured about 1889: Elizabeth, Francis Fellows and David.

sions, was present for the first time. He is a nice man, but he spells kidneys "kidnes," and disability, "dessability." But he may improve.

DEC. 9—A letter from Nelson today states that he is to be baptized tomorrow in the Episcopal Church, a terrible come-down from his ancestral Congregationalism.

DEC. 19—One day last week Francis, David and I were driving together down by the Creek. It became necessary for David to rather suddenly get out of the wagon. The whole proceeding pleased Francis very much and he laughed to himself quite hard. In a few seconds it seemed to dawn upon him that it was improper to laugh, under the circumstances. So he turned to me and said, "I'm not laughing at *Div*id, I am laughing at—," then looking around in the west and seeing Rand Hill, and Lyon Mountain and

174

Dannemora Mountain, he made a wide circling gesture with his hand stretched out and continued, *"I'm laughing at the mountains."*

DEC. 30—I have a slate at the house near the telephone, on which calls are written. If any call has come for me while out, a white cloth is hung in one of the front windows to notify me before driving into the barn. To-day Francis Fellows came to his mother, chuckling and saying he wondered what Papa would say when he saw the cloth in the window. He had made some scratches on the slate and had hung a cloth in the window, the little rogue!

DEC. 31—So ends the year but the mathematicians have convinced us that the century does not begin for another whole year. I think if I could reach the crank that turns the wheel of time I would hurry the rotations and have the century completed under its own name, and not rely on the two figures of the next century.

Notes for 1899

1. A fraternal beneficiary association with local lodges. It took its name from a chivalrous and religious people of Biblical times who, under their great leader Judas Maccabeus, helped the widows, orphans and disabled of their war of liberation.

2. Arriving in Manila on May 1, they were immediately engaged in a long, hard war of conquest. The Filipinos on February 4, when they realized that they were about to be annexed to the United States, revolted under their great leader Aguinaldo.

3. The names of three characters in George du Maurier's popular *Trilby*, published in 1894.

4. The McKinleys and Vice President and Mrs. Hobart spent a month at the Hotel Champlain. Governor Roosevelt, Secretary of War Root and other cabinet officers visited him there.

5. Seven of the Harper's Ferry raiders, including one of John Brown's sons, were moved from their 1859 burial places in Virginia. Two others, buried at Perth Amboy, were also moved, but not in time for this ceremony.

1900

After seventeen years, Doctor Kellogg's work with the Pension Board comes to an end, but he is far too busy with regular and unexpected calls to mourn its loss. At fifty-two years of age, he discovers Lyon Mountain and enthusiastically climbs it twice during the summer. "I have not so well enjoyed myself in years," he writes of the experience.

This year, the Doctor tracks down more of his ancestors and sadly records the passing of Philo Pierson, his loyal old family friend in Vermont. Elizabeth finishes high school, and Robert, now graduated from college, starts to study law in Chicago. Life's satisfactions, which seem to increase with the years, move the Doctor to conclude that he has never really wanted "to live the same year over again."

JAN. 12—Night before last came three companies of the 15th U.S. Infantry to the Barracks from Puerto Principe, Cuba. The company of the 7th Infantry that has been here during the fall left yesterday for Fort Wayne, Michigan.

JAN. 15—Today I received notice from the Commissioner of Pensions that my services as United States Examiner for Pensions would terminate January 18, 1900. I have held this place with about 3 months' intermission since May 1883.

JAN. 26—I got onto a trolley car a little after nine this morning on Cornelia Street to go over the river. The car was going up, and it was nearly an hour before it got to the depot near the Fouquet House. The ice on the rails made it necessary to back and push ahead many times. I think the trolley cars hardly ever had a harder time.

FEB. 22—Last evening while we were seated at the supper table, the hall outside door opened and Robert came in with Levator E. White and Louis Martin, both of the sophomore class. They had come across on the ice from near the mouth of the Winooski River on skates. The broad lake of Burlington is not all frozen over. They walked out on the new railroad bed near to the mouth of the Winooski. They wore sweaters, disreputable tam-o'shanters, knee breeches and long stockings and shoes. They had reached Plattsburgh at 5.15, having been on the ice about 3 hours. They had to return this morning. I drove them down onto the ice as far out as the first crack, outside the breakwater. They got over this and put on their skates

and started back at 9.22. I received this afternoon a telegram signed by
Robert from Burlington saying, "Arrived one fifty five OK not tired."
Robert had to be in Burlington to rehearse in some Gibson play, to be
given tonight.

Yesterday, today and tomorrow are Carnival days here. Many of the
streets have been decorated by placing cakes of ice at the edge of the sidewalks, and into the center of each cake setting an evergreen small tree. Pine,
spruce, cedar, hemlock abound, and the appearance of the walks is beautiful. Flags and red, white and blue bunting abound, and many people are
present. An ice fort or blockhouse has been built on the fair ground, which
is to be "stormed" by "Indians" tonight.

MAR. 4—Drove this afternoon to Salmon River and home on the Lake
Shore Road. The roads were terrible, but Belmont could trot much of the
way to Salmon River. When I reached home I found she had pulled off
a new forward shoe, not even leaving a stub of nail. It required great
strength to lift like that.

MAR. 24—Drove in the night out into North Africa[1] to see a poor sick
woman. It does not seem possible that one could live through what she has
suffered. She may die.

MAR. 28—Robert came home last evening via Rouses Point. Last Saturday morning he and 4 other boys started from Burlington for a trip to the
top of Mount Mansfield. They went on snowshoes, drawing their provisions
on a toboggan. They had 10 pounds of beefsteak, 5 pounds of bacon, 6 papers apiece of sweet chocolate, coffee, chocolate and some other things.
They left the college at 3 o'clock in the morning, going via Essex Junction and Underhill Flats.

About 5 p.m. they reached the foot of the mountains, where they decided to locate their camp. They dug out the snow under a tree in the
woods, cut and placed spruce branches in this dug-out place, made a good
fire, cooked their supper and spent the night there. The next forenoon they
collected better wood and about 1 p.m. continued their trip up to the top
of the mountain, a distance of about 4 miles. They lost their trail and had
to go as best they could up through the woods. They reached the top of
the mountain about 5.

Their descent was rapid, much to the injury of their pantaloons. They
reached their camping place of the night before in due time, made a
fire out of birch logs which lasted all night. The next day they went back to
Underhill Flats. As the snow had become soft, two of them with the toboggan went on the cars and the other three footed it to Burlington in the
slush of the road, carrying their snowshoes much of the way.

APR. 14—A few weeks ago the wife of a man who keeps a little store near the Iron Bridge was very ill. I was called to see her and after prescribing for her I talked with the man in the store for a few minutes. He was really quite successful in his business. I spoke of this and he assented but said, referring to his wife in a nearby room, "I've got a penny-skinner in there." This economy was the greatest compliment he could give his wife. The poor woman, who was his second wife, died in 8 or 9 days, and in less than four weeks the man was married again.

Today a woman was in the office whose sister was recently married after a widowhood of one year and nine months. The sister's first husband had had an insurance on his life of a thousand dollars, but thinking he could not carry it, had let the policy lapse a short time before his last illness began. I remarked to the woman that it was too bad her former brother-in-law had not kept up his insurance. She thought so too and added that if he had done so her sister would not have married again.

APR. 17—Last evening was the last lecture before the Plattsburgh Institute, the seventh season. The course has consisted of nine lectures and all have been excellent. Without disparaging the six previous courses this, I think, altogether has been the best course of all.

MAY 1—About 12.20 this afternoon came a telegram from Dana Pierce asking if Luce Martin and Levator White were here. These two boys had said they were going to make Plattsburgh in a canoe from Burlington yesterday. We were anxious. I drove down to the dock and found the wind so hard from the northwest as to seem to have made it impossible for them to come over this morning, while yesterday the wind had been hard from the south and veering around north in the afternoon. I drove back and Luce and Levy had just reached the house.

It seems the fellows started from Burlington in a south wind about 2 p.m. yesterday in a light canoe, narrow and perhaps 12 feet long. They carried across Colchester Point and with difficulty made Stave Island about 5 o'clock. Then the sea was running so high and they were so wet and tired they concluded to stay over night there. A hospitable Frenchman, a cottage caretaker, kept them in his house, and they continued on their way to Plattsburgh about 9 a.m., reaching Willard's boat livery about noon.

They ate dinner at the house and started back from the place of their landing at seven minutes to three in the afternoon. We tried to have them return on the *Chateaugay* with Nelson, but they positively declined. They borrowed an umbrella and used this for a sail. I saw them start out, and for a mile out their umbrella sail was a dark, moving object on the water.

MAY 2—A telegram came a little after eight this morning from Luce. They got to Burlington about 9 p.m.

MAY 16—About 5 p.m., an old soldier of the Florida War, 1838, a member of the Second U.S. Infantry, was buried in the Riverside Cemetery. He had wanted a salute fired over his grave, and in the quiet of this beautiful afternoon a corporal with a squad of eight men and one bugler marched ahead of the hearse up to the cemetery, and after the Rev. Mr. Hall had finished his part, fired a salute three times. The bugler played slowly taps, and it was all done.

MAY 30—Went over to Essex, Vermont and copied nearly all the inscriptions on the headstones in the cemetery there, of those related to me or connected with, or in whom I had any particular interest. I secured about 60 in all.

JUNE 21—Elspeth is graduated from the High School.

JUNE 27—Robert received the degree of A.B. from the University of Vermont. Elspeth went over on Monday, Bessie and I yesterday afternoon. I came back this afternoon on the *Maquam* and the rest of the family came later during the week. I spent some time in the Probate Court office looking up ancient wills of the Kellogg family.

JULY 11—Yesterday the Medical Society of the County of Clinton had an excursion to Chazy Lake. About 60 people went. As soon as we reached the stopping place, Robert, David, Francis Fellows, Dr. Dare, Dr. McKinney and I started for the top of Lyon Mountain. The trail was most of the distance old wood roads, but a good portion was merely a trail cut through the woods and indicated by blazed trees. Francis F. got tired and Robert carried him. We kept on until at 5.35, or two hours and thirty five minutes, we were on the very top of Lyon Mountain.

We ate our lunch, looked at the long St. Lawrence in the north, the Lake Champlain in the east. We pulled up some tiny spruces as mementoes and at 6 we started down. We had planned to go up for 3 hours, then if we did not reach the summit, we must return. So we spent 25 minutes there and reached the railroad at 7.35, i.e. in one hour and thirty five minutes. I have not so well enjoyed myself in years.

AUG. 2—Theo and her dear baby Martha came this evening for a few week's stay.

AUG. 4—Martha Chase is very winning. She reminds me much of her mother at her age, and of her grandmother all the time I knew her. She is the delight of everyone in the house and especially of Francis Fellows, who has to stop his eating at the table to go and stand by her.

AUG. 9—A telephone message came to the house today announcing the death of Philo Pierson. Poor old man. He had been a sufferer for many years.

179

AUG. 18—This afternoon Nelson and I and many others went up Lyon Mountain, leaving on the 1.10 p.m. train and reaching home on the 9.20. The afternoon did not prove to be so clear as it had at first promised; there was considerable of a view off east and the dense foliage along the trail was of sufficient beauty and interest in itself to repay us for the labor of climbing.

AUG. 30—Robert started for Chicago today at 10.05 in the forenoon. He is going into Russell's office to begin the study of law.[2]

OCT. 6—I went to Troy yesterday with Mrs. Mary L. Olyphant, a widowed daughter-in-law of President Olyphant of the D. and H. C. Co. After getting Mrs. O. safe to her home I went to Albany, got supper, called on Henry Harmon Noble and with him went to the State Library. I worked about two hours on the genealogical records and found some new names of my Atherton ancestors.

OCT. 21—Lizzie is taking a week's vacation. Elspeth made a large cake yesterday which, to say the least, was not a brilliant success. As she brought it onto the table last evening for supper, David said very quaintly, "That is so heavy I don't see how she can carry it."

A German woman last evening, lamenting her daughter's unfortunate experiences, said, "She has had post mortem haemorrhage twice."

OCT. 24—Yesterday a man came for me to go out into the country to see his sick baby, aged 4 months. I was busy then, but told him I would come out when the case I was occupied with should be completed. It might be in the night, and it was. I reached his house about 10.30. The baby had become so much better the whole family had gone to sleep. The house, a comfortable one and quite roomy, was well lighted. I rapped and rapped, eight times in all, at one door or another or on the windows. On looking through the window into the kitchen, I saw a little child on the bare floor, bare below his waist and on his back. After getting the father waked up, I saw him clearing a way by moving the sleeping children onto one side. There were 4 children in this room, thus asleep on the floor, and three in the next room where the baby was sick in its cradle. Not one of the seven had any vestige of bedclothes or pillow or anything other than the hard floor to rest on. Yet they slept as quietly and apparently as comfortably as children in the best bed in the best of houses.

On October 30th Dr. Kellogg took off several days for a visit to Theo in West Roxbury, Massachusetts. He spent much of two days working in the Boston Public Library and the New England Historical Society, still in pursuit of his ancestors. He and Fred Chase did some sight-seeing, in-

180

cluding a trip to Plymouth. As always, he had a wonderful time. He found **1900**
Theo's house just like herself—"as sweet and pleasant as it can be."

NOV. 7—William McKinley was yesterday re-elected President of the United States by an enormous majority and Theodore Roosevelt, Vice-President. This result has seemed so certain during the whole campaign that I had not thought the election of W. J. Bryan among the possibilities.

NOV. 9—Kathleen Ryan goes to the kindergarten with Francis Fellows. He told his mother the other day that Kathleen would really be quite a nice little girl if she were not a Democrat.

NOV. 21—The following are some of the election political jingles which Francis F. has picked up and which so far we have been entirely unable to suppress:

> McKinley rides a white horse,
> Bryan rides a mule,
> And all the dirty democrats
> Had better go to school.

> McKinley rides a white horse,
> Bryan rides a mule,
> McKinley is a gentleman
> And Bryan is a fool.

> Democrats eat dead rats
> And pickled cats.

> Kill the rats and kill the cats
> And kill the dirty democrats.

Later he explains that these desperate deeds are to apply on the democrats in India, not here, as there are some good democrats here.

NOV. 22—Well, we have had a storm!!! About 2 p.m. yesterday, it grew dark and a hard, spattering shower of rain filled the gutters with muddy water. This was accompanied with a heavy wind from the west. After the rain stopped the wind kept on. It blew down a portion of the new brick wall of one of the Lozier buildings.[3] In the evening the wind seemed to increase. I went to bed about 10, and after reading awhile must have fallen asleep for a few minutes, but was roused by the increase of the roaring of the storm. Soon there was a crash of breaking glass upstairs, and at the foot of David's and Francis' bed a scuttle had crushed in the window, a scuttle from one of the Grant houses. We got the boys into another room, but Francis slept through it all.

I took a lantern and went out to look around. The wind was terrific. The elms swayed, bent over almost at right angles, and the awful roaring was increased by contact with the limbs free from leaves. Soon the street lights went out and then the light from the burning buildings in Winooski reddened the southeastern sky. We all went to bed again after a time, and I read the description of the storm at Yarmouth in *David Cooperfield*. I went to sleep again sometime after two, but awoke before 5. The wind had much abated and at 6 I went out with the lantern to look over things. All through town there were fallen trees and broken limbs. There was ruin everywhere, but still not very great. Reports from various portions of the country revealed the same condition of destruction.

DEC. 4—Last evening was the first lecture of the eighth season of the Plattsburgh Institute. Mr. E. F. Botsford gave a fine stereopticon lecture on "The Klondike."

DEC. 6—At length after many years I have found where my great-grandmother, Eleanor Williams, was born, and when and who her father and mother were, and also who her brothers and sisters were, and where they were born, all in Lebanon, Connecticut.

DEC. 21—Last March when I drove to North Africa, I lost my Sigma Phi badge which I had worn since 1866, and have never found it. When I went to Boston last October, I borrowed Nelson's badge to wear and at some time in Boston it became unclasped, and I lost that. Fred advertised in 2 papers and we retraced our steps as much as possible, but could get no trace of it. This morning a note from Nelson announced that it had come back to him through the Williams College Sigs, to whom it had been sent by someone who had found it.

DEC. 25—It seemed queer not to have Nelson or Robert at home today. Nelson is to dine at Chief Justice Brewer's in Washington, and Robert will be at Helen's in Chicago.

We had a nice time. A little tannenbaum was put up in the back sitting room by David and Elspeth, which was trimmed and lighted by candles. There were so many presents I cannot remember them.

DEC. 31—Ends the year and the century. I don't know that ever, at the end of a year, I wanted to live the same year over again.

Notes for 1900

1. A hamlet in the western part of Beekmantown, originally a Negro settlement.

2. A cordial invitation had come for Robert in the spring, if he was not determined to go to law school. He would stay with the Platts, but Russell was sure that he was getting more than he gave in having so dependable a person as Robert.

3. The Lozier Motor Company was persuaded to settle in Plattsburgh in 1900 when its citizens subscribed $100,000 in stock. The Company developed the luxury Lozier automobile and for about 14 years, until it moved to Detroit, it was a leading concern in Plattsburgh.

APR. 10—I had an illustration today of the troubles that superfluities bring. My old reliable pantaloons had faded so and had become so delapidated, I got a new pair. This latter I put on this evening and wore downtown. I found I had left my knives, keys, money and tape line in my other pockets and there I was, desolate and despoiled in my new glory. I am determined to have a bonfire to eliminate one of the pairs.

APR. 23—Just before supper I saw two boys on the street on bicycles, one perhaps 8 or 10 years old and the other 4 or 5 years older. The latter, whom I did not know, said, "A girl can't keep a secret, by Jesus, even if you have her mouth tied up with a string."

APR. 27—According to accounts Francis Fellows is engaged. He asked Ethel Southwick if she would marry him when they are grown up. She said she would if he would not smoke or drink or swear. He agreed not to do any of these things.

MAY 11—Went to Burlington and purchased for seventy five dollars a Concord buggy. I got it from William Smith on St. Paul Street. He made it.

MAY 15—Francis F. broke out with the measles this morning.

MAY 30—At 8.30 this morning David, Seth Sperry and I started for Lyon Mountain. A threatening shower was coming from the west, but we did not stay for that. David picked out the entrance to the road and we started up at 10.10.

The great rule for mountain climbing, for heavy and light people, old and young, male or female is, don't hurry too much. Following that rule anyone can go up Lyon Mountain. For more than half of the way is an old good road. The remainder is a blazed trail. In about an hour it began to rain, and continued to rain more or less hard all the rest of the time. We had only two umbrellas, so there was really no use of trying to be sheltered. I suppose everyone eats on the highest boulder of the mountain, as we did. This is 3,809 feet above sea level. At 2 o'clock we started back. I reached the railroad at 3.45. I had filled my lunch bag with snow to show the people at the lake, because seeing is believing. We reached Plattsburgh at 6.10 p.m., wet, hungry, but feeling better than in the morning when we left home.

MAY 31—I have tried various means to see if I had any perceptible effect left from my wet tramp of yesterday. Possibly, but only possibly, my biceps extensors are a little lame. I should not think of it if I had not been on the lookout for an effect.

1901

The Doctor is called out at 1 a.m. on a moonlit January night when the temperature is below zero. He doesn't get home until five o'clock, but has found reward in the "entrancing" beauty of the night. He notes the death of Queen Victoria and the existence of a small Boer War within his family.

Carrie Nation's evangelistic influence reaches from Wichita to Plattsburgh, and young Francis Kellogg, duly reflecting it, calls his sister "my dear hell-bound sinner." Elspeth is bound, instead, for Wellesley College. Robert, the first son to be earning his living, proudly presents his father with five hundred dollars, "as a sort of rebate" on his college expenses. The doctor, with two children in college and two more to go, admits that the money "will come in mighty handy."

Doctor Kellogg happily climbs Lyon Mountain once more, declaring that it's easy if you "don't hurry too much." This is about the only vacation he has in a hectic year that brings, in September, the appalling news of McKinley's assassination.

JAN. 3—Started at 1 this a.m. and drove out into Beekmantown, 2½ miles west of the Corners, to see a patient with Dr. Swift. I got back at 5 a.m. The night was most beautiful, but it was rather cold. It was 5° below zero when I started, but it was 10° below when I got back. Belmont spun right along and the shadows and moonlight vistas were beautiful. The mountains in the east, the hills and trees, the valleys, all were entrancing. I wonder if such a night is really more beautiful than the day, or is it because one sees it more rarely!

JAN. 14—There is a custom, increasing, I think, for people when speaking to another to speak this other's name. The other evening I saw Mr. Newton on the opposite side of the street and asked him if a car had just gone down. His answer was, "Yes, Mr. McDougal, a car has just gone down and another will be up in about 10 minutes." The other evening I was going down Platt Street and a little girl was running around, a child perhaps about 8 years old. I said something to her and she answered, "Yes,

Uncle." Today while coming in from the Head I met Mr. Albert Hagar driving out. I said "How do you do?" He answered, "Good morning, Mr. Oliver, good morning." So it seems to me this custom may have its imperfections.

JAN. 20—I went yesterday to see a man who had a sore throat, who claimed he had nearly died the night before by choking. If a neighbor had not come in he felt sure he would have died. Questioning revealed that the cause of his choking was what he had taken. He had put together in equal parts *clear alcohol and kerosene*, and swallowed what he could of the mixture.

JAN. 22—Queen Victoria died today.

JAN. 24—Francis F. is strong English and against the Boers. Lizzie is just the opposite, so they have great discussions.[1]

JAN. 30—Last night I was detained at a place on the Peru road until 2.30 a.m. The mother of the woman who was ill was a little, active, old woman, who had had 12 children, ten of whom were living, and all married excepting one son. Some of the children had 8 or 10 children apiece, and the sick woman was the youngest and is 21 years old. This little old grandmother was hustling around, doing whatever was necessary such as fixing her daughter's bed, making the fire better, cheerful and courageous all the time. She also, much of the time, was smoking a long-stem clay pipe. But the delight of her life was "her baby." It seems that a little more than a year ago, a little baby was left on the doorstep of a Mr. Jenkins at Salmon River and this old woman, Mrs. Benoit, had adopted the child and faithfully cared for it ever since. Last night Mrs. Benoit had "her baby" with her at her daughter's, and was as fond of it as any young mother. She hugged and kissed it and fondled it and showed it off with all possible affection. The motherhood in her old heart has not in the least abated.

FEB. 6—There has been a terrible blizzard all around us. Nelson was to come home yesterday. He took a train for the Island Road, just completed, and reached Rouses Point in about 22 hours from the time of starting out. The train got stalled in the snow on North Island and the passengers had to stay in the car all night. In the morning they went to farmhouses and got breakfast. The train was finally shovelled out so as to start about 11 o'clock. There was so much delay after that, they did not get to Rouses Point until about 2.30 in the afternoon. He reached home about 11 p.m. Thirty hours from Burlington to Plattsburgh is a long time.

FEB. 10—Last evening old John Ray, who was a soldier in the War of the Rebellion, and who now draws a pension of 72 dollars per month, was

in the office. He cannot speak, but only makes a peculiar sound. This condition is due to a slight hemiplegia that came on some years ago. His wife was buried in Peru last Wednesday, a paralytic, too. He fully understands what is said to him, and nods emphatically or shakes his head emphatically according as he means yes or no.

Judge W. C. Watson drew up his will for him in my office, and read to him and questioned him very carefully as to how he wanted it ma John fully comprehended and nodded many times in response to questions. I witnessed the will, as also did Mr. Watson. Old John sign his name with difficulty, but still it is legible.

FEB. 11—Prof. Jasper Robertson read a very interesting pa "Woman Suffrage" before the Plattsburgh Institute. His paper wa ously discussed.[2]

FEB. 12—The influence of Mrs. Carrie E. Nation, the Kansan te fanatic, has reached Plattsburgh. In the papers a few days letter from her to the Wichita saloonkeepers which began "M bound sinners." Last night Francis said to Elspeth in most "Won't you please move that lamp, my dear hell-bound sinne

FEB. 28—Robert sent me 500 dollars today, a sort of a college expenses. It will come in mighty handy.

Went to Rand Hill again yesterday. The snow there is al on the level. Today is the 96th day of continuous sleighing be sure, wagons are used in the village between the hotel it is because of the winter accumulations on the snow. ground whatever, and on the bridge, even the packed s under the horse manure.

MAR. 1—In one of my drives out into North Afric lost my Sigma Phi badge, the one I had worn since present of a new one, a Christmas present from Bess It is a beautiful one, plain, and has jets.

MAR. 19—Albani sang in the Opera House las strange to her to come back here, where as a ch practice of singing into her. It is said that he stick and strike her knuckles hard if she made It is also said that her father used to ask peop when they were in so much of a hurry, or for could not stop, he would say, "Well, sometir

APR. 1—I saw a sleigh on the streets to sleighing, to me an unprecedented number.

The top of Lyon Mountain (3,830 ft.), climbed four times by the Doctor and members of his family. Upper Chateaugay Lake is in the distance.

JUNE 11—After long years and considerable money, I have my files of the *Nation* bound and almost complete. Mr. Fred E. Barnum of Utica brought all to me which he took to be bound one year ago, excepting two volumes. These he will complete, bind and forward to me.

JUNE 17—Was called up at 1.40 this morning. Already then the new day was abundantly appearing in the northeast and north. Roosters were crowing, dogs were barking, and the varying undertone of the river was continuous. I walked down onto Margaret Street to make a call, and reached home again at quarter to three. Bess got up to see the morning twilight.

I stayed on the piazza. At ten minutes to three I heard the first robin, over in an elm on Cornelia Street. His first notes were a little scolding for a few seconds and then a full song. At length, a minute or two before three, there came a response similar to his own and a robin flew from the south. The clock struck three, then many other robins joined in. At ten minutes after three the robins prevailed over the roosters and dogs, but the undertone of the river kept on rising and falling, but never ceasing. The new day had come in.

JUNE 20—Helen and her duplicate of 1870 came last evening on the *Vermont*. Little Theodora, a smiling, happy child of nearly 5 years, looks wonderfully as her mother used to at her age.

JUNE 23—Helen and I went over to Essex Center this afternoon to go into the old cemetery there. Things were in better condition than we had expected to find them.

AUG. 6—It seems that many years ago, on the Saranac's banks near its mouth, it was reported that pieces of platinum were found. It was on the land then occupied by William Egan. Egan digged there, and others. At any rate some men, having heard these traditions, obtained an option, the privilege of digging for platinum and of buying the premises for 4 thousand dollars if platinum were found. If not found they were to fill up the hole as good as before and to pay one dollar. Accordingly, some days ago some workmen began to dig. After digging down I am told 18 feet, a man from the State Geological Department told them there was no possibility of platinum existing there, and they filled up the hole again. I am told that they found in the bottom of their excavation a flat stone on which was cut "Michael Egan 1834." Thus was another case of witchcraft made public.

SEPT. 6—The horrible news of the attempted assassination of President McKinley at Buffalo came to us about 5 o'clock this afternoon.[4]
Theo and Martha came last night. Martha is a dear baby, talking much, very beautiful, and is one whom one cannot keep from squeezing.

SEPT. 18—Today on steamer *Vermont* Elspeth left for Wellesley College. She is very happy over the prospects of her college life.

OCT. 1—I have been having a very sick patient for a month. She has been between life and death for a long time, but is much better now and will recover. She told me today that the doctors, her mother and prayers had saved her life. I have learned that she has made a vow to God that she will wear black all her life if He allows her to recover.

OCT. 15—There has been found on Bailey Avenue 11 feet from the surface, a bone 4 3/8 inches long. It looks to me like a clavicle of some large bird. All along in this ditch are layers of marine shells. This bone was about 5 or 6 feet lower than these shells and therefore was deposited there long before the glacial salt Lake Champlain had ceased to exist.[5]

OCT. 18—The evening before last, a little after 6, I was telephoned to go out to George Lafave's, a little beyond West Plattsburgh. I reached there about half past seven, but found that I had been called earlier than was necessary. I waited until 2.30 in the morning and then came home. At 6 last evening I went to Treadwell's Mills, got a boy, and reached home a little after 9. At two this morning I was again telephoned to go to George LaFave's, and reached there at 3.30. The distance to Lafave's is about 7 miles.

OCT. 21—Last Tuesday evening, October 15, I read a paper on Thoreau before the Tuesday Club at the house of Mrs. W. C. Watson. It was well received.

OCT. 24—Nelson came over today. He had been vaccinated and it was working slightly. He said he felt sick, but except for subjective symptoms I could not verify his claim.

OCT. 26—Nelson went back this afternoon. I think he has nearly recuperated. He ate large amounts of potato, bread, butter, milk, pie, cake, steak, salmon and other things, slept until 10.30 in the mornings, took a long drive out into Beekmantown yesterday, and the subjective ones were the only symptoms of illness apparent. It was very windy on the lake this afternoon, and the steamer had to go to the Island and thence to Port Kent. I am desirous to learn how much and how often he fed the fishes.

OCT. 28—A rummage sale is in progress for the Home for the Friendless. Dr. C. E. Bentley found a peculiar old lamp for 20 cents which took his fancy and which he purchased. On investigation it was one which Mrs. Myers, his mother-in-law, had sent down from the house.

Mrs. M. F. Parkhurst by mistake sent down a coat and vest of her husband, thinking it was one of her son George's. Her husband had had the suit made last winter for 35 dollars, it is said. Mr. P. called for the suit a short time after; then she found what she had done. She sent down to the sale room but it had been sold and had gone, no one knew where.

OCT. 29—Another rummage sale incident. A man by the name of Weatherwax from near Valcour went into the sale room, took off his ten-dollar overcoat, laid it down to try on something, and when he came for it, it was gone. Someone came along, asked how much it was. The seller did not know because it was not tagged. It was taken into another room, tagged at $1.50 and sold to the customer. The man himself was pretty mad, and especially as his ten-dollar coat had been sold for $1.50.

NOV. 13—This evening I saw a little girl about 5 years old up on the Miller Road, whose clothes caught fire while her mother was at one of the neighbor's for a moment. The child ran to find her mother and the wind and running increased the flame. She got almost to where her mother was and fell exhausted. They picked her up and carried her back to the house. I saw her in about an hour. From forehead to her knees there was hardly a place that the fire had missed. The skin was burned through in many places and great shreds of it were hanging. The end of one little finger with nail intact came off while I was there, like a thimble, and another was ready to come off. All of the burned surfaces felt like the crust of a loaf of bread. She could talk and see, and was conscious. She only complained of being cold and desired to be covered up! and of an intolerable thirst. She drank several times during the half hour I was there. She did not say once that the burns hurt her. I do not think she will live until morning.

Later. She died at 8.40 p.m.

NOV. 25—Last evening about 7 I started for a place nearly two miles beyond the Wesleyan Methodist Church. I took Belmont and the top buggy. It was raining and snowing. I had on a sweater under my vest and an ulster overcoat. Belmont spun along and I reached my destination in a little more than an hour, in spite of the storm. I found that the side of my ulster coat most exposed to the storm was a coat of ice mail.

The baby was born with 5 pains after my arrival. The mother had held back until I came. I had been with her when her first baby was born, May 14, 1890. She had had all the others alone until this one, and this is the eleventh. All are living and in good health. I wanted a piece of twine for a string. None could be found, for the children rushed for each piece of wrapping twine as soon as it came into the house around a package from the store. It was a rarity for them, an eagerly sought luxury. The people were not poor. They have a good, large, well-built new house, good fuel, a good farm and some money besides.

DEC. 7—I think since Sunday I have done the largest week's work I have ever done in medical work. There are some cases of smallpox in town, and many people have been vaccinated. That is a partial cause of my increased work.

DEC. 21—Elspeth came home from Wellesley and Nelson from Burlington on the cars last evening. I did not know her at first.

DEC. 25—This is the second Christmas that Robert was not at home. I had from Theo Barrett Wendell's *A Literary History of America*, and from Robert *The Cavalier* by Cable.

Notes for 1901

1. There was considerable pro-Boer sentiment in the United States and a vigorous public debate continued during 1900 and 1901.

2. By this time women could vote at school meetings and on bond issues, but annually the legislature refused to extend the privilege any farther.

3. This famous prima donna spent some of her childhood in Plattsburgh while her father, M. Lajeunesse, taught music locally.

4. President McKinley was shot on September 6 but seemed to be improving so that Vice President Roosevelt vacationed in the high Adirondacks. McKinley died on September 14.

5. Dr. Kellogg was instrumental in sending the bone to Albany for identification. The State Paleontologist wrote him that it was the tibia of a seal.

1902

Doctor Kellogg's year begins with an outbreak of smallpox in the community, greatly exaggerated by "out-of-town merchants" who warn that Plattsburgh is dangerous. His own health begins to break down, however, under the cumulative stresses of years of unstinting service to the people of northeastern New York. He goes away on two long trips for rest and recuperation. On his return, he barely misses losing his office in a downtown conflagration.

The Doctor resumes his busy practice and feels sufficiently rejuvenated to climb Mount Mansfield. His journal carefully chronicles the family's progress. David enters high school, and Nelson, graduated from college, starts to train for the Episcopal ministry in New York City. The scattered Kelloggs and Kyles devotedly regroup at Thanksgiving and Christmas.

JAN. 1—I have just completed Wendell's *Literary History of America,* which Theo gave me at Christmas. It is a wonderfully good and exasperating book.

JAN. 8—There are about 40 cases of smallpox in town.

The other day Mrs. F. B. Hall's sleigh tipped and instead of her falling out, she fell down between the two seats and was wedged in there. Two or three men lifted on her and helped her up. When Francis F. heard about it he said, "Perhaps she was full."[1]

JAN. 31—This has been carnival week. The out-of-town attendance has been small because of fear of smallpox. It is said that out-of-town merchants have proclaimed that it was dangerous to go to Plattsburgh now, that smallpox is raging, and that they were burying patients at night in large numbers. As a matter of fact now there are 8 or 9 cases under treatment. There have been 63 cases to date, most of whom have been disinfected and turned out. Not a death has occurred. All of this scare is entirely unwarranted. A large majority of the cases have not been sicker than a hard cold often makes a person. Still, some of them have been sick enough.

191

MAY 5—A long hiatus. I have been to Boston, Providence, Chicago and Sloan, being away for two months, supposed to be on account of my health.[2] I visited Theo, Helen and Robert, and Rebe. Bessie was with me nearly all the time. A friend of mine, George C. Kellogg, gave me one thousand dollars to take the trip.

JUNE 20—Have just returned from a four-weeks' trip to Penacook, New Hampshire and West Roxbury. After getting to Theo's in West Roxbury, I went to Nantasket Beach, Marblehead, Salem, Concord, Concord Junction, Wellesley and Cambridge, and also many places in Boston.

At Concord we visited Sleepy Hollow Cemetery on a beautiful hill, in which are the graves of the Hawthornes, Thoreau, Alcotts and Emersons. We also visited Walden Pond and saw an excavation in the ground where Thoreau's hut is said to have stood. Near this was a large pile of stones, brought there by pilgrims. We went to the pond and took out of the water stones for this pile.

JUNE 23—Went over to Burlington this morning and came back tonight. It was class day. Nelson's oration was "A Plea for the Smaller Colleges." He had by far the best oration.

JUNE 25—Nelson was graduated today, receiving the degree of A.B. David was graduated from the Grammar School here today and enters the High School one half year in advance. He had the closing declamation and place of honor.

"The worst fire I ever saw" was the Doctor's description of the conflagration of July 7th on Margaret Street, Plattsburgh's main shopping area. Fanned by stiff winds, the fire seemed to threaten the whole district and Doctor Kellogg rescued some medical equipment from his office, which was in the path of the blaze. However, the fire was checked through the heroic efforts of firemen and of soldiers from the Barracks. The fire destroyed $125,000 in property, which was incompletely insured. The Doctor's office suffered only from smoke.

Beginning on July 16th David and his father spent several days in Vermont. They took Belmont and the buggy on the steamer to Burlington and drove to Essex Center, where they spent the night with friends. Next day they drove to the foot of Mt. Mansfield, where they left the horse with a farmer. They started climbing the mountain (4,393 feet) at 3.15 and reached the Summit House at 6.40 p.m. The weather and the view were so fine that the Doctor telephoned his wife to join him.

Unfortunately, by the time she and little Francis arrived the next evening, after a trip by boat, train and stage, fog and rain had closed in.

They spent the whole of the following day reading, eating and sleeping. **1902**
*But on July 20, with no break in the weather, they departed as they had
come, David and his father descending the steep northwestern slope of
the mountain. Reclaiming their horse and buggy, they drove into Burlington, still in the rain, in time to meet the train bearing Mrs. Kellogg and
Francis. The Doctor did not refer to it as one of his more successful trips.*

AUG. 25—The other day we were speaking of retreats as getting into
use in the Episcopal Church. Nelson was arguing for them and I was
expressing my disapproval of them. David said that he thought George
Washington established a retreat for Cornwallis that was very suitable.

SEPT. 6—Francis Fellows is 8 years old today. He is a handsome,
hearty, affectionate young gentleman. He is 4 ft. 4 in. tall and weighs 62
pounds. David Sherwood Jr. was 14 years old on Monday the 1st inst.
He is 5 ft. 3½ in. tall and weighs 92 ¾ pounds. If there is any finer
fellow in existence he has never been seen by me.

SEPT. 9—Nelson left on the 12.25 train this noon for New York. He
enters "The General Theological Seminary," an Episcopal school, for a
three years' course in theology. David begins school today, being full-
fledged in the high school. Francis Fellows enters the fourth grade of the
public schools.

OCT. 15—Yesterday the Northern New York Medical Association held
its 32nd annual meeting at the State Asylum for insane criminals and the
criminal insane at Dannemora. About 35 physicians were present. Dr.
Lamb, superintendent of the Asylum, had a sort of clinic, as also did one
of the other Asylum physicians. One big, jolly Negro, short, gorilla-like,
happy all the time, was discoursing on the advantages of being where he
was. He had nothing to worry him. He did not have to pay rent. He did
not have to buy coal. He had plenty to eat, wear, and to make him
comfortable. He said that if he should go out, he "would be like the
fiddler in hell—ostracised."
There is a Holiness preacher in Champlain by name of Taylor who has
a large tent capable of holding 1,500 people. He is so personal in his
remarks that many of the best people are disgusted with him. He pitches
into the Masons, Catholics, other clergymen and many others. Last Saturday evening his tent was attacked by rowdies and somewhat damaged.
Many of the leading citizens of Champlain, becoming so disgusted with
him, published over their own signatures a request for him to leave town
within 24 hours. (This he has failed to do.)
However, last Sunday morning he inveighed against the Masons, claim-

193

One of Plattsburgh's livery stables, from which the Doctor in his later years some-times hired a driver and wagon for his night calls into the country.

ing that a gang of Masons in Champlain instigated the attack on his tent the night before and that hoodlums from Rouses Point executed the attack. Then he said harsh things against the Rev. Mr. Frazer, the Presbyterian clergyman of Champlain, because he was a Mason. After the services were over, Dr. Briggs went to him and told him that Mr. Frazer was not a Mason. Taylor thanked him and said he would correct his error. So in the afternoon he corrected as follows: "I am told that I made a mistake this morning. I am told that the Rev. Mr. Frazer is not a Mason. Even the Masons repudiate him. May the Lord convert him and make his heart as soft as his head."

OCT. 31—Went to Burlington the night before last and stayed at G. G. Benedict's house. Yesterday forenoon I went to Montpelier. Mr. G. G. Benedict gave an account of Stevens, who had died in England during the last year.[3] I had a paper on "Early Mention of Some Events and Places in the Valley of Lake Champlain." There was an audience of 250. Governor McCullough, the Lieut. Governor, ex-Gov. Stickney and others were in the audience.

NOV. 10—I had my sixteenth hundred baby last evening. His name is Charles Edward Herlihy. My back is quite strong, though I consider myself quite a patriarch.

NOV. 26—Nelson came home from New York this noon. His coming was a complete surprise to all of the family excepting myself. I wrote to him last week, telling him that I would send him money for his fare if he would come. I did not tell the family, because if he could not they would not be disappointed. I heard Sunday that he would come and as I had begun keeping quiet, I thought it would do no harm to continue. But not to let the secret out and to account for my being late to dinner, because I met him at the depot at 1.30, I telephoned that a man whom we met in Providence was coming on the train, and I would bring him up to dinner. All of which was literally true, but the family did not get the correct idea of the matter until I drove up to the door with him.

DEC. 18—Bessie has reached her fifty-second birthday. She is much younger than I am.

DEC. 24—This evening a man came for me to go to see his wife. I asked him what was the matter and he said he was quite sure she had a "false reception." I have not been able to determine just what he meant.

DEC. 25—All the family at home. All had nice presents. The family gave me Mr. Wright's *Asiatic Russia*, Rob gave me one of John Burroughs'. Theo gave me two of Thoreau, and there were many other things.

DEC. 26—The man mentioned under Dec. 24 above added another today. He was almost suspicious that his wife's mother had been the means of making his wife ill. He said, "By gosh! If I thought she had I'd go over and lick the whole family."

A few days ago I was called to a house where one of the ladies was ill. I gave her some medicine and told her to take a powder at night on going to bed, and another in four hours, if necessary. Her sister asked, "How shall we know when the four hours are up?" I had not the courage to tell her to look at the clock.

DEC. 29—Today a woman had a new baby. I asked her how many this made her and she said "Eleven." After thinking awhile she said, "No! It's nine. I have had four boys and four girls and this one. What is this one?" As a rule the majority of women remember how many children they have had.

Notes for 1902

1. The unconscious irony in Francis' remark lies in the fact that, far from being "full" Mrs. Hall organized several chapters of the W.C.T.U. in Clinton County.

2. Dr. Kellogg's condition was probably circulatory, aggravated by his strenuous activity and his weight.

3. Benjamin Franklin Stevens (1833–1902), a Vermonter, went to London in 1860 to engage in the rare-book business with his brother. He catalogued American documents in England and on the continent. His most important publication was the 25 volumes of facsimiles of European archives dealing with American history between 1773 and 1783.

1903

The Doctor's rugged routine shows no tendency to become easier as he grows older. He finds compensation, however, in his unflagging interest in the changes of the seasons and the vagaries of the weather. In this year he painstakingly measures spring floods and then the shrinking lake as drought follows, fostering forest fires whose smoke darkens the days and powders the town with ashes.

Doctor Kellogg continues his enthusiastic mountain-climbing and spends a sleepless night in a roaring wind atop favorite Lyon Mountain. He still somehow makes time for lecture engagements and wide reading.

JAN. 8—I am reading Prof. Norton's new translation of Dante. After reading, I am going to compare it with his former translation, issued about ten years ago.

JAN. 14—Yesterday was the annual meeting of the County Medical Society. I went to a minstrel show in the evening and got home a little before 11. I read awhile and then went to sleep. At 12 the telephone whanged me up. A man wanted to make an appointment for me to examine a man for insurance today. I got so thoroughly awake that I lost about an hour's sleep. A little after 4 the doorbell rang. I had to go in a hurry up onto Peru Street. Belmont spun along. Florence Ethel Bennett arrived soon after I did. I reached home a little after 6.

At seven the doorbell called me out again. Just as I stepped down from the front piazza, a man called to me from the back piazza. He had on the street a load of wood to sell, and he would sell it cheap. I did not want to buy. He had started from Rand Hill, about 12 miles away, at 2.30 with this one-horse load. He was in so much pain from rheumatism he could not sleep, so he had driven 12 miles in the night on a load of wood. The thermometer on our piazza then was 3° below zero, and at Rand Hill it must have been 10° colder. He was an example of industry and also was trying what to me is a new method of treatment for rheumatism. I saw him about 9 o'clock downstreet. He had sold his wood for 4 dollars and will come down again tomorrow with another load.

JAN. 27—Read John Fiske's *New France and New England*, which I believe was his last. Of course it is excellent, as all of his writings are.

196

But it seems to me there was no real need of this book. It is another competitor in the lost list of American histories.

FEB. 12—I went to Treadwell's Mills twice yesterday. In the Haseltine swamp the white birch branches were a reddish gray, but the branches of the willows as they appeared in the sunlight were almost red. Within those branches was life, life compressed, hermetically sealed in bark coverings, yet life, life. The 10-year-old pines on the Plains were being cut for wood, but the little ones stood up, not fearing because of the destruction of their elder brothers. After getting back into town, we saw the earliest *sure* sign of spring. A cluster of boys was playing marbles on the sidewalk.

FEB. 24—Went to Shoreham yesterday and read a paper before the Hands Cove Chapter of the D.A.R. I rearranged a paper on the archaeology of the valley of Lake Champlain, paying particular reference to the region around Fort Ticonderoga. Bess went with me and we stayed at Dr. W.N. Platt's house. We took the train here at 9.50 in the forenoon and reached Dr. Platt's house about one. He met us at Addison Junction and we drove with him across the lake.

FEB. 25—Awhile ago I sent a bill to a man out in Beekmantown. The other day an answer came back as follows. The envelope was addressed

> Mrs. D. s. Kellogg
> M.D. – plattsburg
> N.Y.

> feb 20 1903

> ~~Dear Sar i having~~
> Dear Sar i have been ~~work~~
> working ~~a~~ all wenter
> for small wags to surpet
> my famly. But now i
> be geing higher wags
> next moth and i go down
> and see you and try and
> make it all right woth
> yous. excuse me for not
> going down to see you
> before. Your very Respected
> from 2 Jo Ducat. Beekmant
> wn. N.y. to D.s. Kellogg.
> M.D.

Certainly Jo. Ducat 2nd can put his meaning into writing.

MAR. 16—Today came the Kellogg genealogy by Timothy Hopkins, San Francisco, California. I have been waiting for this at least ten years. Its full title is *The Kelloggs in the Old World and in the New*. It contains over 22 thousand names. It is the most complete and best arranged genealogy I ever saw.

MAR. 30—Yesterday afternoon I drove down to the Creek. The water comes up to just 16 inches from the top of the planks on the Iron Bridge. The wooden bridge to the beach has water up to its timbers. The water is over the road just below the Lozier Works, also at the bend just beyond the Creek bridge.

Today I drove over to Cumberland Head, which I found to be an island. The water is continuous from Woodruff's Pond through the swamp to Cumberland Bay. I have seen this so once before. I think this was in 1885.[1]

APR. 3—I had last evening a short paper before the Knights of Columbus on "The Jesuit Relations and Allied Documents."

I have had a portion of the north part of the yard at the house spaded up and the knotgrass cleaned out of it. I am planning to have a garden for flowers there. Perhaps we shall have some cucumbers and tomatoes also. I have had manure spread over most all of the lawn, getting the last on just before the shower this morning.

APR. 22—David and I drove out to the Hartwell swamp after school tonight and got some quite good arbutus. We have sent some to Robert by mail tonight in a tin box. I have each stem wrapped around with moist cotton and the whole surrounded by moist tissue paper.

APR. 26—Today I drove down to the Creek. I measured the surface of the water under the Iron Bridge where I measured it four weeks ago, March 29. Today from the top of the planks, where then the water was 16 inches down, today the water is 56 inches down. In other words, the water in the lake has lowered 40 inches in four weeks.

MAY 6—Tonight at 5.30, I saw what looked like a piece of white cotton cloth taken up into a tree just below Dr. Larkin's house. On getting near, to my surprise this was the bird itself. It had a wholly white back, wholly white wings, wholly white tail, and a moderately red breast. I watched it for three quarters of an hour. It was with robins. It flew like the robins. It was a robin.

MAY 7—I told a number of people about this robin today, among them William B. Mooers. He said, "If you see a white robin you will live to be a hundred years old." He said that old Peter Brucier, alias "Swap

de hoss," always claimed that he should live a hundred years because
when he was young he had seen a white robin. The old man died at the age
of 103.

MAY 20—A young elm near the front piazza has grown up as tall as the
house. For years the cats have climbed this and have gone onto the tin
piazza roof and often thence into the rooms upstairs. The other day I
planned to stop this. So I split a stovepipe lengthwise and David put it
around the elm trunk between limbs quite high up. It had not been up
long before "Poly," Francis's cat, started up, and her kitten after her.
Poly saw the pipe, did not touch it, but it was amusing to see her go out
on one limb, back, then out on another, calling her kitten Thomas, but
wholly unable to get beyond the stovepipe. There is one limb she might
jump up onto, but she has not found this. It is an anomaly that the cat,
Napoleon Bonaparte, should be the mother of a daughter named Thomas.

MAY 22—There has hardly been any rain since before April 4. It is
terribly dry and the fires in the Adirondacks are said to be fearful.

JUNE 1—The new lake steamer *Vermont* made its first regular trip on
Saturday. She takes the place of her predecessor *Vermont* and also her
name *Vermont*. She is a fine boat, but I believe the trip was not wholly
satisfactory. She went from here starting at 8.12 a.m. to Ticonderoga,
reaching Plattsburgh about 8.15 in the evening.[2]

JUNE 4—This morning it was necessary to sweep ashes from the piazza
floor. They had fallen from the heavy smoke in the air. The forest fires
are very severe, and no sign of rain. Last evening when we had supper
at six o'clock, it was necessary to light the lamps to see by, because the
smoke was so dense.[3]

JUNE 9—I measured the height from the top of the plank on the Creek
Bridge to the top of the water, where I measured March 29 and May 30.
The distance now is 100 inches, making a total fall in the water of the lake
just seven feet since March 29.

JULY 10—David has arrived at the dignity of long pantaloons. He
wanted them before school term was completed, but he knew the boys
would guy him so much he preferred to wait till now.

AUG. 2—Sunday. At ten o'clock there was sound of bugles and drums
and of a brass band. This began at the fairground. At 7 o'clock this morning a regiment of Canada-British soldiers came to Plattsburgh, went into
quarters at the fairground and started for church at 10. In front of the
band and buglers was a detachment of artillerymen in helmets and dark
clothes. Behind the band was the main portion with high bearskin caps

Clinton Street, Plattsburgh, in 1903. The village band is giving a concert.

and the typical red coats. The band played while marching the "Star Spangled Banner," "America" and others of our national airs. It was a beautiful object lesson of peace. Eighty nine years ago a portion of the same army marched around on those same streets, but it was war then.[4]

The Doctor's love of the out-of-doors and his enjoyment of activities with his sons prompted a climb up Lyon Mountain late in August. He, David and Nelson started out with a basket of food and three blankets. They reached the summit at 6.30 p.m. and found "complete desolation" from the forest fires of the spring. They also found gale winds, which blew "terrifically" all night.

They ate their supper, collected firewood for the night and, since there was nothing else to do, tried to get some sleep. But the wind blew sparks and fine dust all around. The fire had to be replenished often and the night's supply of wood gave out at 10 o'clock. After that they had to grope for it in the dark, running the risk of being blown over by the roaring wind. David slept about four hours, Nelson one and the Doctor not at all. "After a time," he recorded afterward, "it occurred to me that I was not there to sleep, but rather to keep awake. I could sleep lower on earth. I felt sure there would no sound of a telephone or doorbell reach me."

And so a long, wakeful night wore away. At dawn the visibility was so poor that they decided not to spend the day there. After an early breakfast they started down the mountain at 5.40. They reached home at midday after, as the Doctor wrote, "a most delightful experience of day and night."

Chicago Illinois

Helen and son doing well. Born this afternoon.

H. R. Platt

This is Helen's third son and fourth child.

OCT. 4—This morning at exactly 5 o'clock died the Rev. Francis Bloodgood Hall. He was born November 16, 1827 on Day Street, New York City.[5]

OCT. 13—Went to Saranac Lake to attend a meeting of the Northern New York Medical Association. Left at 8.35 a.m. and got back at 7 p.m.

OCT. 18—Last Wednesday morning Bessie and I started for Boston. Fred met us at the North Station and we reached 174 Bellevue Street about 9. In a short time Elspeth telephoned us from Wellesley. She met us on Thursday afternoon at the South Station and stayed at Fred's that night. The next morning we went over to Wellesley on the trolley with her. Saturday morning I started for home at 8 o'clock, Bessie remaining over until the latter part of the week.

NOV. 16—One day last week a woman was in the office who lives up off the Turnpike. About 6 weeks before, she had had her twelfth child. Her eldest child is 13 years of age. At two of her confinements I have been present. In all of the others she has managed without a doctor.

DEC. 26—Yesterday was Christmas and we had a nice time. All the children were home except Robert. Francis got us all up a little after five. I had a Bible, *Tom Sawyer*, 3 volumes of Carlyle's *French Revolution*, 2 of *Wilhelm Meister*, one of *Heroes*, one of *Past and Present*.[6]

Notes for 1903

1. Dr. Kellogg records this phenomenon on April 30, 1887.

2. The first *Vermont* was built by the Winans brothers in 1808–09 and was followed by others of the same name. The new vessel was 264 feet long and was supposed to be able to make 23 miles an hour.

3. The forest fires were temporarily checked by a late snowfall on May 1 but the drought continued and the fires devastated large areas in the Adirondacks. Rain-making experiments were about to be made when the drought ended on June 10.

4. This was a part of a two-day encampment by the Governor General's Foot Guards from Ottawa. Their visit was taken up with parades, receptions and attendance at a ball game.

5. See footnote 21 for 1886. The church did not survive its only pastor for it was closed almost immediately.

6. This refers to Goethe's *Wilhelm Meister's Apprenticeship and Travels*, and Carlyle's *Heroes and Hero Worship* and *Past and Present*.

1904

*A new winter brings a furious storm and the coldest weather that the
Doctor has ever recorded on his porch thermometer. As the year moves
on, he continues to find great pleasure in the sayings and antics of his
youngest son, Francis. He also continues his observations of wildlife, even
engaging the great naturalist John Burroughs in correspondence over
curious sparrow behavior.*

*He returns to Sorel, Quebec, after a lapse of fifteen years to pursue his
search for traces of the infant Riedesel, who died in 1783. He has a good
time but no better luck than on the first trip.*

JAN. 1—Went to Salmon River in a sleigh. A little before noon, just
after I started back, the wind changed to the north, and for a few minutes
there was a terrible blizzard. The wind was furious and a dry snow fell.
I could not see many rods before me and the snow drove into the cloth of
my overcoat. Before I got very far the snow stopped, but the wind
increased. Once many years ago, one Thanksgiving Day, I was similarly
honored. I drove to Salmon River in a hard south wind, remaining about
20 minutes, and on my setting out to return as now, the wind changed
into the north, hard, and I had to face the storm both ways.

JAN. 15—Went to a dinner tonight at the Miss Smiths', who live on the
old Bailey-Platt place. While we were gone Francis had the two little
Angell girls to play with him. They were having a fine time running and
playing. Francis took some perfumery water in a cup or bottle and held
it over Louise's head. He said: "Louise, I baptize you in the name of the
Great Jehovah and the Continental Congress." Then he dowsed the water
onto the top of her head.

JAN. 19—Last evening at 9.30 the thermometer was 18° below. Within
an hour it was 21° below. At 7 this morning it was *26° below*. This is the
coldest that I remember it ever to have been on our piazza.[1]

FEB. 5—At 12.30 this morning O. T. Larkin telephoned me that there
was a small fire over Percy's store and that the hose came up my stairs,
and he thought I would like to know it. I dressed, harnessed Belmont and
with David came down. A full hose was on the stairs and extended through

into Percy's. Another hose had been brought up onto the roof from Durkee Street behind, and the water was coming down the stairs in torrents. The fire continued until after three o'clock and was finally put out. The necessary water did more damage than the fire. I was only discommoded by the smoke and water.

FEB. 21—Francis was in Lizzie's room looking at a picture of Christ, where he is holding one hand up and one finger extended. He asked some questions about it and then after looking at the hand more closely he said, "He used to bite his fingernails, all the same."

MAR. 9—I measured some ice which had been cut from the lake. It was 27 inches thick.[2]

APR. 7—Bessie has been very sick, sicker than I remember to have seen her. She fainted three times in the night. She is tired out.

MAY 26—This forenoon I went over to Cumberland Head, coming back by the sand beach. Some men drew a seine at 10.15. I got two good pike from them. The man scaled them and, cutting them open the whole length of the abdomen, took out the entire viscera. I put both fish in a paper and laid them in the bottom of the wagon. These fish were flopping around at least until I got as far as the Lozier works, for certainly 20 minutes.

JUNE 6—Nelson came home from New York Saturday night. He finished his second year at the General Theological Seminary about two weeks ago.

JUNE 11—I received the following this afternoon:

Boston, Mass.

Fine boy this morning nine o'clock both doing well

F. H. Chase

JULY 7—David and I drove over to the Head this forenoon. On our way back we got one of the fishermen to take his boat over into the old creek, where was an abundance of beautiful pond lilies. We got, I presume, as many as two hundred. After getting into town we gave lilies to 8 different ladies, and now at night we have almost none left.

JULY 16—This forenoon I saw a dead sparrow lying on the walk in front of the entrance to the office. Another sparrow came up to it with food in its mouth and tried to make the dead one eat. It took the food to the beak of the dead one and put it close to the dead mouth a number of times. It flew away and came back again with the food at least three or four times.

AUG. 1—Mrs. Kellogg and Francis have been spending a few days at camp at Long Point. Today she caught while trolling a six-pound pickerel that was just 30 inches long.

AUG. 12—The other day I wrote to John Burroughs, telling him of the sparrow incident of July 16, and this morning I received an answer, of which this is a copy:

West Park, N. Y.

My dear Sir.

Thank you for your letter of the 8th. Your English sparrow incident is very curious. I wish I could accept your invitation to visit your city this season, but I fear I cannot. My plans will not admit of it. I thank you all the same.

Very sincerely yours,

John Burroughs

AUG. 28—Yesterday David, Francis F., Seth Sperry and I left on the Chateaugay train for Lyon Mountain. We reached the old barn in just an hour, but we got out of our trail in some way and did not reach the summit until 2½ hours more had passed. We saw where we had our night fire one year ago. The foliage on the mountain was being renewed. Even in the descent we got out of the trail a little and were thus delayed. But the path through the raspberry bushes and life everlasting and the sedge under the dark green trees on the lower part of the trail, the glimpses of Chazy Lake, and above all the woodsy odor, made the whole excursion as delightful a one as we ever had.

Ever since 1889 Dr. Kellogg had wanted to return to Sorel and resume his search for records or the burial place of Canada Riedesel. At the end of August he and his wife made a two-day trip by train to Montreal and boat to Sorel.

At the English rectory they met a lady who was moving to Ontario. Sorel, once partly English, had almost entirely "gone over" to the French. She was the owner of a large quantity of goods once the property of the Duke of Kent, father of Queen Victoria, when he lived in Sorel.

But nowhere was a trace of the Riedesels to be found. The Baroness Riedesel recorded that upon her return to Germany "the officers promised me that they would place such an inscription on her tombstone as would restrain the inhabitants, who were fanatical Catholics, from removing her as a heretic child from consecrated ground." But the Doctor found the Protestant cemetery "in a sad state of dilapidation," although he discovered the grave of Dr. Wolfred Nelson, one of the leaders of the Papineau Rebellion.

He paid two dollars for their lodging and meals, and his wife thought "it was cheaper than staying at home."

Cady's Drugstore, a leading Plattsburgh dispensary in Dr. Kellogg's day.

1904 SEPT. 6—Francis F. has his tenth birthday today. He came downstairs rather earlier than usual. He said to me, "You can't spank me," and then sort of backed around to me as if challenging me to make the attempt. He had a large, thin board crowded down into the seat of his pantaloons as a protection.

SEPT. 17—Yesterday at 6.50 a.m. David and I started on the train for Ausable Forks and Whiteface Mountain. We got a horse and buggy at the Forks and drove to Everest's hotel in Wilmington. Everest had lunch done up for us and sent a young man to show us the way and to drive our horse back. This man got lost once and when he refound an old trail it proved to be no trail at all. So we failed to reach the summit, though we went up very high. We walked down and as many as eight different people, including Everest himself, told us that we did not even go on the right hill that had the trail up to the mountain top. But they told us this on our way *down*, not *up*. The pseudoguide used the expression "By Crimus" so many times that David and I named him Crimus.

OCT. 13—A letter came from Robert today from Springfield, Illinois. He was to take his examination for admission to the bar yesterday and the day before. We hope he will succeed.

The following is a copy of a telegram received this morning.

Passed examination O K

R. D. Kellogg.

NOV. 4—Nelson came up from New York yesterday morning to vote next Tuesday. He and I went to Burlington yesterday afternoon to attend the Sigma Phi initiations last evening. There were 5 members of the freshman class initiated.

DEC. 20—Two weeks ago tomorrow I started for Boston. I went to West Roxbury, Providence, New York, where I stayed over Sunday with Nelson. Reached home at 6 last evening. Robert came at 10 via Montreal.

DEC. 29—I have been asked to read a paper at Malone on local archaeology before the Franklin County Historical Society, I believe. I am making plans for a trip to California in a few weeks. It seems like quite an undertaking.

Notes for 1904

1. This record-breaking cold spell brought temperatures of 50° below at Saranac Lake and 52° below at Paul Smith's.
2. Dr. Kellogg was one of two doctors appointed by the County Medical Society to see that no impure ice was cut. Together with the Plattsburgh Health Board they directed cutters to avoid the currents that carried village and river sewage into the bay.

1905

By far the most memorable experience of this year in the overworked Doctor's life is a seven-week trip to California, beginning in mid-January. He describes it in rich and enticing detail. It is his first journey to the Far West. He visits his son Robert and niece Helen and her family in Chicago both on the way out and on his return. In California he stays mostly with his sister Mary and her husband, neither of whom he has seen for about fifteen years. Although Doctor Kellogg does not say so, this trip is apparently for the sake of his health. For some time his Journal has been declining in legibility, and as the year opens he doubtless is suffering at least from deep fatigue. At home he can never avoid the pressing demands made on him by telephone and doorbell. Here, at last, is the chance to get away entirely from routine responsibilities, and he responds to the opportunity with boyish enthusiasm. Upon his return, though, he plunges right back into his strenuous professional life.

In this year, too, Nelson completes his seminary training and begins the work of a curate in Philadelphia, while Elspeth graduates from Wellesley. The two sons still at home figure prominently in their proud father's Journal.

JAN. 2—Rob went back to Chicago this morning. I took him down to the 5 o'clock train.

On January 16th, Doctor Kellogg set out for California. The trip lasted until March 6th and was a success in every respect. Upon his return home, the Doctor wrote a full account of his experiences, as was his habit after every journey of note. The following long excerpt from that account opens with his westbound train's arrival at the California border, and he proceeds to paint an alluring picture of the Golden State as it was in the tranquil days before expansionism had got a grip on it.

After a good night's sleep, about 6 in the morning, our train had a long wait. We heard someone say "The Needles" and we knew that we were just entering California. A stroll outside gave us the first glimpse of a tropical summer. There were rows of great palms and of green pepper

207

trees. There was green grass and many indications that we were in a land of perpetual summer. The railroad men filled our water tanks and supplied us with ice, as they had done at Albuquerque. The people of the place curiously walked up and down and looked attentively at our train and its occupants.

I do not recall that any experience during the whole trip gave me such an impression as this early morning at The Needles. I expected palms, and pepper trees, and flowers like calla lilies, and green grass, and tall eucalyptus trees from this time on would be the *common* things. Therefore I was not prepared for the great barren land—more than 200 miles long and I do not know how wide—that was before us. There were wide valleys opening out from us, and high mountain ranges on either hand, without a green tree or leaf upon them. There were great black masses of rock which we learned were volcanic. I saw mountain cones that must have been made by volcanic eruptions. One of them was very perfect but the apex was sliced off. Think of mountain ranges 8 to 10 thousand feet high, so young and so dry that not a leaf nor blade of grass ever appeared on them. It was pleasant to recall that our eastern mountains were old enough and moist enough to grow green trees and flowers and even dwarf spruces. Arizona and New Mexico were fertile and abounding in luxuriant growth compared with this wide valley of desolation. The whole land was as bare as a newly-plowed field.

There were indications of freshets that had done much gullying, and dams and sluices had been made to turn the water, but rarely did any water appear. We passed large gangs of Mexicans who were working on the railroad or on the dry dams and sluices. Once we stopped for quite a long time, and we learned that a man had found a broken rail and had flagged the train. He said that about a week before an inch of rain had fallen, and that accounted for the gullies and washouts. We saw numerous mirages that looked so like water that we could hardly credit our own eyes. We were not surprised that thirsty horses and men hurried down to these phantom waters, only to meet death after a most terrible disappointment. We thought the houses in New Mexico and Arizona to have been unfit for human beings to dwell in, but here a duck hunter's shack would have been palatial. We could not realize that for most of the year this was a land where no rain fell.

At length we reached a height of land from which we looked down into the valley of San Bernadino, or "San Berdoo," as it was called. Our train now began a rapid descent, and swinging rapidly round on curve after curve, so as to make one almost hold on to his seat, we pulled into the city of San Bernadino. We were in a land green with palms, pepper trees, eucalyptuses, and long rows of lemon and orange trees, trees that were yellow with golden fruit and green with beautiful leaves. And this anomaly was frequently met with afterwards—i.e., the same tree holding a great multitude of shiny smooth leaves interspersed with most fragrant blossoms, and great clusters of green and yellow and fully ripe fruit. We slid through town after town and several small cities, Pasadena among the latter, and there was a great abundance of tropical growth.

Though I had passed out of winter and deserts and was in a land of perennial summer, I had only to look back to some high mountains and see perennial snow. But we learned that advantage had been taken of conditions here to build large reservoirs, and the waters from these high mountains had been penned up for irrigating these broad valleys, and thus make productive this naturally beautiful land.

Finally our train entered the City of the Angels and reached the Santa Fe depot at 5 P.M., only about three hours late. Henry was at the depot, and although I had not seen him for nearly 15 years, I recognized him at first glance. We took a trolley to the new depot on Sixth Street and thence by a large, elegant and swift trolley car we went to Whittier. Henry telephoned for Mary to come up with a horse—he lived about a mile distant—and thus began my first night in Southern California.

It was not long before the white coat of "Old Puss" could be seen coming on the street, and Mary was driving her. She had not changed much since I last saw her 13 or 14 years ago. We drove up Pennsylvania Street and then Painter Avenue to her home, where I had supper. I was hardly expecting ripe strawberries, but they were on the table and I ate freely of them. I went to bed early and had a good night's sleep. After breakfast Henry and I drove into town and I gradually became acquainted with the locality.

Whittier is about 17 miles southerly from Los Angeles. It reaches high hills on the east and is called "The Hillside City." The soil is chiefly of an adobe nature, and is cut through by deep gullies with vertical sides. These are called *arroyos* and correspond to our *brooks* and to the Canadian *discharges*. They are mostly dry, but a heavy shower quickly makes roaring torrents. It is wonderful how quickly the water all runs out of these gullies, which are 15 or 20 feet deep. In Henry's ranch were long rows of thrifty orange and lemon trees in leaf, blossom and fruit. There were also some English walnut trees, pepper trees, magnolias, and rubber trees. Roses, morning glories, nasturtiums, calla lilies were all around, while the tall, rapid-growing eucalyptus trees were in a schoolhouse yard across the street. The eucalyptuses are their chief wood, and in four years from the time of setting, these trees will grow up 30 or 40 feet or more and are in a condition to be profitably cut into stove wood for market or for home use.

As rare a growth as any was *grass*. But the grass lawns are as hard to obtain as any other growth. All growth of whatever name or nature would die without *irrigation*. Without irrigation this whole region would be an arid desert, a thing hardly comprehensible to people from the watery East.

The earth-covered mountains on the east are tipped with derricks, where are pumps for petroleum. Much of the refuse oil is burned near the wells. In the daytime a dense smoke rises from these fires; at night I saw very bright lights which I at first thought were low planets. This crude oil often washes down the arroyos, and where the wash spreads out over the land a dark crust exists, which is not very agreeable to one's nose. While some of the streets in the central part of the city are asphalted, and others have a coating of dry, gravelly earth, yet many of them have been sprinkled with crude oil, and so the whole city reminds one of an old kerosene barrel. This same condition also appears in the streets of Los Angeles.

My cousin George Whitney Sibley tents on his walnut ranch about a mile from Mary's. His pretty, 21-year-old daughter keeps tent for him, and they live in genuine open-air style. Whit's tent has a board floor and is near his barn. This part of the barn has a stove in it and also furniture. They eat in this part. A *ranch* here is a farm. It may contain 5 acres or 5,000 acres, but it is a ranch just the same, no matter what its size.

During this week I received letters from my friend Chauncey Stoddard at Pasadena, and then came a telegram asking me to spend a week with him and Mrs. S. Accordingly on Saturday I took a trolley at Whittier and went to Los Angeles and took a car to Pasadena. It puzzled me at first to know whether to take the "short line" or the other to Pasadena. "Pasadena Short Line" meant by the ostrich farm, and I never happened to go by that route. I had seen a group of ostriches a little out of Whittier, and I did not think it a very great sight. So I went up to Pasadena and soon was at the hotel, Le Casa Grande, where Mr. and Mrs. Stoddard were staying.

That afternoon they showed me the city. The drives were beautiful, also the streets and houses. Here were even large palms and more grassy lawns and roses and other flowers than in Whittier. This city is older, and there has been much more time for improvement than at Whittier. Pasadena is a city of hotels, automobiles and millionaires. The hotels are the Maryland, the Raymond, made because of the Raymond excursions, the Green, because of Green's August Flower, and Le Casa Grande. Mr. Stoddard took me around to all of these. In this city of perhaps 12,000 people, there are said to be between 90 and 100 millionaires. But it was pathetic. I never saw so many Grand Army buttons as here and in Los Angeles and Whittier. The inhabitants were thus shown to be old people, and they had come West to live in order in their old age to avoid the rigors of a winter in the far East. As the mercury was in the daytime often 84° in the shade,

it seems they had chosen well. The automobiles were numerous and dan-
gerous. The guests from the larger hotels were also largely from the East, and probably averaged more than 70 years of age.

On Sunday Mr. Stoddard took me to a Presbyterian church, where I heard the Rev. Malcolm McLeod preach. It seemed strange to have to wait at the church door in order to get a seat. Mr. Stoddard, being so nearly blind, was specially favored and the usher gave him and me a seat near the pulpit. I think the church would hold 5,000 people, and it was *packed.* Mr. McLeod was what a minister should be—an earnest, scholarly, sincere man. His sermon would make one think, was convincing, appealing to the reason as well as to the sympathies. I felt that if there were no other way possible, it would pay me to go from the house to the church on my hands and knees in order to hear such a sermon. At the close the whole con-gregation sang "Just as I am." It was wonderful.

My room was on the ground floor overlooking a tennis court. The lawn was covered with shaven grass, and one morning I went out and put my hand on it and found there was really a white frost, and this in spite of the hot days. This is supposed to be practically a rainless and lightningless coun-try, but many days there were heavy showers, and one afternoon a church was struck by lightning and burned to the ground. These anomalies were attributed to the presence of so many Eastern people.

The next day Mr. Stoddard took me up Mount Lowe. There were certain trolley cars that went to the foot of the mountain, where we took a cable car and were drawn up a long incline. This went near the Mount Lowe Observatory, and thence we went by another trolley to the Alpine Tavern. Here our trolley was chained to a tree so that by no possible chance could it get away and roll back of its weight. This Tavern looked much like pic-tures of Alpine houses. It had pointed roofs and gables, and there was a wide and deep fireplace in its main room where a brisk wood fire was burning and such a fire was not only a luxury but a necessity. For the air was raw, and the clouds resting on the mountain made a damp fog.

We had passed ravines and canyons, had come through groves of stately yellow fir trees—trees that were often 150 feet high and straight, their slowly tapering sides made graceful by long drooping limbs. I found one of these trees cut down and secured some of its bark and cones to take home with me. There were numerous gray squirrels running all around, fat and sleek and so tame that they would come nearly to us when we stopped and held our hand out to them. The clouds had closed in, but occasionally they would open for an instant and then we could see not only Pasadena and Los Angeles but the Pacific Ocean itself. The mountains around had a growth of green tufts called, I think, *mesquite* wood. I asked an Irishman—a rare growth, even an exotic there—what was the

1905 name of this growth. He said it was greasewood and was used as "shrib-
bery" in some of the cities. That shibboleth betrayed him; he could not
say shrubbery.

One evening Mr. Stoddard took me to the Y.M.C.A. building, where we
heard and saw Mr. Burton Holmes in one of his "Travelogues." This one
was of Russia and one of his moving pictures was of Tolstoi walking
around in his farmer frock. It gave me the impression of a much taller
man than I had supposed him to be. In one of our drives around the city
the residence of Mrs. Pres. James A. Garfield was pointed out to us, and
once we saw her walking. During this week also Mr. and Mrs. Stoddard
took me down to Ocean Park. We went and came by trolley. At one place
I picked up some flint that was Indian-chipped. We saw the swells rolling
in from the broad Pacific and could only wonder at the "beyond."

One afternoon the Stoddards took me to the San Gabriel Mission, a few
miles from Pasadena. We went all through this old church. I went across
the street and had a taste of *tamales,* my first and only. This was warm and
baked in corn husks, but I did not go deep enough to get the real taste of
this famed delicacy—I was perfectly willing to forego that privilege. On
our way back we passed an old Mexican woman by the roadside, who
seemed afraid that we might see her face. She was short and enormously
fat, resembling a small haystack. She turned her back directly towards us
and held an apron or shawl or cloak up like a sail, which entirely occluded
us from her, and stood in this ridiculous position until we had entirely
passed by her.

Wednesday morning, February 8, we left on the steam cars for Los
Angeles and Santa Catalina Island. The ride was a little less than two
hours, to San Pedro, and thence by boat 30 miles to Cataline Island. I
copy letters written from there.

HOTEL METROPOLE

"My dears—I am here, 30 miles out at sea, where I never expected to
be. The passage over was like a warm, clear, summer day from Plattsburgh to Burlington. We saw porpoises and the whole trip was delightful. We are going out in a water boat, that is, a boat with a glass bottom,
through which to look at the life under water. We go back tomorrow, and
I shall be in Whittier at night, where I hope to find letters. Will write later.
D.S.K."

The next letter is from the same place and of the same date.

"My dears. This has been a most wonderful day. As I wrote you awhile
ago, we reached here from San Pedro at 12.30 on the staunch steamer
Cabrillo ("Cabreyo"). There were over 200 passengers. We came direct
to this hotel, where we had a fine dinner. At 3 p.m. we started on a "glass

212

bottom boat" for *seal rocks* about 4½ miles away. Previously I found a few barnacle shells for Mr. Hudson. This boat was a moderate-sized steamer with something like boxes arranged in a frame. The bottoms of these boxes were of plate glass, and there were seats all around where people could look to the bottom of the sea, sitting on easy seats.

"The boat steamed out and followed the shore for 4 or 5 miles. I saw what I never expected to see in my life. I never dreamed of any such wonders and beautiful things. We could see to the bottom, easily 30 or 40 feet, and the captain said we could see in places 125 feet. There were long stems of seaweed 30 or 40 feet long waving gracefully back and forth as if swayed by a gentle wind. Sometimes these long growths came up to the boat and we would go through them like pond-lily leaves, only softly and easily. Often there were broken masses of rock that had fallen down from the high, adjacent shore. These rocks were covered more or less with mosses and wavy growths.

"Then, all through the water were fishes, great yellow ocean gold-fishes, others as spotted as trout, others a deep dark blue, some with two white spots on their back near the dorsal fin, all swimming in their native element utterly unconscious of any foreign eyes, and each attending to his own affairs. They made me think of a crowded street in a city where Chinamen, Indians, Japanese, Mexicans and Americans were walking along, each attending to his own affairs, and not in any way interfering with one another. I saw one fish about a foot long, boring a hole in the sand with his nose by turning himself around and around. The hollow that he made was funnel-shaped, with the apex at the center. There were quantities of sea cucumbers that lay flat on the rocks or on the ground, resembling great cucumber pickles. They are said to be about the lowest form of life, between animal and vegetable. There were many shells, mostly "Abalones." You know when we got to the top of Poke-O-Moonshine Mountain, and looked down on the forest tops, that we wanted to sail off through them. This is what we imagined ourselves to be doing in going through these seas today. Certain of these areas are called *marine gardens.*

"At one place high up on the island mountains we saw wild goats feeding. They were white specks in motion. Just before reaching the Seal Bay, we saw an enormous eagle perched on the apex of a high rock close by the sea. On our return an eagle's nest was pointed out in a high crevice. I did not see it, but saw many eagles flying. The south end of the island, close to the water, was lava resembling a regular pudding stone.

"But soon we were at Seal Bay. The seals lay massed on the shore, in a V-shaped cluster, the apex extending up to a little cave. Their heads were all one way and they reminded me of fish in a stream of running water with their heads all pointing upstream. I think there must have been 200 of them, but others of the party said there were not so many. By whistling to them as one does to a dog, they would turn and start waddling or flipping down towards the water, barking like dogs. I wish you all could have been there today.

"Just above the desk I am writing on in this Hotel is a large oil painting of a four-seated carriage drawn by three spans of horses, going along at a brisk pace. There are ten people in this conveyance. The most suitable thing the artist could find to paint in this beautiful island was a stagecoach!   D.S.K."

That night my room was in front overlooking the bay of Avalon. The barking of the seals close by disturbed me somewhat. Had I not known what they were I should have supposed them to be dogs. The sun rose in the wrong place next morning. I walked around the city and saw new buildings going up. One was the Boston Club house. But the houses that people lived in, and also the tents with board bottoms, would have been very inadequate in our eastern climate. But here they were sufficient.

There was a street shaded by double rows of pepper trees that was beautiful. Along its sides were board floors which later, when the visitors are very numerous, will be covered with cloth tents that will be sufficient protection. The mosquitoes had feasted on my blood in the hotel during the night and people were bathing in the waters of the bay, even though it was February. I went to some stores and bought a few things, and saw men polishing moonstones that had been brought from Moonstone Bay. I also went to the aquarium and saw more wonders of the underworld swimming around in tanks. Finally at three we started back on the *Cabrillo,* which had come over in the morning again and had brought 240 passengers.

San Pedro has a long railroad breakwater, and the great amount of redwood lumber in the city revealed to some extent the vastness of this port as a lumber center. The steam cars soon took us to the Santa Fe depot in Los Angeles. Before taking the trolley for Whittier I went out and telephoned to Henry, telling him what time I would reach Whittier. Soon I was buzzing along on a rapid car, but before reaching Whittier the car had to wait on a switch for a coming trolley. While waiting, there seemed to be a swamp nearby, in which there was a great multitude of frogs peeping. Frogs in February were a new thing to me, but there they were.

I reached Whittier quite late and in the dark. Henry missed me so I started to walk, carrying a heavy satchel. The rains had gullied the streets and sidewalks and, not being familiar with the locality, in the dark I really did not know where I was. But I knew the general direction of the

214

house, and just before reaching it Henry overtook me. He had driven
around and around.

In a few days I went to Ocean Park again. Mary and I went together. We stayed at Tena Sibley's home. Their hired house was on the top of the high sand ridge that forms the beach of the Pacific. In the night, when a heavy sea came in, we could only hear its beginning, then it would break off and the sound cease immediately. It was as if a very heavy rain suddenly began and as suddenly stopped.

The next day Anna Sibley and I walked along on the shore and picked up shells that the sea had thrown up. We watched the gulls and ducks ride over or under the heavy seas. At times they would watch and when the high wave had almost reached them, they would make a dive down and let the great mass of water go over them, when they would appear in the next trough.

At one time in Whittier there was a "Santa Ana." About noon there suddenly came up, filling the whole atmosphere, what looked like a smoke or a fog or heavy cloud but which was not any of these. The sun shone through it for a time and then was occluded altogether. It was whiter than smoke and one could hardly experience any more than the sight of it, but it could be tasted, and I was told that at times there was a perceptible deposit from it on smooth surfaces. The explanation was that a heavy wind on the desert blew up a heavy dust, and this was the finest part of the dust that was carried far beyond the immediate wind. I heard afterwards that this Santa Ana extended down to Ocean Park and far out over the Pacific. It is so called because it came through the Santa Ana Pass.

One day at Redlands we drove down to Mr. Henry Fuller's and saw the finest orange ranch I had seen. Mr. Fuller had recently made a journey around the world. His whole route was 38,000 miles. He had brought home many interesting things and talked very entertainingly of his experiences. I heard that he had written a book about his travels. He told me that his oranges *netted* him last year 10,000 dollars. He said that now when he wanted some money, he picked from his own ranch and shipped a *carload* of oranges.

Finally on Thursday at 6 o'clock I started on a trolley car for San Bernardino, where I was to take the California Limited for Chicago. To my surprise my train went the wrong way, yet it really took me to Chicago. I might say that during my whole journey, east was west and north was south. I was turned around all the time. In the night whenever I could see the Great Dipper or the North Star I recognized direction.

The journey was three full days and three full nights. All day Sunday I was going through Missouri and Illinois. There was snow here and the numerous rivers, large and small, were covered with ice. I was due in

Chicago at 2.15 p.m. but it was nearly dark when we passed through Joliet, about 40 miles from Chicago. At length we got there, a little after seven. When I got out the heaped-up snow was so dirty I could not believe it was snow. I had been so long in midsummer I hardly could trust my eyes. However, a man told me it *was* snow! and my thin raincoat was not enough to deceive me into thinking that I was in Southern California.

The next day there came letters from home and I found that Bessie might come out and either go to Sloan or go back with me. I telegraphed her and she reached Chicago at 8 a.m. T8hursday, March 2. She left Plattsburgh at 5 a.m. March 1, coming via Montreal and Laenia. She did not go to Sloan, but we started for Plattsburgh at 11.58 a.m. Sunday, March 5 on the E8rie road. We reached home at 10.20 p.m. Monday, March 6.

After leaving Albany the weather grew colder. The sun set, and there was the purple evening twilight of a winter afternoon in the valley of Lake Champlain. The thermometer was below zero, the car windows were thick with frost, and we were where winter is the *proper* thing, as *summer* had been the proper thing in Southern California.

MAR. 24—Last night was called out at 1 a.m. and got home at 3 p.m.

MAR. 25—Went down to the Creek at 1 this a.m. and got home at 4 a.m. It was raining hard.

APR. 1—Went to the Head yesterday at 3 p.m., got home at 12.30 a.m. Was whanged out of bed at 1.30 a.m. Got home at 3 a.m. Was whanged out at 3.30 a.m. and got home at 5 a.m., bringing Elspeth up from the depot, where she arrived from Wellesley.

MAY 19—David went up to Wolf Pond yesterday to fish for trout. He and his guide brought to the house 75 trout, of which he brought home 38. He fished in a hard snowstorm but had a good time.

JUNE 10—Nelson was graduated from the General Theological Seminary, New York City, on Wednesday of this week.

Last evening died in New York City Dr. George F. Bixby, editor of the *Plattsburgh Republican,* a friend of mine for 30 years. In many respects he was probably the most valuable man in Plattsburgh. I do not know who will carry on his work. He was the only *real* editor in Plattsburgh.[1]

JUNE 23—Nelson left Wednesday for Philadelphia, where he goes to begin work in St. Clement's Church as a curate.

JULY 31—Henry Russell Platt, Jr. came to visit us. He is a nice little fellow and needs to get out of the city to grow up strong and vigorous. His mother and sister have gone from Shoreham to West Roxbury to visit Theo.

AUG. 14—Today David, George Daley, Phillip Guibord and Franklin Palmer have gone up to Wolf Pond to be gone a few days. They are going to camp out and make themselves as miserable as possible under the guise of happiness.

AUG. 25—A note from Evanston says that Russell had a severe hemorrhage from the lungs the day before. He had been having a cough for 2 or 3 months, but he was thought to have become better. It is very ominous.

SEPT. 13—Russell and Helen have gone to Wyoming, near Sheridan. A letter from Robert today says that Henry and Mary were at his office. They will soon reach here, I hope.

SEPT. 22—A letter came from Helen yesterday from Clearmont, Wyoming, where she and Russell are on a ranch. Russell seems much better, but still coughs.

SEPT. 25—I spent the day yesterday at the Macdonough farm on Cumberland Head, coming home in the rain at 9 o'clock last night. The great rains this fall have spoiled nearly all of the potatoes. They are rotting terribly.

OCT. 5—Henry and Mary came this forenoon. They came via Burlington and steamer. It is good to see them once more.

OCT. 16—Francis Fellows has the care of Harry Martin's little dog, "Spotty." When he wants to make Spotty go anywhere he says, "Out, damned Spot." This is not original with Francis, that is, that use of that quotation is not original with him.[2]

Schuyler Larkin, Dr. Larkin's little four-year-old, was riding with his father and mother the other day and he said, "Dad, this gosh damn bridge ain't safe."

OCT. 28—Last evening I drove to Pt. au Roche in the dark. Dr. LaRocque rode with me and Dr. McKinney drove his own horse. We three went to see a patient with Dr. Fairbank, who met us there. The patient had improved so there was really no need for a consultation. I had been out to see the same patient Tuesday with Dr. Fairbank.

DEC. 7—Went to Albany yesterday with Mr. A. Guibord to consult Dr. Vanderveer. Left in the morning at 8.15 and got home at 10.15 at night. 'Twas a dark, gloomy day.

Notes for 1905

1. Dr. Bixby died at the age of 75 from the effects of an operation in New York City. As editor he had been known particularly for his Democratic politics and his widely-read Historical Department. His daughter, Helen S. Bixby, became editor.
2. Francis here quotes Lady Macbeth of the guilty conscience.

1906

Early in his fifty-ninth year, the Doctor writes a characteristic journal entry revealing that the pace of his hard life is still unchecked and that his appreciation of nature remains as fresh as ever. After spending half a night delivering a baby, while son David tends his horse for him, the Doctor finally heads for bed "reluctant to leave the beautiful moonlight."

In this year, he parts with twelve hundred of his prized Indian relics, presumably for much-needed cash. He has provided college educations for two nieces, a nephew, and three of his own five children. There are two to go.

It is a year of important beginnings for his family. Robert starts practicing law in Chicago. Nelson is ordained into the Episcopal priesthood at Albany. Elspeth comes home after graduating from Wellesley. David enters the University of Vermont, and Francis, with precocious skepticism, goes to grammar school.

JAN. 1—This evening there was a Sig gathering at Judge W. C. Watson's. We had a nice time. Sang Sig songs.

JAN. 6—Last night between 9 and 10 o'clock, I drove out toward Salmon River three miles. It was a beautiful moonlight. The distant Dannemora hills were very distinct, also Rand Hill. The nearby pines rose up dark from the white snow. The sky was of varying lights and shades of color. The bright stars twinkled. It looked to me like a night in California, only many degrees colder.

On reaching home at 10.30, the signal lamp was in the window, indicating that a call to go somewhere was awaiting me. David then came and he held the horse for me until 1 o'clock, at which time a little baby girl had come into the world. We got home and to bed about half past one and even then were reluctant to leave the beautiful moonlight.

FEB. 6—Bessie has sold the Ticonderoga relics and has received 125 dollars for them. This does not deplete the collection at all. These had been packed away in the back closet and never exhibited. There were a little more than 1,200 of them.

MAR. 9—Yesterday afternoon I was paid 30 dollars by Miss Marsh at her home on Broad Street. I put the money into my pocket, drove down to the post office, and my money was gone. I can get no trace of it. I put an advertisement into the paper this morning.

Tonight Moses Greenlaw and Fred Fontaine brought my money to me.

They found it in the post office about 3 yesterday afternoon. The police told me that the Greenlaw people they would have thought the very last people to pay it back.

APR. 4—Went to Wolf's Pond on the afternoon train yesterday to see Mrs. John Bailey, who is ill. I got 15 dollars for my trip.

APR. 12—The Y.M.C.A. has its gymnasium up the stairs back of my office. The rabble goes up there and comes down with great noise. It is a great nuisance. Just now the young people are rehearsing for some operetta and the noise is frightful.

APR. 13—Had a telephone put into my office today. It is Clinton No. 417R and is to cost me one dollar per month.

APR. 16—David, Franklin Palmer, George Daley and Hibbard Purdy left this morning for Wolf Pond. They took a lot of stuff and expect to stay a week to fish in the brook there.

APR. 19—The *Chateaugay* made its first trip today, though it was here on Tuesday to carry Sousa's band to Burlington.

APR. 21—The boys came down from Wolf's Pond yesterday. They caught more than 400 trout. They stayed in an old abandoned house belonging to John Bailey. They were all brown and dirty.

APR. 30—Went out to Daniel Thornton's beyond the Wesleyan Methodist Church last night, leaving here at 8 p.m. and getting home at 5.15 this morning. Mr. and Mrs. Thornton had their 14th descendant last night, all of whom are living.

MAY 14—There is a curfew bell and a horrible siren whistle at 8.50 p.m. every evening. E. J. Marks has perpetrated the following. Connors is the chief of police and Senecal is an ordinary policeman.

Connors Soliloquizes
The curfew shrieks at 9 p.m. each day,
The frightened roosters from their perches flee,
The kids in terror take their homeward way,
And leave the street to Senecal and me.

MAY 18—This morning Bessie left at 8.15 for Albany to attend Nelson's ordination at the Cathedral there tomorrow.

MAY 26—Yesterday afternoon went nine miles out on the Turnpike, to Napoleon Chauvin's. The case detained me so I did not start home until dark. I heard whippoorwills and frogs, and often in the dark the pungent odors of the Balm of Gilead trees filled the air. On nearing the Miller Road, the light from the city looked like an evening twilight. I had borrowed a lantern from Pat Knowles, which enabled me to see the road.

1906   JUNE 11—At 5 this a.m. the doorbell rang and Leonard Harper wanted me to go up to his house on the Turnpike at the Wesleyan Methodist Church. He carried me in his buggy and brought me back.

JUNE 21—Today David was graduated from the Plattsburgh High School, classical department. He is in his eighteenth year, and is every inch a fine fellow.

JULY 23—Went to Chicago last Wednesday and got back tonight at 10. Went to see Helen, who is sick. She lives in Evanston and has a pleasant home. I found her better than I expected. She has a complete nervous breakdown. Little S.K. is a sturdy fellow with ringlets all over his head. Theodora is as interesting as ever and so is Henry Russell.

SEPT. 4—Francis began school today, his first grammar school. A while ago his mother was telling him something and said, "The Bible says so." Francis replied, "Well, you know, Mamma, you don't believe much in the Bible."

SEPT. 7—Yesterday afternoon, drove up to Rand Hill. We reached the top a little after 3 p.m. We went into the open meadow back of Leonard Sanger's, which forms the very summit. The view was as grand as ever. Lake Champlain and its valley were far beneath us. On coming back we met Leonard Sanger and his family. He has sold his farm and expects to move away from his sightly home. I spoke about the beautiful view and he said, "Yes, but a fellow has got to have something to eat."

SEPT. 24—David left this morning to enter college at Burlington. He went on the boat and Nelson was with him. He seems happy in the prospects of college.

OCT. 1—A letter last week from Henry stated that Mary had had a stroke of apoplexy.

OCT. 16—David is to be initiated into the Sigma Phi tonight at Burlington. I am sorry I could not go over.
A letter has come from Mary, written by herself. She is much better.

OCT. 25—Rainy, blue sky, wet, cold and muddy. Lonesome. Business dull.

NOV. 10—David came over last night and went back this afternoon. This is the first time I have seen him wearing a Sig badge. It became him well.

NOV. 30—Yesterday was Thanksgiving Day, Mrs. F. B. Hall took dinner with us. Elspeth, David and Francis F. were all at home. In the evening about 9, the telephone bell rang and Nelson telephoned from Philadelphia. His voice was clear and distinct as though he were in the same room.

220

1907

Doctor Kellogg writes vividly of a confinement case in a shack shaken and chilled by January winds but housing at least one undauntedly happy occupant.

He takes Francis to California for a stimulating spring visit, but through the rest of the year he has intermittent worries about his wife's health. Francis Kyle brings home a wife for the family's pleased inspection, and Elspeth proudly flashes an engagement ring.

On the last night of the year, the Doctor rides through a stinging snowstorm to assist at one more birth. The stars are bright on the homeward journey, toward dawn, but the Doctor reports disappointedly that he couldn't persuade his phlegmatic driver to look up and admire the Big Dipper.

JAN. 3—Nelson left for Philadelphia this forenoon. Robert and David left last night, the former for Boston, Providence and New York, the latter for Burlington.

JAN. 10—I had an interesting experience yesterday. I was at a confinement case at the Creek. A hard north wind was blowing. Mercury was going down all day from 28° in the morning to zero at night. The hard wind rattled everything—house, windows and everything movable. There were two wood stoves in the room, both with fires, but it was almost impossible to keep warm. The chimney to each was a stovepipe going straight up through the roof through an opening in the sheet-iron guard. But there were also additional openings in this sheet iron to admit much sunlight. The roof itself was boards covered with paper nailed on, and was about 10 feet above the floor. The windows had curtains nailed to the frames, which curtains rattled and shook. The floor extended up to about 4 inches of the side walls, and the space between the floor and the side walls was all open. To be sure, the house outside was banked up with sand. When the fires in both stoves were burning hard the room would warm up somewhat but soon would become cold again, and it was difficult for the patient and also for me to keep warm. Between this lean-to-room and the main body of the house where the family lived was hung an old quilt for a door. The house had only these two rooms.

The grandmother of the new-coming child was a young-looking woman of less than 40 summers, the mother of 9 children and quite pretty. She was what might be called ignorant. She did not know her age—"her brother had it in a book." She could not tell when her father died nor when her own children were born. Yet I doubt if any woman in Plattsburgh were any happier or more contented than she.

FEB. 1—Grip has gripped me for the last two weeks. Headaches, fever, pain and discomfort have prevailed.

FEB. 19—Francis Fellows and I are to start today for Chicago and go thence to California. We go via Grand Trunk to Chicago and thence on the Santa Fe to Los Angeles.

Until April 23, Doctor Kellogg was away on this trip, his second to California. He took Francis with him but had to leave him behind in Chicago for a few days on the return when a sore throat developed.

The two saw much of southern California, with headquarters at his sister's in Whittier and his cousin's in Ocean Park. His brother-in-law had ten acres set out to fruit and nuts. His cousin lived on the seacoast, and the Doctor was fascinated by the moods and wildlife of the ocean. "It was a delight to see and hear the waves come in from the broad Pacific," he recorded. Interested and enthusiastic as he invariably was, the Doctor was everywhere welcomed and entertained so that he later exclaimed, "I never knew of any such hospitality."

JUNE 3—Elspeth came back from Burlington this morning. She is quite jubilant. She has a fine diamond ring, which she is very proud to wear. She has to show it to everybody.

JUNE 15—In the *Plattsburgh Republican* of today under the head "Golden Wedding, Mr. and Mrs. J. D. Everest of Schuyler Falls celebrate the 50th Anniversary of their Marriage" is the following: "Mr. and Mrs. Everest are of the good old-fashioned stock when people *married for a purpose and for comfort.*"

JULY 3—Was whanged out of bed this morning at 3.45 to go out into Beekmantown, 5½ miles. It was a false alarm and there was not a cent of money in it. But the day was beautiful, the sun coming up over the eastern mountains at 4.15. The Lord's grass was a dingy blue in the morning dew. The cattle and even the sheep in the pastures and the horses were made wild by the mosquitoes. They jumped around, stamped, shook their tails, ran, to get away from the pests. Belmont, when I stopped at my destination, had hundreds of mosquitoes on her neck, back and sides.

JULY 20—At 2 p.m. Dr. Arthur telephoned me to go up to Redford with him starting at 3, to examine an insane man. Of course I told him I would. He would come after me with a span of horses. Before the appointed time there came up a most terrific thunder shower. But the storm abated, and a little after 3 Dr. Arthur drove up. After leaving Cadyville it was evident that a new storm was making up and coming down toward us from Dannemora Mountain. We had to put the boot up and fasten the side curtains and let the rain beat in, as it would in spite of us. The wind blew cold, and gloves and raincoats came into good use. We reached Saranac Hollow about 6 and Redford about 7.

The little 10-year-old son of the man whom we had gone up to examine, a bright little fellow, asked frequently how his father was—was he any better. We could not tell the child that his father must go to the asylum at Ogdensburg and might never be any better, or was likely to die soon. The moon was shining all the way back and the roads were most of them very wet. We reached home at 12.30 in the morning, cold and somewhat tired.

Today I received a letter from Francis Kyle, the first one in about two years. He is married to "a lovely woman," he says, and has a son named Kellogg Warriner Kyle, born July 4.

AUG. 16—Ever since July 30 I have been planning another trip to Redford. So this morning I had a team come from the livery at 7.30. The team was at the door and I was about to go out and get in when the telephone whanged and a woman's voice said I had better not go. She thought she might need me, and she did. Her baby was born about 12 p.m. and she had a terribly hard time, but she got along all right.

AUG. 17—Well, we made the Redford trip yesterday as we had planned for the day before. Mrs. Kellogg, David, Francis and I. We started about 8 in the morning and reached Barnaby Goking's hotel in Redford at 12.30. We had a good dinner at an expense of 25 cents apiece and the same for each horse.

After dinner we drove onto the hill and saw the old glass works. These were of stone, roofless and in great decay. A man took a shovel and dug out a place where glass had been stored. In this way we got some good fragments of "bull's-eyes" and edge pieces. They called it *crown* glass.[1]

After this we went out into an old cemetery on the very top of a high hill overlooking the country for miles around. The view was magnificent. But we must hurry back. We wanted to see the gorge made in the river at the High Falls. We turned off to our right on the way down to Saranac. David and I spent two hours following down this gorge and then did not get to the lower end of it. In fact, I doubt if we really saw the best part of it. But we hurried back to the team and started again for home, which we reached at 8 o'clock.

SEPT. 23—For the last two weeks Bessie has been quite ill with pain in epigastrium. It has been on several times like gastritis, but she has vomited

High Falls of the Saranac River, explored by Dr. Kellogg and David while his wife and Francis F. waited in the carriage.

only once and that was some weeks ago at the time she was first taken. 1½ grains morphine sulph seems to remove it all.

SEPT. 30—Last evening about 5 the telephone bell rang and a strange voice came through the phone. It was Francis Kyle on his way to Troy from Saranac Lake with his wife. They came right up to the house and had supper. We had never seen her before and we all liked her. She seemed the right sort of a woman for Francis.

OCT. 14—I have a case of typhoid fever, one of diphtheria and two of miscarriages. This morning at 5, I had to go down to Bailey Avenue to see a child with meningitis. So I have been quite busy.

OCT. 28—Mrs. Kellogg went back to Philadelphia with Nelson Oct. 18, and has been visiting her cousin, Mrs. Julia Mather Turner. Bessie is much better than she was when she went away. She is to go to West Roxbury tomorrow to visit Theo.

NOV. 7—Bessie was planning to go to West Roxbury last week Tuesday but the pain came again and she had to wait over until Wednesday. Nelson went with her. She has had the pain several times since. We hear from her irregularly. She is at Theo's in West Roxbury. Her difficulty is gastritis.

224

NOV. 17—I left Plattsburgh last night on the train. I got to Boston at 8 this a.m. and thence by trolley to West Roxbury, where I found Bessie in bed but really much better. She had no recent pain and the doctor there had diagnosed her trouble as "gallstones," and he may be right. I stayed at Theo's until Tuesday, Nov. 19, when Bess and I started for Troy on the Fitchburg, going through the Hoosac Tunnel. Francis Kyle and his wife's sister, Miss Warriner, met us at the depot. The family seem to worship Francis, and the baby is a fine fellow, strong, clean and jolly. In the evening Francis insisted on giving me a bath—said that everybody who had been through the Hoosac Tunnel ought to have a bath, and I think he was right. Wednesday at 1.20 p.m. we took the train to Plattsburgh, where we arrived at 7.15 p.m.

DEC. 14—Mrs. Kellogg is much better but had more pain tonight, the first since Nov. 17.

Tonight it is snowing hard. While sitting at my office window, I saw a man walking in the snow. He raised up one foot, lighted a match on the bottom of his boot and, in turn from that, lighted his pipe, all without really stopping.

DEC. 31—Last night a little before 12, the telephone rang and word was received that I was wanted at Silas Chauvin's, about 8 miles up the Turnpike. I telephoned to Justin's and had a man come with a horse to take me out there. It was snowing hard and a hard north wind was blowing. The man came with a one-horse open buggy. We had to face the wind all the way. The snow cut my face and made my eyes sting. The driver did not spare the horse, but kept it on a good trot all the way. It was a relief when we turned into Chauvin's yard and thus away from facing the wind.

The house was warm and after about 3 hours a new baby boy came. As this was the first boy, the people were delighted. They already had two girls and this boy was what they had long wanted. Their last baby, born Oct. 14, 1906, a beautiful rosy-cheeked little angel, lay in the cradle, fast asleep.

Finally, as I had finished my part of the work about 4 o'clock, we started for home. The wind was at our back now, so the return drive was not so cold. The stars were bright and I tried to have the driver see the Dipper, but I could not get him to look at it. Finally at 5.30 I reached home, but the excitement of the case and the ride kept me wide awake until night, with a little short nap.

Notes for 1907

1. Redford glass was made during a 25-year period before the middle of the 19th century. It had a typically pale blue color and is today a collector's item. The bull's-eye was once considered a useless by-product of the successful blowing of other pieces.

1908

There are now long gaps in the Doctor's journal as declining health takes its toll of his time and energy. He struggles on, however; early in the year he writes of several upsets in the snow on nighttime calls into the country. The man's ready humanity is reflected in his willingness, when six other doctors have refused, to deliver a baby for an unmarried woman. His lively wit belies his own condition, for not once does he refer to his health. In the fall, however, he suffers a stroke, and the journal, which has long shown an unsteady hand, becomes almost illegible.

JAN. 22—At 1.50 a.m., Jan. 20, my telephone bell rang and I was asked to go to So. Platt Street. I went and found a young unmarried woman in confinement. She had had the town doctor engaged but he could not come to attend her. Five *other* doctors had refused her for one reason or another and it was impossible to get a woman to assist. The woman she boarded with was inefficient, but finally Mrs. Francis Glancy came and was of great value. Finally about 5 the baby was born. It came hard but things ended all right. I was promised my pay all right, but up to now none has come.

This morning my telephone rang at 4 a.m. and I was wanted at Thomas Lawliss's, about 2 miles north of Nip City. I got a horse from Justin's and a driver, and we started. It was −6°, but no wind. The sky was cloudy and we could not see the track. As a result we had one fine tip-over. I fell into the snow and the driver on me. But neither was hurt. We reached Lawliss's about 5.30. It was a principarae and finally at 12 noon I put on the forceps and delivered her a fine boy, both in good shape. I got home about 2 p.m., having received 10 on account with a promise of 5 more.

FEB. 18—Mr. L. L. Smith was buried last Saturday. He was very rich and gave a lot of money to Plattsburgh and Plattsburgh people. Mr. E. J. Marks said to me today, "Devil Hell Smith: There are two individuals who cannot be bought with money, God and the Devil. Men think if they throw over a tub in a storm that that will save them," i.e. that no matter what their life has been, a little change at the last will save them.

226

A family group pictured in 1909. Rear row: Mrs. Kellogg, Mrs. Francis Kyle, Robert Kellogg. Front: David Kellogg, Francis Kyle holding his son Kellogg, and Dr. Kellogg.

FEB. 26—Last night at 7.30 the telephone rang and I was called out to Patrick Thornton's at West Beekmantown. They had a new baby boy and were happy in consequence. The night was very windy and the snow was flying. We tipped over 3 times but were not hurt. My elbows were lamed but not enough so that I could call for accident insurance. It was a wild night. I got home about 3 a.m. I was so excited that I could not sleep for some time. It was an *experience*.

The other day John B. Gallagher told me that he often read in the evening paper to a man who does not know how to read. John read to him about our fleet being now in Peru and on its way to the Pacific Ocean.[1] The man [innocently thinking of the nearby town of Peru, New York] said that he could not understand how the fleet could get up the Salmon River, *especially in the wintertime.*

APR. 10—Much time has passed since I have written in this record. Spring has come and the robins. The ice has left the lake and river, the south wind blows, the dust flies.

Robert and Russell Platt are no longer together. Robert has started in business for himself in Chicago.

227

AUG. 7—Tonight on the 10.20 p.m. train Rob came. Francis went down for him and I did not know he had come until the next morning.

AUG. 10—Went to Isle St. Michel, Crab Island. In Mr. Willard's boat, the *Ko Ko*, went Rob, David, Elspeth, self, Mrs. K., Helen Barber and Mr. Willard. We had heard of cannon having been seen in the water. We supposed they were the ones sunk in 1759. Mrs. Willard had written for us: "Crab Island cannon lying in 14 to 18 ft. depth of water northeast of Crab Island half imbedded in the sand; muzzle and band of silver plainly seen resting, cannon resting between two boulders in a slanting position in a rocky part. First seen by Justin Wheeler of the 21st Infantry, who watched through the transparent ice from noon until 4 o'clock one wintry day, peering down into its translucent depths. Capt. Will Forkey afterward took a party out on his iceboat to Crab Island, who verified the fact it was also seen in low water in a calm day in the month of August."

AUG. 12—The horse Belmont died of a colic tonight after an illness of 20 minutes. She was a fine animal.

NOV. 26—Nelson came over Tuesday and went back yesterday. He seems to enjoy Poultney.[2]

NOV. 29—Last Wednesday E. J. Marks got to sleep in bed and set the clothes on fire. He was reading and said he fell asleep in the French Revolution and "waked up in the flames." He is original if nothing.

DEC. 1—Pearl Pope came over Saturday and went back yesterday. She imagined that she was ill but no one saw any signs of illness about her. It is dreadful to be so notional.[3]

DEC. 4—Little Nixie Platt has had a serious operation. An abscess developed in the Wolffian bodies and formed about 7 ounces of pus. A second and third operation have been deemed necessary. The little fellow is better.

Notes for 1908

1. This was the American navy's noted trip around the world, ordered by President Roosevelt to demonstrate the navy's coming of age.
2. Nelson had become rector of the Episcopal church in Poultney, Vermont.
3. This entry was made after the Doctor had been invalided by a stroke.

1909

*The sole entry in the Journal for 1909 follows. Dr. Kellogg died on
December 18, 1909.*

AUG. 16—Have sold all of my Indian relics to Amherst College and
got my cash, 6,000 dollars. Prof. F. B. Loomis came and helped pack them.
There were 40 boxes all together. It makes me very lonesome to have
them gone.

229

APPENDIX

Fee Bill of Clinton County Medical Society
Adopted May 1st, 1867

1. Visit within one half mile	$1.00
2. For every additional mile travel, ...	.50
3. Call in when passing, ...	1.00
4. Vaccinating one person with subsequent attendance	2.00
5. Opening abscess in office, ...	50 cts. to 1.00
6. Cupping in addition to visit, ...	1.00
7. Fracture Reduction and Dressing, ...	$5.00 to 20.00
8. Capsular Fracture of Thigh, ...	50.00
9. Subsequent dressing of same, ...	5.00
10. Dislocations of upper extremity, ...	5.00 to 10.00
11. " " lower "	10.00 to 40.00
12. Accouchement normal eight hours, ...	10.00
13. Every extra hour detained, ...	.50
14. Applying Forceps, ...	15.00
15. Craniotomy, ...	25.00
16. Extirpation of Tonsils, each,...................	5.00
17. Amputation, Arm, ...	15.00 to 20.00
18. " Leg, ...	25.00 to 50.00
19. " Fingers or Toes, ...	5.00
20. Each subsequent dressing, Arm or Leg, ...	2.00
21. " " " Fingers or Toes, ...	1.00
22. Introducing Catheter, first time, ...	2.00, sub't, 1.00
23. Operation for Hydrocele, ...	5.00
24. Paracentesis Abdominis, ...	10.00
25. Trephining the Skull, ...	25.00
26. Ligating the Femoral or Brachial Arteries, ...	15.00 to 25.00
27. Branches of " " " "	5.00 to 10.00
28. Hernia reduction by taxis, ...	5.00 to 10.00
29. " " " operation, ...	30.00 to 50.00
30. Application of Truss and advice, ...	3.00
31. Consultation, (mileage not included), ...	3.00 to 5.00
32. Fistula-in-ano operation, ...	10.00
33. Examination in office, prescription, ...	2.00 to 3.00
34. Tracheotomy, ...	25.00
35. Introducing Seton, ...	2.00
36. Leeching, each, ...	.25
37. Post Mortem Examination and giving evidence before Coroner's Jury, ...	25.00
38. Before Court and Grand Jury, ...	50.00
39. Visit Small Pox cases within half mile, ...	3.00
40. Night Visit, extra, ...	1.00

Index